A Quick Index to Twenty Essential Questions

BUILDING TYPE BASICS FOR

justice
facilities

Other titles in the
BUILDING TYPE BASICS
series

HEALTHCARE FACILITIES
Michael Bobrow and Julia Thomas; Thomas Payette;
Ronald Skaggs; Richard Kobus

ELEMENTARY AND SECONDARY SCHOOLS
Bradford Perkins

MUSEUMS
Arthur Rosenblatt

HOSPITALITY FACILITIES
Brian McDonough; John Hill and Robert Glazier;
Winford "Buck" Lindsay; Thomas Sykes

RESEARCH FACILITIES
Daniel Watch

OFFICE BUILDINGS
A. Eugene Kohn and Paul Katz

COLLEGE AND UNIVERSITY FACILITIES
David J. Neuman

BUILDING TYPE BASICS FOR

justice facilities

Stephen A. Kliment, Series Founder and Editor

TODD S. PHILLIPS

MICHAEL A. GRIEBEL

WILEY

JOHN WILEY & SONS, INC.

Published by John Wiley & Sons, Inc., Hoboken, New Jersey
Published simultaneously in Canada

For general information on our other products and services or for technical support, please contact
our Customer Care Department within the United States at (800) 762-2974, outside the United
States at (317) 572-3993 or fax (317) 572-4002.

Wiley also publishes its books in a variety of electronic formats. Some content that appears in print
may not be available in electronic books. For more information about Wiley products, visit our web
site at www.wiley.com.

Library of Congress Cataloging-in-Publication Data:

Phillips, Todd.
   Building type basics for justice facilities/ by Todd Philllips, Stephen Kliment,
Michael Griebel.
     p. cm.
   Includes bibliographical references and index.
   ISBN 0-471-00844-3 (cloth)
     1. Prisons—United States—Design and construction. 2. Correctional institutions
—United States—Design and construction. I. Kliment, Stephen A. II. Griebel, Michael.
III. Title.

  HV8827.P55 2003
  725'.6'0973—dc21

CONTENTS

PREFACE

STEPHEN A. KLIMENT *Series Founder and Editor*

Few building types involve such challenges in programming, planning, and design as the buildings that house the nation's justice system. Changes in demographics, definitions of crime, and social attitudes have added to the hurdles in recent years. It has not been an easy road, but a body of expertise has emerged, along with experts with sound, practical ideas on dealing with these challenges. Two of those experts are Todd S. Phillips and Michael A. Griebel, the authors of this book. They point out key trends likely to drive the planning and design of today's and tomorrow's justice system facilities:

- *Statistics.* There has been a sharp rise in judicial caseloads. More than 30 million cases are filed each year in state and county courts—one for every 8.5 citizens. Citizens in custody comprise 0.65 percent of the U.S. population, and these include much larger numbers of women, juveniles, and inmates with special needs than ever before.

- *Information technology.* From courtrooms to command and emergency operations centers, justice facilities of all types are becoming more technology-intensive. Traditional physical adjacencies are being taken back to the drawing board on new projects, and rapid adoption of wireless technology is opening fresh possibilities for older buildings in need of retrofit.

- *Multi-occupancy and networked systems.* Although mixed-use facilities embracing law enforcement, detention, and the courts are not uncommon, many new facilities are larger today and more likely to include an array of public and sometimes private sector occupants, both justice and non-justice related.

- *Good design.* We see a greater focus on the value of good design in the public realm generally. The role of good design in justice facilities is increasingly recognized for its value in developing and giving new life to communities.

To deal with these challenges and opportunities, this book has been organized into eleven chapters, including an introduction. Six chapters present the key subtypes that make up the justice system: law enforcement, adult detention, the courts, corrections, facilities for juvenile and family justice, and multi-occupancy facilities to house a combination of these.

The remaining five chapters discuss the consultant expertise required to make the buildings viable. The topics covered include lighting and acoustics; selection of structural, mechanical, and electrical systems; specialty systems unique to justice facilities such as escape prevention; building security; and economic factors such as costs and financing.

PREFACE

This book follows a format that has become the hallmark of Wiley's "Building Type Basics" series. The subject matter is tightly organized for ease of use. The heart of the series is a set of twenty questions that designers, as well as first-time owners, most frequently ask about a particular building type. The Twenty Questions cover predesign (programming); project delivery process and management; site problems; unique design concerns; codes, ADA, and security; the four principal engineering systems; environmental challenges; special systems and equipment; acoustics; lighting design; special interiors issues; materials; wayfinding; preservation issues; operation and maintenance matters; and financial issues.

A unique index organized according to these twenty questions is printed on the front and back endpapers to help readers zero in quickly on their areas of interest.

Finally, note that this book, like the preceding ones in the series, is not a coffee-table book, heavy on color photography but light on usable content. Rather, it is a hands-on resource that architects, their consultants, and clients need in the early stages of a project when time is scarce. Students, too, have found the series helpful in solving a design problem.

I am confident that this book will serve you as guide, reference, and inspiration.

ACKNOWLEDGMENTS

The community of planning and design professionals who specialize in justice facilities includes numerous experts whom the authors are pleased to regard as both colleaques and friends. Many of these contributed substantive reviews, additional materials, and practical advice as this book was being prepared.

Two colleagues, Elizabeth Heider and Eduardo Castro, contributed as the primary authors of portions of the book. Elizabeth Heider brought her expertise to Chapter 12, dealing with costs, financing, and project delivery. Eduardo Castro generously developed the discussion of structural systems, as well as the section that addresses blast resistance and force entry protection, in chapter 9.

Among the many architects, engineers, and other design and justice-system professionals who helped along the way, the authors are especially grateful to: Fred Geiger, David Goldenberg, Don Hardenbergh, Hunter Hurst, Dennis Kimme, Peter Krasnow, Alan Latta, Howard Leach, Kristina Feller, Rob Fisch, Jeffrey Foster, Michael McMillen, Tony Nuciforo, Peter Obarowski, James Robertson, Conrad Rushing, Robert Schwartz, John Sporidis, Patrick Sullivan, Scott Sullivan, William White, and Cliff Wilson.

Special thanks are owed to Steve LaHood, our graphic artist, who prepared new line art specifically for the book. In addition, there are literally dozens of people in design firms throughout the U.S. and Canada who gave up many hours to assist with the compilation of photographs and graphics. Without their friendly cooperation, the book could not have been completed.

Associates of the authors who served as a continual source of encouragement include Devertt Bickston, Brian Conway, Hans Ehrlich, Henry Pittner, Charles Short, and Patrick Winters.

Finally, our deepest thanks go to our families for their patience and support.

INTRODUCTION

The justice system in the United States is supported by a variety of facilities at each level of government—federal, state, and local. The facilities are designed to enable the system to affirm and administer the rule of law on a fair and equal basis for all citizens.

Two branches of government, the executive and the judiciary, are involved. They work together to preserve the balance between individual rights and the common good. The system is at the core of American life; it is central to the fabric of society. Its workings are rooted in bodies of law and shared values born in the past and carried forward to today.

A hallmark of the system is its evolving nature, as new societal demands call for new ways to ensure timely justice for all. Another hallmark is its openness. The administration of justice in America is intended to be a process for all to see. The presence of spectator seating in many courtrooms is an apt metaphor for this spirit.

Many different types of professionals are involved in the U.S. justice system. Police officers, lawyers, judges, prison officials, administrators, and others work alongside an array of allied professionals from the public and private sectors. There are educators, health care providers, forensic scientists, records management experts, and so on. The system also includes elected and appointed officials and public review bodies, as well as community-based volunteers and not-for-profit organizations.

MAIN ELEMENTS OF THE JUSTICE SYSTEM

The main elements of the justice system consist of law enforcement, adult detention, courts, adult corrections, and juvenile and family operations. Each element comes in many forms, and these can vary further according to the level of government involved. The operations and the brick-and-mortar infrastructures are likewise varied.

NOTEWORTHY CHARACTERISTICS OF JUSTICE FACILITIES

Justice facilities involve structures whose architectural prominence varies from type to type, complicated functional programs, unusually substantial building materials and demanding design techniques, and a context that often includes other buildings constructed at earlier times.

Architectural Prominence

Some justice facilities are highly visible. They are major civic projects in central locations. Others are less visible and may be sited in remote areas. Courthouses, for example, are often landmarks or anchor points in communities. They are the focus of design attention that tries to convey an appropriate judicial image to people entering or just passing by on the street. Prison facilities, in contrast, may not strive for an attention-getting image; the emphasis in the design may be to make them appear unobtrusive and bland. Some juvenile and family facilities are distinguished by a smaller, more residential scale that deemphasizes an institutional appearance in favor of a design that may fit easily into a neighborhood.

The full spectrum of justice facilities represents a variety of types at every scale and with every kind of architecture. Some facilities are places where freedom is celebrated; others, for those persons who have been convicted of breaking the law, are places where freedom is denied.

Complicated, Mission-Driven Programs

Justice facilities are mission driven and programmatically complicated. Each set of justice operations—law enforcement, detention, courts, corrections, juvenile and family—has demanding functional requirements. Careful planning and design to ensure fitness for purpose are critical. Ill-conceived facilities may not work and can be unsafe.

Achieving fitness for purpose means developing facilities that meet today's purpose, using currently available equipment and staffing, as well as accommodating tomorrow's needs when the equipment and staffing may be different. The challenge is to combine long-range flexibility and durability in ways that remain finely tuned to operations.

Appropriate Materials and Methods

Most justice facilities are intended to do more and to last longer than conventional buildings. A standard commercial office building is a simple and short-lived affair as compared with a courthouse that may have a projected life span of 80–100 years. High-quality materials and assembly methods that are functionally and aesthetically appropriate, and that do not degrade substantially under heavy use, are the norm.

Justice facilities are also increasingly packed with information technology. The ability of a facility to support the needed technology—and to adapt to the changing space requirements of emerging technologies—presupposes a level of planning, design, and construction beyond that which is commonplace in the building industry.

Presence of Existing Facilities

All new design and construction for justice facilities takes place directly or indirectly in the context of existing facilities. The bricks-and-mortar of justice in the United States has grown up over many decades in an additive and sometimes ad hoc fashion. New facilities are inevitably part of something bigger than their own footprints. They are often physically tied to other buildings, because they can be located on sites containing long-existing justice operations. Sometimes the existing buildings are architecturally or historically distinguished. Even when a new project is undertaken as a stand-alone on a remote site, it is placed with an awareness of how it fits within a larger jurisdiction-wide network.

SOURCES OF INFORMATION AND DESIGN GUIDANCE

Numerous sources of information can be tapped to assist with the task of planning and designing a justice facility. Each major field of justice operations includes professional organizations (e.g., the American Bar Association, the National Association of Chiefs of Police, the National Sheriffs Association, the American Jail Association, etc.), many of which have published materials that should be consulted as appropriate by anyone starting such a building project.

The American Correctional Association (ACA) has published sets of standards for detention, corrections, and juvenile training schools. Similarly, court facilities now benefit from design guidelines prepared by the federal government for its system and those developed by the National Center for State Courts, as well as various individual state guidelines. There are also materials that address some specialized issues, such as the U.S. Marshals Service standards for security.

Much of the material is a mix of physical design and operational matters. The ACA standards, for example, speak primarily to such things as staffing levels, required services, and prescribed procedures inside a facility. Compliance with the standards may or may not be mandated by the state or other licensing authority having jurisdiction. Other information focuses on architectural and engineering issues, and some of it is impressive for its ability to remain current in an environment of rapid change. The work of the U.S. General Services Administration (GSA) is noteworthy in this regard.

Both the strength and the weakness of the available information is its piecemeal nature. Each publication addresses one type of justice facility, or subpart of it, only. The strength of a tight focus on one type is that it allows some subjects to be addressed in greater depth. The weakness is that there is no inclusive overview of the system as a whole—no easy-to-find design guidance that helps with the question that often arises, "What happens when different kinds of justice operations are joined together in the same project?"

Also, not all the published information is equally up-to-date and consistent with current best practice. It is often remarked that "One can meet the code but not meet the need." The design decision maker is therefore encouraged to conduct intensive research, including tours of built projects that have had to resolve comparable problems. Going into the field to see what works is important.

ORGANIZATION OF THIS BOOK: CHAPTER SEQUENCE AND EMPHASES

The organization of this book aims to provide a broad overview of the planning and design issues associated with each of the main facility types within the justice system. Each main type has its own chapter. The sequence of the chapters corresponds to a typical sequence of actions in a criminal matter, beginning, for example, with an arrest by law enforcement and the pretrial detention of an individual in a jail, followed by an adjudication process in a court and, if necessary, sentencing to a correctional facility. This law enforcement-detention-court-corrections progression follows the path through the system that a convicted lawbreaker would take.

The complicated arena of juvenile and family justice has its own chapter, which is organized around special courts, detention, and training schools. A short chapter then addresses the widespread phenomenon of multi-occupant facilities in which different justice and non-justice operations may be combined under the same roof or co-located as part of the same project. The remaining chapters focus on technical subjects.

Each chapter about a facility type stresses an awareness of its program, its functions and operations, key operational and organizational concepts, major areas and spaces, and architectural design. The information provided is intended to introduce the reader to the program-driven nature of the facility and to the important planning and design concepts and possibilities. The discussions do not attempt to be definitive; each facility type can be the subject of intensive study on its own.

DISTINCTIONS

The organization of this book encourages the reader to notice the interrelatedness of the various operations and associated facility types, as well as some vital differences. Foremost among the distinctions is the issue of judicial independence. The courts are at the heart of the system; at the same time, they exist within it as the third branch of government whose independence must not be compromised.

Another vital distinction is that between adults and children. The justice system encompasses everyone. Every imaginable type of person may be involved, either through a process as ordinary as requesting a form or through proceedings that may entail the loss of property or freedom. Facilities that deal with children or young people—or with the often volatile domestic relations cases, for example, that involve children —have planning and design considerations that set them apart.

DESIGN DECISION MAKING: TEAM AND PROCESS

The planning and design of justice facilities is a multidisciplinary process. The issues to be worked through are too complicated for any single set of skills. Within the group of design professionals, experts with engineering and specialized technologies play central roles. At the same time, architectural knowledge that includes a command of space and form is arguably more necessary today than ever before.

Beyond the architects and engineers, the design decision-making team must include key representatives of the user

groups. Often, there is an imperfect link between design professionals and justice system professionals. A facility's users and its owners tend not to be the same. The voices of the users may not be heard enough in the planning and design stages. Or only one dominant voice representing the primary occupant may be heard, and contributions from other users are neglected.

The most consistently missing voice in the process is that of the individual citizen. He or she generally has no designated champion at the table. This is unfortunate in the case of facilities that should have inviting and effective public spaces. The lobbies, corridors, waiting areas, and counters that can play a big part in the experience of the citizen are vulnerable to false economies and short-sightedness as participants in the process argue for other priorities. Consideration of citizens' interests and needs is essential.

Adequate time for planning and design is the other critical piece. If the ability to study the problem and explore alternative solutions is hampered by time pressures, the process and its end result will be flawed.

TRENDS

The vast scope of the system means that it is subject to different kinds of trends. Law enforcement in the United States, for example, comprises 18,000 agencies working at all levels of government, from the sheriff in a small community to the policeman on patrol in a big city to the director of the Federal Bureau of Investigation (FBI). The 1990s saw emerging trends toward some "integrated justice" operations that enable law enforcement agencies to work more closely with each other through advanced

Participants in Project Decision-Making Process

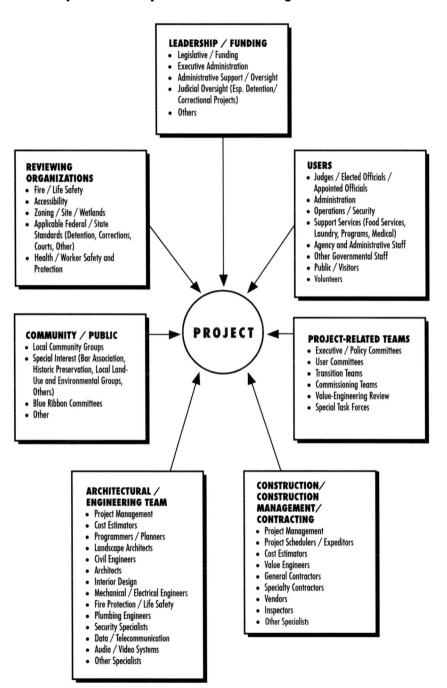

LEADERSHIP / FUNDING
- Legislative / Funding
- Executive Administration
- Administrative Support / Oversight
- Judicial Oversight (Esp. Detention/ Correctional Projects)
- Others

REVIEWING ORGANIZATIONS
- Fire / Life Safety
- Accessibility
- Zoning / Site / Wetlands
- Applicable Federal / State Standards (Detention, Corrections, Courts, Other)
- Health / Worker Safety and Protection

USERS
- Judges / Elected Officials / Appointed Officials
- Administration
- Operations / Security
- Support Services (Food Services, Laundry, Programs, Medical)
- Agency and Administrative Staff
- Other Governmental Staff
- Public / Visitors
- Volunteers

COMMUNITY / PUBLIC
- Local Community Groups
- Special Interest (Bar Association, Historic Preservation, Local Land-Use and Environmental Groups, Others)
- Blue Ribbon Committees
- Other

PROJECT

PROJECT-RELATED TEAMS
- Executive / Policy Committees
- User Committees
- Transition Teams
- Commissioning Teams
- Value-Engineering Review
- Special Task Forces

ARCHITECTURAL / ENGINEERING TEAM
- Project Management
- Cost Estimators
- Programmers / Planners
- Landscape Architects
- Civil Engineers
- Architects
- Interior Design
- Mechanical / Electrical Engineers
- Fire Protection / Life Safety
- Plumbing Engineers
- Security Specialists
- Data / Telecommunication
- Audio / Video Systems
- Other Specialists

CONSTRUCTION/ CONSTRUCTION MANAGEMENT/ CONTRACTING
- Project Management
- Project Schedulers / Expeditors
- Cost Estimators
- Value Engineers
- General Contractors
- Specialty Contractors
- Vendors
- Inspectors
- Other Specialists

◀ *The numerous participants and types of expertise involved in a typical planning and design project for a justice facility.*

information technologies. A number of states, notably Pennsylvania and Colorado, have led the way with their own integrated justice procedures.

More interagency information sharing is being encouraged by antiterrorist measures, including a new Department of Homeland Security. One newspaper noted, "In federal law enforcement, 'all the walls are down.'" A "Strategic Information Operations Center" has been developed at the FBI to create a "system of systems" with the Departments of State, Defense, and Treasury, the Central Intelligence and National Security Agencies, and "allied nations." Integrated justice efforts on this scale may speed up trends toward closer informational ties at the state and local levels. The implications for the design of facilities that can support such technology-intensive ties are potentially far-reaching.

In the arena of corrections, the period of the 1960s and 1970s saw the development of more progressive supervision methods and rehabilitation programs. Since then, changes have included the appearance of new drugs on the street, prison populations with many more women serving longer terms, increases in the number of violent juveniles, stiffer penalties and "three strikes" sentencing, and a lesser commitment to humane corrections environments in which offenders are encouraged to rebuild their lives for reentry into society. This arena is rife with different points of view.

Courts, too, reflect many trends. The federal courts construction program launched in the early 1990s has reinvigorated an appreciation of high-quality architecture in the public realm. The Design Excellence program sponsored by the U.S. General Services Administration (GSA) has raised the level of awareness of architecture and, increasingly, building performance.

The planning and design of courts at the state and local levels are also being affected by different conceptions of the courts' role in "therapeutic justice" and "restorative justice," as well as the growth of new kinds of courts, such as drug courts. Alternative dispute resolution processes, and more pretrial and postadjudication involvement by courts in some cases, demand designed space. Trends toward mediation, for example, are leading to the provision of more space for confidential meetings and small conferences, as well as greater flexibility in traditional areas, especially courtrooms.

The justice system as a whole is being challenged by the increasing pace and complexity of American life. As the United States population grows and becomes more diverse, large concentrations of people speaking many different languages in urban areas are becoming commonplace. The traditional categories of "family" and "household" are no longer as clearly defined as they were a generation ago. Many people are transient, and their interests and property may cut across numerous geographic and jurisdictional boundaries.

A lot of the work performed by the justice system is unchanged from former times, but its volume has increased. At the same time, there are new kinds of work for the system that did not exist even 10 years ago. The protection of intellectual property rights, for example, can involve more complicated litigation today than it did prior to the advent of the Internet.

International developments that entail new patterns of competition and cooperation are also affecting the system.

Immigration laws, treaties, trade agreements, multinational business dealings, drug trafficking and other crime that crosses national borders—these add further to the mix of challenges facing the U.S. justice system. Some problems are compounded when law enforcement or the courts have to deal with cases involving foreign countries that do not have stable legal and judicial systems of their own.

SPECIAL ISSUES

There are four broad issues that deserve special consideration: technology, security, accessibility, and sustainability. The first two—technology and security— have the potential to overwhelm other considerations that are priorities as well. The other issues, accessibility and sustainability, are easy to underestimate.

Technology

Information technology has become increasingly pervasive. Its impact on operations and staffing patterns, and on the physical spaces that support them, suggests that major changes in the bricks-and-mortar of justice may occur over the course of the next generation.

Much is still unknown about how technology may affect the justice process. It would be unwise to reconfigure facilities automatically according to what technology alone might make possible. Not all face-to-face interaction, for example, can be replaced by a video screen. Justice professionals and policy makers still must determine the most desirable roles for technology to play.

Security

Security will test the skills and convictions of everyone involved in a project. Threats to people, to buildings, and to other critical assets can range from calculated and politically motivated actions to random, spontaneous outbursts by individuals who lose self-control. They may involve explosive devices, biochemical weapons, computer viruses, handguns, pocketknives, or a piece of furniture that is not secured to the floor. Security threats may originate outside or inside a facility. The threat assessment process on every project must identify and rank the possibilities.

Planning and design principles for security, and specific technology-based security systems, are discussed at length in the following chapters, especially in Chapter 11. There are subtle, psychosocial dimensions to the issue, and optimal security is not a function of hard physical barriers, firewalls, and filtration systems alone. A facility that is designed to bristle with surveillance cameras and uniformed authority may or may not have achieved its security goals. Skillful design that goes beyond functionality alone to create environments that encourage good behavior is an essential piece of the puzzle.

Accessibility

One in five Americans has a physical disability, and since the Americans with Disabilities Act (ADA) began to highlight the problem of barriers to and within buildings, justice facilities planners and designers have developed innovative techniques for improving access. Moreover, the concept of accessibility itself has been enlarged to extend beyond the physically disabled to the poor, the elderly, the non-English-speaking, and indeed every citizen.

The question of accessibility no longer turns solely on the problem of physical obstacles. There are also growing numbers of self-represented, or *pro se,* litigants, many of whom require the assistance of interpreters, and who need to be able to make their way through the system's procedures and corridors as easily as possible. Good design anticipates the navigational needs of people who approach and enter a facility to find a public information desk and guidance that they can understand.

The system must also be able to open some of its files, as well as many of its doors, to the public. Citizens are entitled to access to many of the records contained in justice facilities. The ability of the system to make records available presupposes many things, including policies governing information that may fall in the uneasy zone between the Privacy Act and the Freedom of Information Act. This is a serious issue for many courts, as the pace of information gathering outruns the ability of policy makers to keep up.

Meanwhile, the facilities themselves must be able to support state-of-the-art records management and office automation systems, as well as efficient and safe interaction with the public. Accessibility, then, means many things that are essential to the preservation of public trust.

Sustainability

Sustainability is a term long used in connection with "green" design that addresses environmental issues, and it now extends to new knowledge about enhanced building performance that has been developed in recent years. Designs for improved building operations and maintenance, reduced energy consumption, and higher-quality space for occupants feature more complete integration of building systems, from structure to shell to basic services. Yardsticks for evaluating individual systems and whole building performance, notably the LEED rating system, are continuously being refined.

The emphasis on sustainability is growing, and numerous public sector projects are in the lead. For the design process, coordination across disciplines is critical. Architects and engineers need to collaborate throughout a project, beginning with its earliest phases. For design and construction budgets, old rules of thumb for estimating costs may be replaced by new life cycle and trade-off calculations.

Sustainability criteria have the potential to affect the image of justice facilities. Sustainable design solutions that respond to site-specific environmental conditions will necessarily vary by region. Sustainability may drive and diversify architectural formmaking in new ways and cause us to rethink the traditional symbolism of justice facilities.

LAW ENFORCEMENT FACILITIES

Law enforcement agencies are established to uphold the nation's Constitution and to enforce its laws and those of its governmental subdivisions.

Law enforcement responsibilities in the United States consist of overlapping jurisdictions and coverage areas. Key law enforcement groups include local (specialized units, community/city, and county—typically a sheriff's department), state (state police and others), and federal (the Federal Bureau of Investigation, the Drug Enforcement Administration, and others).

The facilities required to support these organizations and their functions are diverse, ranging from small local outposts for daytime operations only, to 24/7 operational centers designed as the nerve centers for national and international investigations and coordination/communication for worldwide law enforcement efforts.

Police facilities are often integrated with other services—community services, local and municipal governments. The location of police facilities is particularly important, because the presence of uniformed personnel has a deterrent effect on criminal activity. Since the widespread adoption of community policing approaches and with increased numbers of police officers nationwide, statistics in most states reflect a decrease in overall reported crime.

STANDARDS

Standards associated with observation, arrest, and procedures were developed to respond to issues of security and safety in dangerous and emotionally charged situations. Effective law enforcement operations are driven by the need to maintain control in a wide variety of situations, provide leadership in emergencies, and to respond appropriately during both typical and atypical situations.

As a result, state and national operational standards are primarily written to define legal and practical issues related to law enforcement. Unlike the standards for detention and correctional facilities, law enforcement standards only loosely define the physical requirements of spaces associated with law enforcement activities, except in areas that are designed for short-term holding of in-custody prisoners. Standards that apply to short-term holding include the American Correctional Association (ACA) Standards for Short-Term Detention, state standards for municipal and police facility lockups, and national law enforcement standards.

Principal standards include the *Standards for Law Enforcement Agencies,* published by the Commission on Accreditation for Law Enforcement Agencies. The Commission on Accreditation was formed in 1979 to establish standards and develop an accreditation process. The standards manual contains more than 400 standards and 40 topic areas that reflect optimal professional requirements and practices. In addition, the International Association of Chiefs of Police (IACP) has recently published *Police Facility Planning Guidelines: A Desk Reference for Law Enforcement Executives (2002).*

PROGRAM REQUIREMENTS

There are many variations in the organization and operations of local law enforcement agencies in the United States. In

▲ *Elgin Law Enforcement Facility, Elgin, Illinois. OWP/P Architects. Photo: Howard Kaplan, HNK Architectural Photography, Inc.*

broad terms, the functions provided by most agencies include the following:

- Administration (administration, legal, planning/research, training/personnel, fiscal/support, and community relations)
- Operations (patrol, investigations, traffic, juvenile, and specialty teams)
- Support services (records, communications, property, evidence, and lockup)

The workload and staffing for local law enforcement agencies is driven by the size of the overall population served, court and prosecutorial activity, local policy and attitudes regarding crime and enforcement, and economic and environmental factors in the community. In addition, state and national grant programs may provide support for specific programs and efforts. Typically, law enforcement facilities must be developed with provisions for growth and increased staff to support population and service increases for 20 years or more.

Large cities today may have staff sizes in excess of 14,000 (such as the Chicago Police Department); small municipalities may have only a few staff members. A city of 150,000 may have an overall law enforcement staff of 250–300, including more than 200 sworn personnel. In smaller organizations, functions and responsibilities overlap, and thus staff have multiple responsibilities. In larger organizations, each function is served by separate staff and units, with specific operational and facility requirements.

Reserve officers may be used to assist full-time sworn personnel in the day-to-day delivery of law enforcement services and during emergencies. Reserve officers, if authorized by law, may require law enforcement powers equal to those of full-time officers, including limitations and restrictions on authority and discretion.

KEY OPERATIONAL AND ORGANIZATIONAL CONCEPTS

24/7/365 Operation
Police facilities provide support to law enforcement personnel 365 days a year. The facilities serve as the central reporting and staff location—the "home base" for operations, the control center, radio/communications center, and training center.

Law enforcement agencies operate 365 days each year. Although specific schedules vary by agency, 24-hour operations are maintained in patrol and communications, and larger agencies may maintain 24-hour operations in patrol, investigations, juvenile unit, records, communications, property/evidence, and lockup. Because each shift represents a "use cycle" for spaces, furniture, and equipment, the impact of 24-hour operations on facilities should not be underestimated, especially when considering energy, wear and tear, and durability.

Multiple modes of operation
It is important that the design of most law enforcement facilities, regardless of the specific jurisdiction and operations, support three modes of operation:

1. Standard operations, as needed for most day-to-day functions.

2. Peak period operations, such as at shift overlap points, peak conditions, and regular, predictable, peak operational periods.

3. Emergency and special event operations, which may occur during periods of natural disasters, major events, or catastrophic events. During these periods, the law enforcement facility must serve as the nerve center, often for an entire community, and must be coordinated with other emergency operational centers in the county or state, acting as a network center.

All planning and design must respond to the needs of the organization during both routine and emergency operations. Many emergencies can be predicted and should be considered in planning, design, and selection of systems and materials. The design process should include a review of various emergencies and a careful assessment of how the facility will provide reliable, dependable, and sustained support for the organization during an emergency or series of concurrent emergencies.

Written policy and procedures should govern the response of the agency and staff to unusual occurrences and special operations. Emergencies can result from natural or man-made disasters, including floods, hurricanes, earthquakes, explosions, and tornadoes. Special events and civil disturbances can include riots, disorder, and violence arising from political gatherings, marches, disputes, and conventions.

Potential and actual attacks on law enforcement facilities, correctional and detention facilities, court facilities, and other governmental buildings (e.g., bomb threats) must be considered as part of comprehensive planning, which should include plans for traffic control, evacuation, medical assistance, equipment requirements, and coordination between multiple agencies and large support groups.

Security zones

Security plans for law enforcement facilities must address a wide range of threats and risks:

- Facility security—attack against the facility
- Personal security for staff—attack on law enforcement staff moving between vehicles and staff areas
- Determined escape attempt
- Personal safety for the public—requires deterring, detecting, and responding to attacks on persons coming to the facility for assistance (domestic disputes, threats to personal safety, etc.)
- Natural disasters
- Fire and other emergencies.

Key security concepts include the following:

- The design should minimize the need to rely on electronic surveillance of the site and building, especially reliance on closed-circuit video equipment (CCVE) systems.
- In many ways, the critical security requirements in law enforcement facilities relate to the control of unauthorized access to specific information, material, and equipment, whereas in detention and correctional facilities the intent is to control access to and between people.

- The design should provide a normal appearance for the facility, despite the need for appropriate physical, operational, and electronic security features.

Physical separation of public and staff areas is a key design requirement in a law enforcement facility. Historically, police facilities were designed with secure office and work areas, and small reception areas from which the public would be admitted. Arrestees in many facilities were brought to interview and holding areas through unsecured areas, often through public entrances and lobbies.

Today, police facilities are designed with separate zones and circulation for the public, staff (secure private), and persons in custody (secure detainees). Prisoner security areas should be controlled, separated, and designed to provide appropriate access. Every point of entry or access between public areas and staff areas requires controlled access and positive verification of identity. All openings in the perimeter, leading to the exterior or the interior, should be secure.

The public should enter the building through a single entrance into a public lobby, and public circulation should be restricted to the lobby and any public counters, community rooms, or shared areas. Shared training areas may be located so as to provide access from public areas, allowing them to be used for other functions and multidepartment training but minimizing disruption of the staff areas. Direct access to community or neighborhood relations or drug-abuse resistance education (DARE) staff may be provided from the public lobby and entrance area. Some areas, such as those for internal affairs, may be provided with

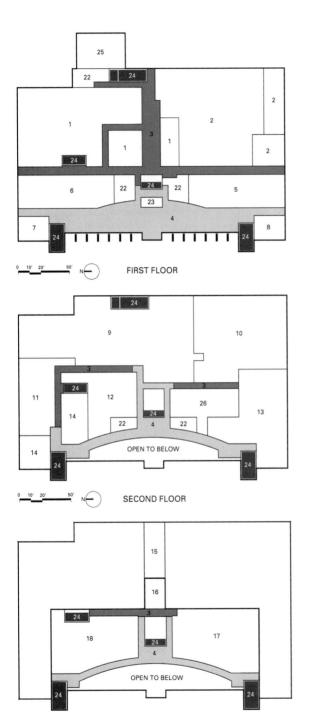

FIRST FLOOR

SECOND FLOOR

THIRD FLOOR

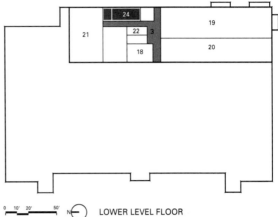

LOWER LEVEL FLOOR

KEY:

- ■ VERTICAL CIRCULATION
- ■ SECURE CIRCULATION
- ■ PUBLIC CIRCULATION

1. PATROL
2. PROPERTY/EVIDENCE
3. SECURE CIRCULATION
4. PUBLIC CIRCULATION
5. RECORDS
6. COMMUNITY RELATIONS/CRIME PREVENTION
7. COMMUNITY ROOM
8. PRESS BRIEFING/COMMUNITY ROOM
9. LOCK UP
10. INVESTIGATIONS
11. TRAINING
12. TRAFFIC
13. JUVENILE INVESTIGATION
14. FITNESS
15. OUTDOOR BREAK
16. STAFF BREAK
17. OFFICE OF THE CHIEF
18. COMMUNICATIONS
19. MECHANICAL ROOM
20. FIRING RANGE
21. STORAGE
22. SUPPORT
23. FRONT DESK
24. VERTICAL CIRCULATION
25. SALLY PORT
26. SWAT/USA TEAM

▲ Floor plan diagrams, Elgin Law Enforcement Facility, Elgin, Illinois. Note the generous public lobby and community rooms on Level One, firing range below, and staff training and break areas above. OWP/P Architects.

direct access from both the public and staff areas of the building.

In all areas used by the staff, including patrol areas, investigation areas, and support areas, access to secure private (staff) areas is limited to police department personnel (sworn and civilian). Admittance to the secure private areas of the facility must be controlled and, in most police facilities, should be monitored by the records counter, watch commander, or communications center.

Typically, the primary staff entrance should be monitored and operated by a card access system with or without a keypad. The public entry or entries to staff areas from the public lobby should be observed and should require that staff release electric strikes and/or greet visitors prior to admission to the secure private areas. Provisions should be made for separate access to staff areas for confidential witnesses, victims, and undercover personnel.

Design for accessibility

All areas of police facilities should be designed to accommodate persons with physical, mental, and emotional disabilities. All areas, including rest rooms, telephone stations, offices, interview areas, staff stations, and public areas, as well as all equipment, should be designed to accommodate persons with disabilities.

Prisoner holding areas should also accommodate all individuals, and search and interview areas should be designed to allow searches of people and equipment (such as wheelchairs) when persons with disabilities have been arrested.

AREAS AND SPACES

The basic components of a local police facility include the following:

- Administration areas
- Operations areas
- Support areas

Administration Areas

The public entry should be open and visible from both the front desk and the exterior parking areas. The exterior areas near the public entry should be well lit (5 fc minimum) and designed to prevent hiding or concealment of contraband or weapons. After entry from the exterior, the interior doors of the public entry vestibule may be designed to lock during after-hours operations. An intercom and camera to the records counter, watch commander, or the communications center can allow the public to approach the building, enter a weather-protected area, and ask for assistance without being allowed farther into the building during nonoperational hours.

Public lobby

The public lobby should be designed to be open and visible from the front desk, with limited seating provided for waiting visitors. The lobby should serve as a circulation hub for access by the public and for official visitors to training and community center areas, to report-taking rooms, or to administrative staff. Public toilets should be accessible from the lobby.

The records center or communications center should visually control and supervise the public lobby, public toilets and phones, access to any training and/or community rooms, the public entrance, and any public service centers (emergency shelter, warming/cooling centers, and the like). These functions should be adjacent to the public lobby and waiting areas, with duress alarm and entry door remote release switches and CCVE monitors of entry areas. The front desk should control access to the secure private (staff) circulation areas. Interview, report taking, and lineup rooms should be located in close proximity to the public lobby.

Community policing units

In larger police facilities, community policing (CP) units may be provided with spaces for special meetings, training and educational sessions, and the like. These spaces may be equipped with audio-video conferencing systems and equipment for special presentations.

Crime analysis unit/staff

Crime analysis staff collect, analyze, and distribute general and project-specific information regarding crime patterns. Crime analysis is a scientific process; it involves collecting and analyzing readily available crime data and making the analyzed information regularly available to line officers and investigators. Staff work spaces include office and workstation areas designed for computer use and

▼ *Public entrance lobby, Elgin Law Enforcement Facility, Elgin, Illinois. OWP/P Architects. Photo: Paul Schlismann.*

▲ *Interior at second level, Elgin Law Enforcement Facility, Elgin, Illinois. OWP/P Architects. Photo: Howard Kaplan, HNK Architectural Photography, Inc.*

administrative function. Some accommodations should be made for the press and media near the lobby and/or the records center. Access to these areas should be provided from the lobby, outside the staff (secure) areas of the facility.

Administrative offices

In most police departments, the offices of the chief and top administrative staff should include work areas designed to support administrative and hands-on operational work. Although coordination and management (internal to the department and with other city or governmental groups) are the primary functions of administration, there is a strong relationship between administration and day-to-day operations in most police departments. To support both, the administrative offices and work areas should incorporate individual and team-work environments that are carefully designed to provide acoustic and visual privacy as warranted by the activities performed therein.

For example, assembly areas and staff work areas for routine matters should incorporate appropriate open desk, cubicle, and closed office areas (with and without glass) to support both practical teamwork and privacy for concentration and private discussions (phone and in-person) as needed. Provisions should be made for secure and confidential personnel files in administrative areas. Support areas that can be shared by administrative staff and operational groups include library and conference spaces.

General shared support spaces provided in administrative areas should include spaces for computer support: printers, copiers, shared computer stations, and special research workstations.

analysis of printed reports. Areas designed for report writing and coordination should include writing surfaces with layout spaces and computers, with some acoustic separation, and should be designed to allow concentration and minimize visual distraction.

Press and public information areas

Public information assistance, dissemination, and coordination, including provisions for releasing information at news conferences, constitute an important

Crime prevention/community relations units

Neighborhood and community relations/crime prevention staff are responsible for community awareness and alertness programs. Crime prevention programs may include neighborhood watch projects, child safety programs, employees-on-patrol programs, child identification programs, rape prevention, and residential security survey programs.

Offices and work areas for neighborhood and community relations staff should be visible and located near the public entrance to the facility. Support areas typically include public reception, computer workstations, video monitors, and storage areas for public information pamphlets and program flyers. Training areas and areas for community groups should be located near public areas.

Other units

In some police departments, special programs may include mental health units (with personnel specially trained in handling and transportation of mentally ill persons and in dealing with mentally ill citizens in the community), although many departments transfer these responsibilities to other programs and facilities.

Operations Areas

Patrol

Patrol staff are responsible for maintaining public order, enforcing the laws of the state and municipality, and serving the public through prevention, detection, deterrence, and intervention. Patrol staff are typically involved in handling citizen complaints when individuals come to the police facility.

Patrol, or field service, units almost universally provide 24-hour coverage and may be divided into three shifts (day, evening, late night, or other designations). Shifts may follow eight-, ten-, or twelve-hour patterns, with four- or five-day schedules. Typically, patrol groups work under shift supervisors (sergeants or lieutenants), and patrol coverage is assigned by sector, beat, zone, or district.

Most areas associated with patrol functions are shared work, storage, and assembly areas designed to serve the staff who perform the field work 24 hours a day, 365 days a year. Shared support areas and equipment include the following:

Roll call/assembly areas

Report writing areas

Conference/work room(s)

Storage areas (clean and dirty uniform storage, equipment storage, equipment issue/radios, armory)

Staff rest room and locker areas

Exercise and training areas

Roll call/briefing room

Roll calls are held to accomplish several tasks: to brief officers regarding daily patrol activity and coordinate with investigations and unusual situations, to notify officers of changes in schedule or new directives, and to evaluate readiness to assume patrol. The briefing/roll call/assembly room should be planned to accommodate typical peak numbers of officers during roll call/briefings, based on current and anticipated staffing.

Support equipment should be provided for routine presentations and discussions, including marker boards, a mailbox for each officer, and bulletin boards. Video display systems are typically provided for digital display (presentations, digital photos, and access to Internet information), and projection and display systems may

▲ Briefing room, Elgin Law Enforcement Facility, Elgin, Illinois. OWP/P Architects. Photo: Paul Schlismann.

▲ Conference room, Elgin Law Enforcement Facility, Elgin, Illinois. OWP/P Architects. Photo: Paul Schlismann.

include monitors for use of the room for major briefings and/or distance learning (remote instruction) programs.

Other support areas

Other patrol support spaces near the roll call/assembly areas should include staff lockers, rest rooms, and exercise areas. Space should also be provided for radios and a charger and for special storage of additional uniforms, outerwear, and the like, as needed. Provisions may be required for the storage of incoming and outgoing uniforms, depending on policy and procedures regarding uniforms.

Supervisory offices

Office areas should be provided for the watch commander or patrol supervisor, with adjacent secure storage for shared common tactical weapons. Office areas may be provided for administrative and shift personnel, with office support equipment and shared workstations, including copiers, video equipment, space for training and report writing, shelving, a mail distribution area, and bulletin boards.

Training

Training functions are a critical aspect of law enforcement; these include academy training, in-service and roll call training, advanced training, specialized training, and civilian (and reserve officer) training programs.

Training spaces include training rooms, audiovisual storage, libraries, and storage for training materials and for files and computer records of training. Training/ multiuse spaces should be provided in midsize and large facilities. Additional space should be provided as part of the patrol assembly and roll call area for in-service computer training of staff before or after shifts.

Training areas constitute one of the topics for which the Standards for Law Enforcement Agencies give specific requirements: "33.2.2 If the agency operates an academic facility, the facility includes, at a minimum: a) classroom space consistent with the curriculum being taught; b) office space for instructors, administrators, and secretaries; c) physical training capability; and d) a library."[1]

Training spaces must accommodate groups as well as individuals. Virtually all law enforcement agencies and published standards require that all personnel assigned to tactical teams engage in training and readiness exercises, and access to appropriate training areas is an important requirement.

Special investigation and enforcement (tactical squads/gang units)

Provisions should be made for special enforcement teams, including squad rooms, areas for special assembly, briefing areas, and storage. Following assembly and briefing, access to special equipment, supplies, and vehicle storage/parking may be required. Because of the nature of their work, undercover staff may require private access to the facility. In addition, there may be extensive requirements for coordination between agencies, and access to some areas by other law enforcement agency personnel (outside agencies, state and federal staff, and the like) may be needed.

1. Law Enforcement Agency Accreditation Program, *Standards for Law Enforcement Agencies* (Alexandria, Va.: Commission on Accreditation for Law Enforcement Agencies, 1994), p. 33-1.

Special investigation and enforcement units may be provided for major crimes, white-collar crimes, gang-related crimes, and so forth. The activities of these staff members include intelligence gathering and follow-up investigations. Support areas can include special interview and workroom areas, including spaces for ongoing/major cases and rooms for long and multijurisdictional cases; records storage, office, and office support areas; special equipment and supply storage; and operations rooms. In some locations, where an emergency operations center (EOC) is planned in conjunction with the office, the EOC can serve as a temporary ongoing/major case room.

There are wide variations in the requirements for staffing, policy, operations, organization, storage, and support for these units. In larger jurisdictions, spaces may be required for office and assembly functions and for general and secure storage of electronic equipment and vehicles (possibly including special assault vehicles).

Special weapons and tactics (SWAT) units are frequently tactical response teams assembled from personnel from a number of operational groups. The necessary support spaces include office areas and equipment rooms; and access to roll call/assembly areas is also required. Special vehicle storage areas may be required, and these areas may be enclosed and heated, depending on climatic conditions.

Juvenile units

In mid- to large-size agencies, juvenile units may be responsible for processing youth arrests, conducting investigations involving juvenile offenders, presenting and coordinating court cases, and working with alternative and prevention programs. Juvenile records, fingerprints, and photographs should be stored separately from other records and should remain confidential, according to the statutes and guidelines of many states. As a result, juvenile units may be physically separated from other investigative units. Special access may be provided to assist in maintaining confidentiality and ensuring that the constitutional rights of juveniles are protected.

Traffic enforcement

Traffic units may be created with specific responsibility for maintaining traffic and parking operations through planning and enforcement. Activities include both routine work and special investigations regarding major accidents (both response and reconstruction). Other activities may include providing emergency assistance to injured persons, protecting accident scenes, handling special events, and conducting at-scene and follow-up investigations.

Space requirements for traffic units can include public reception and workroom areas, interview rooms, and storage of special supplies (e.g., traffic control and crossing guard supplies).

Other enforcement units

If an agency uses special-purpose vehicles, horses, or canine teams, special policies and procedures are developed for use, authority, maintenance and care of the animals and equipment, and designation of positions or persons authorized to work with them. Special facilities are required for these units, which may include kennels, stables, and other animal care and housing facilities, running and exercise areas, storage and supply areas, and staff offices and work areas.

Special vehicle warehouses, docks, hangars, maintenance areas, and supply and fueling areas may be required for specific units, and these areas often involve planning for operations at locations away from the police station or headquarters.

Support Areas

Lockup area

In some situations, police officers bring arrestees to the police station for questioning and short-term holding. After questioning, a decision may be made to release or to hold a person. A detained person may either be held at the police facility lockup or transported to a local (county or regional) detention facility for intake, booking, and holding prior to a court appearance.

The lockup area provides space for booking, processing, and holding in-custody persons. The design of secure in-custody areas includes provision of a vehicular sally port (for one or more police vehicles), with a property/evidence drop-off point; gun lockers for securing weapons prior to moving prisoners; and movement through a pedestrian (secure) sally port to a "pre-processing center," an area for fingerprinting, digital or traditional photography, short-term holding (group or individual seating, secure or open—based on behavior and the preference of the police department), prisoner property areas, and access to interview rooms.

Lockup and short-term detention space requirements and staffing-related issues are described in Chapter 3, "Adult Detention Facilities." In mid-size or larger police departments, jail or lockup operations are typically under the command of a facility administrator, and jail personnel are organized into rotational teams with assignments for custody and control of the operation during specific eight-, ten-, or twelve-hour shifts. Personnel assigned to these units are responsible for the immediate supervision of personnel and in-custody defendants, for making regular safety and security inspections of the jail, for maintaining accurate counts, and for ensuring that medications are distributed as directed.

Lineup or identification room

A lineup or identification room should be provided in or near the lockup. Access to this area should be provided from distinct areas—from the public lobby for public access, and from the prisoner lockup area, with direct access and adjacency to the holding cells.

Support staff

Support staff may be assigned to booking operations, responsible for receiving, processing, and handling releases and transfers of all prisoners, and responsible for the supervision and safety of all prisoners in the area. Bond personnel may be provided in support of lockup or jail operations. These clerks receive and process bonds posted at the lockup or jail and are responsible for full and accurate accounting of all transactions. The bond payment and reception/release function of the lockup are important, and such areas should be designed to allow payment and release at virtually any time without affecting or disrupting other functions of the facility.

Depending on the size of the operation and the length of time prisoners are held, officers may be assigned to supervision of housing units, control center operations, and handling other operations (phones; door control; preparation and distribu-

tion of food, supplies, and medication; and access to recreation). Medical staff (registered nurse and contract physician or psychologist/psychiatrist), who may have regular and "on-call" hours, attend to sick call and routine and emergency medical needs.

Depending on the size and nature of the facility, holding areas may be provided for male and female adults (if both are provided, they must be separate in sight and sound), groups and individuals, and particular areas may be provided for sobriety holding and special needs (e.g., padded cell). In most states, provisions for juveniles must have complete sound and sight separation through the use of separate holding rooms or areas.

If holding areas are designed for use beyond 24 hours, state and national standards for short-term detention must be followed, including provisions for access to natural light, appropriate area allocations, and required detention spaces, such as dayroom areas.

Additional support areas for a lockup facility include storage areas, control rooms, laundry areas, employee/staff areas and rest rooms, and general multipurpose rooms. Because lockup facilities may be used to hold prisoners until their initial appearance in court, a lockup may include a fully functional arraignment court or a holding area for prisoners making an appearance via video arraignment. The design of arraignment court holding areas may include provisions for access to private defense counsel or public defender staff, depending on the policy and requirements of the state and local court jurisdiction.

Preprocessing activities can include initial observation and report preparation and the use of sobriety or other testing equipment. In large facilities, where holding for more than eight hours may be anticipated, booking and intake functional areas may be provided with contact and/or noncontact visitation booths and interview rooms (with direct and separate access from public circulation).

Records

Records staff process and maintain police report files, warrant and arrest files, fingerprint cards and systems, traffic records, master name indices, and weapons registration files and records. In large facilities, these units operate for extended hours. Records staff and file areas should be adjacent and accessible to the public lobby (with public counters) and to the patrol roll call/report room.

Typical spaces provided in a records area include the following:

File and record storage units (open or closed shelving, file cabinets, and vaults)

Office and workstation areas for staff

Public counter/reception areas

Copy areas/equipment

Shared/specialized computer workstations

Microfilm readers and printers

Archive storage

Worktables and processing areas for incoming and outgoing records

General storage

Because of confidentiality requirements, most records units include provisions for commercial-type shredders and storage of outgoing shredded documents.

Firing range

Training in the use of weapons is an important aspect of a police department's training programs. A variety of systems and facilities are used, ranging from com-

puter-aided firearms training systems designed for use by individuals or small groups, to actual firing ranges. To accommodate various work schedules, ranges must be accessible during extended hours throughout the week and often on the weekend. Issues related to access and use by outside agencies, if any, should be addressed early in planning.

Specific requirements for room design, acoustics, lighting, security, ventilation systems, and toxic waste handling (spent ammunition) are defined in several national standards (e.g., the standards of the National Institutes of Safety and Health, NIOSH) for firing range design and hazardous materials handling. Typically, a range area includes the firing range, range control room, supply room, armorer's room, and an interactive video training area. Interactive video training must accommodate audio-video equipment that tests responses and decisions. Provisions for such rooms should be coordinated with the simulator equipment and systems.

Communications center

The communications center (911 center, emergency control center) is responsible for receiving and processing requests for police, fire, and medical assistance 24 hours a day, 365 days a year. Communications center personnel provide communications support for police and fire department field units. The communications center is functionally the nerve center for operations and should be designed to promote staff alertness and responsiveness at all times.

In smaller facilities, communications units frequently handle radio dispatch and lobby reception. In larger facilities, these centers are typically "buried" with-

◀ Communications center. Elgin Law Enforcement Facility, Elgin, Illinois. OWP/P Architects. Photo: Paul Schlismann.

in the facility, rather than located near the public entrance, because their function is crucial to operations. If such a center is located in a secure area, natural light and views may be provided. Within the center, staff receive calls for services, dispatch appropriate units for response, maintain communications between department staff and other law enforcement agencies, maintain records of all radio transmissions and calls for assistance, and access the state and federal criminal identification networks (National Crime Information Center— NCIC—and others).

Personnel may work eight-, ten-, or twelve-hour shifts, with four- or five-day rotations, depending on departmental practice and policy. Assignments and the number of consoles operated vary according to the shift and the day.

▲ Communications center. Robert A. Christensen Justice Center, Castle Rock, Colorado. Hellmuth Obata Kassabaum Architects. Photo: Timothy Hursley.

Typically, communications centers are designed with multiple console positions for shift dispatchers and switchboard operators, with an adjacent but separate shift supervisor's office (with direct view of the communications center), break room, locker areas, rest rooms, file cabinets and records areas, equipment room (for computer and communication equipment and panels). Department-wide computer systems, including file servers, may be located in the communications center equipment room as well.

Because of coordination requirements and requests for information, the communications center should be adjacent to the records department, but in a controlled and secure environment. Various public and student groups tour police facilities, and because their presence inside the actual communications center would be disruptive, a public viewing area of the communications center may be provided.

Property and evidence

Property and evidence staff are responsible for the receipt, processing, and secure storage of stolen or seized property and evidence. This function is a 24-hour activity, and staff may operate on an "on-call" basis in smaller departments.

The design of the receiving, processing, and storage areas must ensure that the "chain of evidence" is maintained and that practice and policy can demonstrate that evidence was properly handled. Typically, evidence and stolen or seized property are brought to a reception area, and field staff place such property in a locked evidence locker. Properly stored, the lockers can be opened only by property and evidence officers, typically only from within the property/evidence room, where the property or evidence is marked, processed (if/as required), tagged, and stored for future retrieval and use.

Evidence areas must be designed for logging, packaging, and labeling property for storage. Extra security measures may be needed for exceptionally valuable or sensitive items of property, including the use of card reader and access control systems to monitor access and provide a clear audit trail for demonstrating the preservation of the chain of evidence.

Typical support areas and equipment include the following:

- Property/evidence storage and drop-off areas.
- Evidence lockers, which may have to accommodate larger firearms, and evidence preparation areas (including fume hoods and other processing stations).
- Storage areas (general storage).
- Special vaults (for drugs, valuables, weapons, and special items).
- Bulk storage areas (for bicycles, large equipment, or furniture). These areas may or may not be located in the same area as general storage.

Many departments operate a vehicle impound area and operation. In some situations, a multiple-vehicle sally port can be provided, and one or more spaces can be used as needed for vehicle impound and detailed searches. Security is a high priority in this area, and special design requirements must be met for controlling access, monitoring the area, architectural construction, and engineering systems for ventilation and plumbing for processing areas.

The property/evidence drop-off areas (with lockers) must be available 24 hours a day, 365 days a week, although property/evidence room staff in smaller agencies may not be present at all times. The property/evidence areas should be adjacent to staff entry areas and (if provided) to the vehicular sally port, or areas with highly controlled access points. In addition, public access should be provided to this area (for a public "claim" counter for recovered property).

Investigations

Investigation staff are responsible for conducting police investigations of crimes, especially major crimes as defined by the FBI index: robbery, homicide, assault, fraud, and drug offenses. Investigation units typically provide 24-hour service, or an "on-call" schedule of investigators is assigned.

Investigation work includes information development, interviews and interrogation, collection and preservation of evidence, surveillance, background research, and analysis. Background investigations are critical, and record keeping systems and files are essential to this work. Investigation staff are involved in both preliminary and follow-up investigations; their activities include direct observation, interviews and coordination of victims and witnesses, maintenance and protection of crime scenes, coordination of evidence analysis, and preparing cases and giving testimony in court cases.

Criminal investigation staff, who have specialized training in criminology, conduct crime scene searches and are involved in the collection, preservation, and testing of evidence. In many police departments, investigation staff are responsible for coordination with forensic laboratories (that perform analyses of evidence) and must transport evidence to and from various locations for analyses.

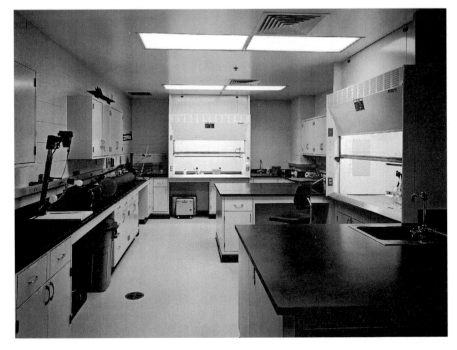

◀ Evidence lab equipped with fume hoods. Robert A. Christensen Justice Center, Castle Rock, Colorado. Hellmuth Obata Kassabaum Architects. Photo: Timothy Hursley.

Office and support areas for investigation staff include the following:

Individual and team work areas, with provisions for private conversations (phone and in-person)

Conference and interview rooms

Equipment and supply storage

Copying equipment

Records areas

Dedicated computer workstations and printers

Video monitors and work counters

Because they are required to coordinate with special investigations and other activities, the investigations unit should be located near patrol and special investigation units, with discrete access from public lobby and entrance areas that are used for access by victims, witnesses, and observers. Provisions should be made for parking and confidential access by victims, undercover staff, and informants. Good access to evidence storage and processing areas is required.

Victim/witness services

There is an increasing trend among police agencies to accommodate and support victims and witnesses. The role of victims and witnesses is crucial to law enforcement, since:

In a free society, we are absolutely dependent upon the aid of these victims to hold the criminal accountable. In return, the victim deserves support and fair treatment. As often the first to arrive on the scene of the crime, the [officer] is the initial source of protection for the victim. The manner in which [the officer] treats a victim at the time of the crime and afterward affects not only [the victim's] immediate and long-term ability to cope with the crime, it can

determine his [or her] willingness to assist in prosecution.[2]

In addition to assistance services, space may be provided for victim and witness entry and waiting areas, and the appropriate separation of these entry and waiting areas from general public circulation and waiting areas may be required.

Warrants and civil process

Warrant units may be provided for the service of warrants and the interstate and intrastate transfer of fugitives. In addition to field staff, clerks may assist in the research process, identification of last known addresses, entering and clearing warrants on NCIC and other systems, and responding to inquiries from other jurisdictions on outstanding warrants.

Civil process units provide immediate service of papers received from the clerk's office, through the mail, or directly from attorneys. Prior to service, papers must be verified for accuracy and correct fee amounts, and each paper must be tracked and reports prepared after the return of the process server.

Other support areas

There are many other support areas that should be included in the planning and design of law enforcement facilities. These include building support areas, such as emergency generator rooms, mechanical and electrical rooms, and incoming service areas for data/telecommunications equipment. These areas should be indoor spaces, and designed with appropriate service entries and clear-

2. Ibid. Preface to Section 55, quoting Assistant Attorney General Lois H. Herrington, chair of the President's Task Force on Victims of Crime, p. 55-1.

◀ *Staff locker room, Elgin Law Enforcement Facility, Elgin, Illinois. OWP/P Architects. Photo: Paul Schlismann.*

ance to allow easy access and replacement of equipment and parts while keeping the facility operational.

In addition, provisions for staff locker rooms, rest rooms, and break areas are critical. Lockers for sworn personnel must be provided, and these should be 24 in. wide, full height, and designed to accommodate the needs of modern law enforcement personnel (sufficient space for briefcases, helmets, and other gear). Locker areas are frequently provided for reserve and visiting personnel as well, and in some locations staff lockers are provided for nonsworn personnel. Classrooms and physical training areas should be located near rest room and locker areas, well designed, and appropriate for heavy, but professional, use.

Law enforcement facilities should be treated like "staging facilities," with space for emergency equipment, supplies, storage of the tactical gear and supplies for various units, and good

access to a loading dock or a large vehicular access point.

SITE SELECTION

Determining the location for a local police facility (station or substation), a headquarters facility, or specialized facilities and support areas (lockup, evidence storage/processing center, 911/Communications Center, etc.) involves these critical requirements:

- *Adequate site size.* Site development should consider the need for ground level operations, particularly access and parking for pedestrians and vehicles (members of the public, official visitors, staff, arrestees; special vehicles, and vehicle support facilities; including provisions for preprocessing and booking activities).

  Planning must consider the need for multiple parking areas with separate circulation, access, and security areas. Primary issues to be considered include convenience and support for functional flows, particularly because most law enforcement functions have a need to be located on the first floor.

Planning for expansion is critical in developing a new facility, inasmuch as the functional requirements of a growing law enforcement operation typically expand in all areas at the same time. Thus, the site must be planned to accommodate the immediate building program with provisions for expanding the building and parking areas—including options for shell areas (space designed to be fitted out later when the need for it arises with future growth) and areas for special operations and teams (for unique/high-profile cases/multijurisdictional operations, etc.). In addition, ground space (and appropriate air clearances) may be required for a number of critical support elements, such as radio antennas, gas tanks/pumps, utilities, water detention/retention, and other special items.

- *Sufficient parking.* Overall parking requirements for a police department include provisions for administrative staff, visitors, official vehicles, and all operations staff at the facility (including patrol and investigations personnel and others). Parking for staff and the public should be separated. Parking requirements for patrol and other operations staff vary according to the specific operational practices of the department, such as whether staff members take official vehicles (marked or unmarked) home. In general, parking counts should accommodate peak staff periods, including full shift overlap periods.

In jurisdictions where staff come to the station in personal vehicles, staff parking areas should be provided. Staff will then enter the facility by means of a secure staff entrance, go to lockers and/or exercise areas, and assemble for roll call. After roll call and briefing, staff pick up equipment and supplies and go to the squad car parking areas. In jurisdictions where staff arrive and depart in assigned official vehicles, the process is similar, but after roll call/briefing, staff return to their assigned vehicles. Although the operational patterns and flows in the two instances are similar, this procedure can have a dramatic impact on the required parking counts for staff parking.

- *Appropriate linkages.* Local police facilities may be located near a number of other city or governmental facilities. In many locations, because of the amount of movement (staff, prisoner handling) and communication between agencies, police stations should be close to the following:

  - First-appearance/arraignment courts, for prisoner transport. There are many concerns involved in moving prisoners to court, including separation of the flow of inmates, the public, and court staff; provisions for safety/security in transport and at the courthouse; provision of appropriate temporary holding and support services (e.g., food services during lunch hours).

    Because of the importance of this process, planning for new facilities (in large jurisdictions) should carefully explore links to the courts, including provisions for a first-appearance court (a court at which a prisoner makes his or her first appearance) or room at the lockup.

- The county detention facility. In many cases, only minimal short-term holding of arrestees will be accommodated at local police facilities, and if it is likely that an arrestee will be held pending first-appearance court, law enforcement personnel in most municipalities transport the arrestee directly to the jail (booking/intake area).

A properly designed jail intake and booking area includes places for initial interviews by arresting officers and spaces for report writing by arresting officers, and these functions may be moved in their entirety to the local detention facility.

- Other governmental facilities and services. It is not uncommon to locate police headquarters on the same site as or near the administrative facilities of the local municipality. Police facilities are frequently located near emergency response centers. With the increased emphasis on neighborhood policing and crime prevention through environmental design (CPTED) principles, a growing number of police stations and substations have been located within the communities they serve. These stations, which can serve as 24-hour-operation centers or may be more limited in their hours, provide a base for law enforcement operations.

- Transportation and access (roads, public transportation, air) for staff and visitors. Traffic flows on and off sites for functions not related to law enforcement should be carefully planned to prevent or reduce opportunities for accidents or interference with police matters.

UNIQUE DESIGN CONCERNS

Whereas detention and correctional facilities are functional, often utilitarian, in terms of their image, law enforcement facilities should promote the image of the community government—significant, dignified, solid, businesslike, approachable, safe, and pragmatic—a wise use of public expenditures.

Design for Staff

As with other justice facilities, the single most expensive element in the budget associated with law enforcement activities is the cost of staff. Various studies have concluded that the construction costs of a new law enforcement facility will equal less than 10 percent of the combined cost of operations and construction over a 30-year life cycle. Of the 90 percent for nonconstruction costs, more than two-thirds will be the cost of staff. Designing a facility that supports efficient operations and provides effective support for staff during all operational modes makes good sense.

In practical terms, this means that police facilities should be designed with reasonable office and staff areas, with appropriate and careful use of natural (controlled) skylight, comfortable work areas, and appropriate support equipment and storage areas (lockers, break areas, and the like).

See Chapter 11, "Security Systems," for more information on effective visible and unobtrusive design measures for ensuring the security of a site.

▶ *Deputy chief's office, Middletown Police Headquarters, Middletown, Connecticut. Jeter Cook Jepson Architects, Inc. Photo: Woodruff / Brown Photography.*

Building Organization

A number of different physical models for law enforcement facilities have emerged over the years. In general, most facilities have a need for:

- A controlled public access area
- An administration area (designed for public access and interface)
- A central core of support areas (conference, training, and other areas)
- Functional team areas, which are treated as related but separate "destinations" within the building, each with specific and unique requirements based on functional needs

Separate functions housed in the building often are provided with specific and unique work areas and environments. For example, patrol areas are frequently separated from investigation areas, and each area is designed to provide appropriate spaces and access to support its respective operations. Patrol areas, including staff lockers, briefing/roll call, report writing,

and administration areas, are often provided with direct access to vehicle areas. Investigations areas require controlled access to public areas of the facility and provisions for discrete access for confidential interviews and undercover staff and informants. Both require access to evidence check-in and storage areas, and some staff areas (conference, training, and locker/shower/physical training areas) can and often should be shared by various staff.

The Building Exterior

The building's design and orientation should provide employees with light and views, with minimum adverse effects on shading, heat gain, and operational costs. Exterior wall designs should consider wind, sun, and water. Suitable cladding materials include limestone, granite, precast concrete, and face brick. The use of curtain wall or other all-glass glazing systems is appropriate for public entrance areas or other featured areas.

◀ Public entrance. Middletown Police Headquarters, Middletown, Connecticut. Jeter Cook Jepson Architects, Inc. Photo: Woodruff / Brown Photography.

▼ Elevation with street-level retail space beneath awnings and law enforcement functions above. Middletown Police Headquarters, Middletown, Connecticut. Jeter Cook Jepson Architects, Inc. Photo: Woodruff / Brown Photography.

Exterior windows and doors should be distributed to maximize views and minimize negative heat gain, with appropriate shading systems accounting for sun angles, shadows, and glare from nearby buildings. Main entry doors should be of excellent quality and appearance and designed for heavy use. Balanced-type doors or doors with concealed automatic swing-type closers should be provided for the handicapped-accessible route into the building. Clear glazing should be used in the glass wall and entrance doors of a lobby, with windows and entrance doors designed with insulated glazing (shatter-resistant and/or special security) in accordance with good design and security practices.

Roofing materials should be designed to provide an excellent appearance and low maintenance, and an area of the roof should be planned for current and future placement of antennae and microwave dishes. Various roofing materials may be used, but any roofing system should have designated walkways for the required routine maintenance of the roof and the items located on the roof.

Interior Design

The interior design of the main public entry areas (lobbies, etc.) should be consistent with the exterior design in the use of materials, detailing, and proportioning. Color schemes should be conservative and muted, as the facilities will be required to provide many years of service. Entry areas should be attractive and durable, while providing a sense of accessibility through the orientation and openness of the lobbies.

There are a variety of consoles used in a law enforcement facility. All console positions should be designed with appropriate clearances to all sides to allow quick access and easy repair and replacement of equipment as necessary. Specific design requirements for console positions and communications centers include provisions for display of visual maps detailing service areas, officer status indicators, written procedures, duty rosters, and phone numbers. Typically, communications centers are designed as computer centers, with access flooring and temperature and lighting controls. Wherever possible, provisions should be made for natural light and views in this area (that are controlled and secure) to promote a sense of time and provide relief during breaks.

Design requirements for a communications center include special provisions for uninterruptible power for equipment, lighting, and dedicated mechanical (heating, ventilating, and air-conditioning, HVAC) systems and self-contained rest rooms and break areas. The communications center should be designed to remain in operation through virtually any emergency, including natural disasters and unexpected and rare events. The center must be safe and secure, and access to the center should be limited. To accomodate internal staff, however, such areas should be pleasant and designed to support alertness and reduce fatigue. Workstations should be comfortable and properly lit for computer monitor and status board viewing.

Security measures for a communications center should limit access to appropriate personnel, protect equipment and backup resources, and provide security for power

▶ ▶ *Plans, Middletown Police Headquarters, Middletown, Connecticut. Note lower level sally port and holding cells, and upper level operations space. Jeter Cook Jepson Architects.*

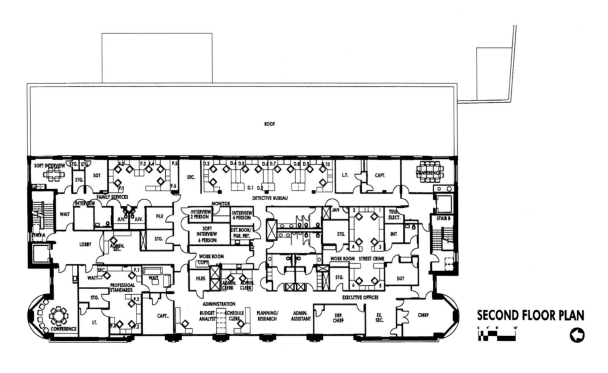

SECOND FLOOR PLAN

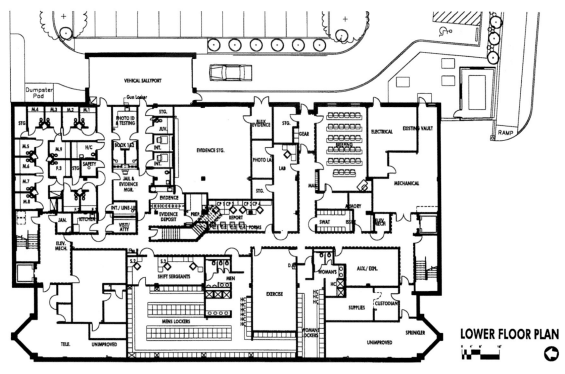

LOWER FLOOR PLAN

sources, transmission lines, and any satellite or antenna systems. Protective measures for the center will vary, but may include locating the center in a secure area of the facility and installing bullet-resistant glazing at public access areas.

Interior construction should meet specific functional requirements (acoustical performance, durability, ease of maintenance, and fire code or resistance requirements). Special attention should be given to construction and finishes in areas where there are large numbers of people, such as lobbies and entrances, to ensure high durability, long life, and ease of maintenance. Particular attention must be provided at corners, where abuse can be substantial and appearance is crucial.

Ceilings
Accessible suspended acoustical ceilings ensuring appropriate acoustical performance should be provided in most areas of the facility.

Walls
Painted or stained woodwork and wall coverings may be provided in special office and support areas, but painted gypsum wallboard or drywall with vinyl wall covering is provided in most office and general support areas. Materials and construction in prisoner holding and accessible areas are described in Chapter 11.

In general, special finishes are required in:

- Public areas, which should feature the use of durable permanent flooring. Ceiling heights should as great as possible. Appropriate directional and locational graphics, directories, departmental emblems, and display cases should be incorporated into the design.

- Conference rooms and areas, with appropriate special features and lighting.

- Rest rooms, which should be designed with ceramic wall tile on wet walls and vinyl wall coverings on other wall surfaces. All finishes and materials should be designed for durability, ease of maintenance, and water and chemical resistance.

- Storage and utility areas, which should be designed for low maintenance and high durability.

- Prisoner holding, detention, and processing areas, which typically should feature the use of glazed or epoxy-painted concrete masonry units (CMU) and lath and plaster ceilings (or other security ceilings). See Chapter 11, "Security Systems," for additional information on design features for prisoner holding and processing areas.

Flooring
Carpeting with a wood or rubber base is provided in most public and staff areas of the facility, with special flooring provided in several designated areas, including entrance and elevator lobbies, rest rooms, department storage and workrooms, food service and vending areas, evidence processing and storage areas, and prisoner processing and lockup facility areas.

Furniture
Workstations and furniture should be durable, of above-standard quality, well built, and designed for long and continuous operation. A number of chairs without arms should be selected for staff areas to accommodate staff members with weapons.

CHAPTER 3
ADULT DETENTION FACILITIES

The purpose of detention facilities is to provide secure detainment of prisoners remanded to the custody of the controlling official, typically the county sheriff. The goals are to provide for the secure and safe intake, processing, housing, and support needs of the detainees.

Unlike corrections, detention generally involves short-term periods of confinement. The average length of stay in county detention facilities in the United States is only a few days. Many detention facilities also provide housing for inmates who have been convicted of lower-level felonies or misdemeanors and sentenced to serve terms, typically of one year or less, but the majority of persons held are there for shorter periods.

This emphasis on short-term holding means that certain activities, notably visitation and escorted transfer to court, play a larger role in detention than in correctional facility planning and design. The U.S. courts have defined minimum levels of services, programs, and activities that must be delivered to provide constitutionally acceptable conditions of confinement. The conditions must not constitute "cruel or unusual" punishment. The local, state, national, and international standards that have been developed for detention facilities specify physical standards and operational requirements that affect all manner of activities. Such standards typically represent *minimums*.

The standards state:

Inmates must be housed in a facility where their constitutional rights and safety are ensured, and where they are protected from each other and from themselves.

Inmates must be observed, and regular communication must occur between staff and inmates.

Staff must respond to inmate calls for assistance.

Inmates must be classified and separated.

Required inmate activities, services, and programs must be provided (medical, visitation, religious, exercise, and others).

Security systems and procedures must be implemented in jails.

Female inmates must be appropriately processed and supervised.

Electronic surveillance equipment must be monitored.

Effective emergency response plans must be developed and implemented.

Principal standards include the *American Correctional Association (ACA) Standards for Adult Local Detention Facilities* (3d ed.), by the ACA in cooperation with the Commission on Accreditation for Corrections.

PROGRAM REQUIREMENTS

The primary focus of a detention facility is the housing of prisoners and the provision of services and programs that keep them properly fed, clothed and cared for medically, if need be, while in custody.

The greatest activity involves the intake, transfer, and release functions. The ability to handle a steady or sporadic influx of persons in custody, and to transport them to and from courts and other facilities, is a distinguishing feature of detention facilities.

Frequently, detention facilities in the United States feature integrated services with sheriff's department operations (administration, patrol, community ser-

▲ Milwaukee County Jail and Criminal Justice Facility, Milwaukee, Wisconsin. Venture Architects. Photographer: Howard Kaplan, HNK Architectural Photography, Inc.

vices, emergency services, and investigations). Such operations, in turn, are sometimes located with or near a court. Detention and sheriff's department operations may be small or large. Most jails house fewer than 100 prisoners and are centralized within a county (or geographic region) with local autonomy and political support. Each facility tends to have unique requirements and needs.

KEY OPERATIONAL AND ORGANIZATIONAL CONCEPTS

Three considerations influence the physical layout of a detention facility:

Classification and separation of prisoners

Type(s) of supervision methods

The facility's approach to the delivery of basic services and programs

Classification and Separation of Inmates

Detention facilities are required to accommodate a wide variety of detainees, including large groups, small groups, and special populations. ACA standards today specify that facilities should provide separate management of the following categories of inmates[1]:

Females and males

Other classes of detainees (witnesses, prisoners in civil cases)

Community custody inmates (work releases, weekenders, trustees)

Inmates with special problems (alcoholics, narcotics addicts, mentally disturbed persons, physically handicapped persons, persons with communicable diseases)

Inmates requiring disciplinary detention

Inmates requiring administrative segregation

Juveniles[1]

The classification process considers such factors as detainees' arrest status (violent offenses, drug- or alcohol-related charges), problems at time of arrest (intoxication, health problems, psychological or mental condition, need for medical treatment), and history of arrest, incarceration, or alcohol or drug abuse.

Classification plans address specific needs for separate housing of different types of prisoners. Providing physical separation of detainees from each other in both housing and service and pro-

gram areas is a design and operational necessity. Appropriate physical, sight, and sound separation should be ensured.

Small jails respond to the same variety of inmates and classifications as large ones. In small facilities, however, there may not be sufficient numbers of inmates in most classification categories to properly separate prisoners. One method of solving the problem is to create larger inmate populations by combining the needs of several jurisdictions into one larger multicounty or regional facility. This approach can create other problems, however, associated with transport and visitation across greater geographical distances.

Alternative Supervision Methods

ACA standards require correctional officer posts to be located in or immediately adjacent to inmate living areas, so as to permit officers to hear and respond promptly to emergencies. The assisting officer should be physically available or within sight or sound of the officer entering a unit. There are four basic approaches to supervising inmates. Of these, two require the constant presence of staff; the other two do not. Each has implications for how the elements of the facility may be configured.

Direct supervision

Jail staff are assigned within each housing unit and are in direct and constant contact with inmates. In this system, staff are expected to actively manage and supervise, not just watch and react. The staff is present within the housing unit at all times. In many facilities, direct supervision works in self-contained units, thereby reducing the need to combine units with shared control positions.

1. American Correctional Association, *Standards for Adult Local Detention Facilities,* 3d ed. (Lanham, Md.: American Correctional Association, 1991), p. 79 (3-ALDF-4B-03).

Direct supervision is regarded as the most desirable way to manage general population inmates. It may not be appropriate, however, for inmates requiring disciplinary separation. The direct supervision method can allow for merging some populations that might not otherwise be housed together. Placing staff within small pods for direct supervision and separation of prisoner groups may increase the staff-to-prisoner ratio.

Indirect supervision

Unit designs are based on the idea that remote and enclosed control centers are positioned with direct lines of sight to cells and activity areas. The housing control center is constantly occupied by detention staff, who maintain continuous but remote observation of the inmates. Remote surveillance designs can create sight line and acoustic problems when several housing pods or areas are supervised by a single post. To handle these problems, the housing clusters for different classifications of prisoners should be isolated from each other.

Intermittent supervision

Intermittent supervision designs assume that staff will observe housing units, typically, at 15- or 30-minute intervals.

▼ *Indirect supervision station in housing unit. Milwaukee County Jail and Criminal Justice Facility, Milwaukee, Wisconsin. Venture Architects. Photo: Howard Kaplan, HNK Architectural Photography, Inc.*

Units designed for intermittent surveillance (such as linear units) can be separated, inasmuch as there is no inherent requirement to group the housing around a control position. Units may be located across from each other, back to back, or next to each other in one common cell block area. While staff patrol and monitor the housing, the inmates are largely responsible for their own behavior.

However, according to the *Small Jail Design Guide,* "intermittently monitored facilities have greater operational problems in the areas of assaults, suicides, escape attempts, and damage."[2]

If intermittent surveillance units are used, the density of each housing area must be kept low and the prisoners posing security risks should be clearly separated from others. Intermittent surveillance may be a good approach for participants in work release programs, for example, but may not be appropriate for high-security-risk prisoners or for those held in administrative or disciplinary segregation housing.

Electronic surveillance audio/ video systems

Closed-circuit video equipment (CCVE) and audio surveillance systems are used to conduct remote surveillance of housing and activity areas in some facilities. Such equipment is effective only when staff are assigned and available to monitor it, and when other staff are available to respond when summoned.

An important question in the design of staff post positions for housing or supervision control is whether a post should be enclosed or left in an open counter-type workstation. Open counters can be versatile and allow freedom of movement to perform activities other than staffing the post. They are not effective, however, without support from Central Control, which should be designed as a secure, enclosed, 24-hour position. This position should have complete override capability on all security systems and full control of the perimeter of the prisoner area.

A challenge in detention facility design is to match classifications of inmates to preferred supervision approaches. Although some facilities and operations use one supervision approach for all inmates, it is not always feasible or recommended to use a single approach. Each method has advantages and disadvantages.

Prisoner Services and Programs

A major issue facing the designer involves the location of services and programs in relation to housing. There are two alternatives: Services and programs may be either centralized or decentralized.

If services and programs are centralized in the facility, prisoners must be moved there from the housing units. This approach entails extra measures for

---

2. Dennis A. Kimme, et al., *Small Jail Design Guide: A Planning and Design Resource for Local Facilities of up to 50 Beds* (Washington, D.C.: U.S. Department of Justice, Office of Justice Programs, National Institute of Corrections, 1988), p. 3–33. See also Kimme and Associates, Inc., *Jail Design Guide: A Resource for Small and Medium-Sized Jails* (Washington, D.C.: U.S. Department of Justice, Office of Justice Programs, National Institute of Corrections).

ADULT DETENTION FACILITIES

▶ *Aerial view, Curran-
Fromhold Correctional Facility,
Philadelphia, Pennsylvania.
DMJM Architects. Photo: Bo
Parker.*

▼ *Plan showing housing
unit pods across from
programs and services
areas. Curran-Fromhold
Correctional Facility,
Philadelphia, Pennsylvania.
DMJM Architects.*

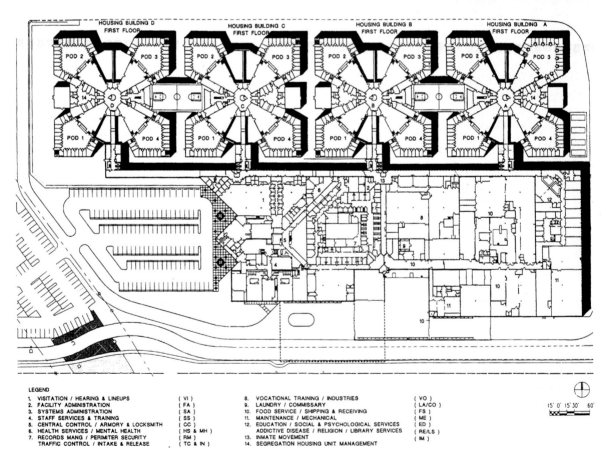

LEGEND

1. VISITATION / HEARING & LINEUPS	(VI)	8. VOCATIONAL TRAINING / INDUSTRIES	(VO)
2. FACILITY ADMINISTRATION	(FA)	9. LAUNDRY / COMMISSARY	(LA/CO)
3. SYSTEMS ADMINISTRATION	(SA)	10. FOOD SERVICE / SHIPPING & RECEIVING	(FS)
4. STAFF SERVICES & TRAINING	(SS)	11. MAINTENANCE / MECHANICAL	(ME)
5. CENTRAL CONTROL / ARMORY & LOCKSMITH	(CC)	12. EDUCATION / SOCIAL & PSYCHOLOGICAL SERVICES	(ED)
6. HEALTH SERVICES / MENTAL HEALTH	(HS & MH)	ADDICTIVE DISEASE / RELIGION / LIBRARY SERVICES	(RE/LS)
7. RECORDS MANG / PERIMITER SECURITY	(RM)	13. INMATE MOVEMENT	(IM)
TRAFFIC CONTROL / INTAKE & RELEASE	(TC & IN)	14. SEGREGATION HOUSING UNIT MANAGEMENT	

15' 0' 15' 30'   60'

security and control by detention staff while moving prisoners and, once they are at the service or program location, may increase the potential for conflict between different classifications of prisoners.

In recent decades, there has been growing interest in facility designs that minimize the movement of prisoners by providing decentralized services and programs in spaces located inside the housing units or directly adjacent to them. This approach allows the staff who supervise the housing areas to see and control other activities. It delivers services to the inmates, rather than delivering inmates to the services.

The decentralized approach can reduce the problems associated with prisoner movement and allow the designer to increase space utilization and efficiency by locating service and program areas for shared use between housing units.

▼ Aerial view, Federal Detention Center, Sea Tac, Washington. NBBJ Group. Photo: Assassi Productions.

ADULT DETENTION FACILITIES

Section and plans showing vertical organization of housing above programs and services areas. Federal Detention Center, Sea Tac, Washington. NBBJ Group.

Northeast- Southwest Building Section

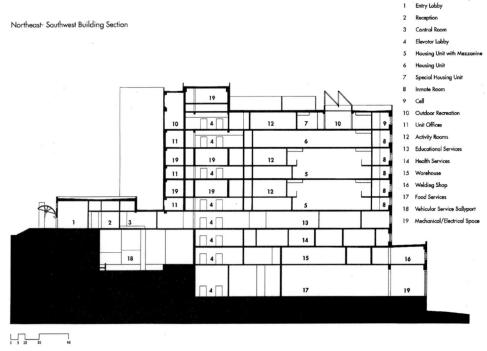

1	Entry Lobby
2	Reception
3	Control Room
4	Elevator Lobby
5	Housing Unit with Mezzanine
6	Housing Unit
7	Special Housing Unit
8	Inmate Room
9	Cell
10	Outdoor Recreation
11	Unit Offices
12	Activity Rooms
13	Educational Services
14	Health Services
15	Warehouse
16	Welding Shop
17	Food Services
18	Vehicular Service Sallyport
19	Mechanical/Electrical Space

Floor Plan - Level B

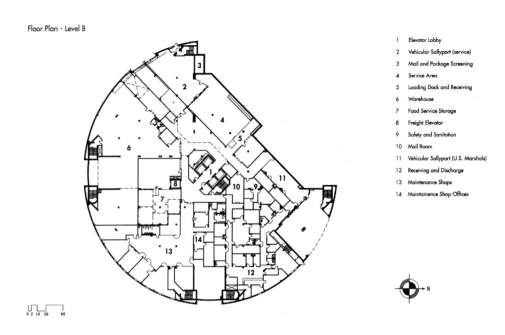

1	Elevator Lobby
2	Vehicular Sallyport (service)
3	Mail and Package Screening
4	Service Area
5	Loading Dock and Receiving
6	Warehouse
7	Food Service Storage
8	Freight Elevator
9	Safety and Sanitation
10	Mail Room
11	Vehicular Sallyport (U.S. Marshals)
12	Receiving and Discharge
13	Maintenance Shops
14	Maintainence Shop Offices

Floor Plan - Level 6

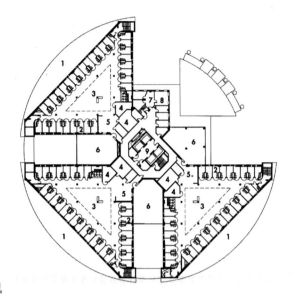

1	Typical Small General Hous Module
2	Typical Inmate Room
3	Dayroom
4	Activity Room
5	Food Preparation
6	Outdoor Recreation
7	Offices
8	Conference Room
9	Elevator Lobby

Floor Plan - Level 1

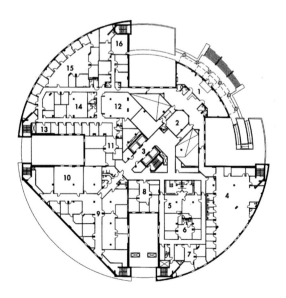

1	Entry Lobby
2	Control Center
3	Elevator Lobby
4	Visitation
5	Staff Assembly
6	Lieutenant's area
7	Associate Warden
8	Psychology
9	Education
10	Multi-use
11	Executive Offices
12	Hearing Room
13	Human Resources Management
14	Employee Development
15	Financial Management
16	Correctional Services

Services and programs that may be provided at the housing units include the following:

- Passive recreation (in dayrooms and multipurpose rooms adjacent to housing)
- Active recreation (in exercise areas, both indoor and outdoor, if located adjacent to housing units; these areas may be shared between two housing units)
- Educational programs (with activities conducted in classrooms and multi-purpose areas adjacent to housing)
- Program spaces for religious and general programs (in multipurpose rooms)
- Visitation (provided at the housing units in facilities designed with a discrete and separate circulation system for visitors, and increasingly provided by means of video)
- Food service (with meals prepared in a central kitchen and food delivered to the housing unit)
- Medical and mental health care services (including sick call and pill call visits, typically conducted by medical staff at the housing units to limit the movement of inmates through the facility and to reduce trips to the central medical area to those requiring special examinations, testing, treatment, or infirmary care)

AREAS AND SPACES

Central Control

The ACA Standards for Adult Local Detention Facilities require that each facility maintain a control center (Central Control). The standards specify that Central Control be staffed around the clock, that access to it be limited, and that it should monitor and take responsibility for inmate counts, key control, and coordination of the internal and external security network. The ACA standards note that the functions to be accommodated within Central Control include:

- Monitoring all security perimeter systems
- Control of and communication with people at all entries to, and exits from, the primary security perimeter
- Control of and communications with people at many key access points between various security zones within the facility
- Monitoring building systems and security/safety systems and equipment
- Handling facility control, monitoring shift changes and identification checks
- Communication with facility staff at all posts, whether fixed/stationary or moving

In small and mid-sized facilities, Central Control may function as a staffed supervision point for monitoring special holding or housing units or other processing, public, or inmate activity areas. In some facilities, it may be combined with the law enforcement dispatch function and may monitor or assist in public reception.

Central Control should be designed as its own security zone, with a security vestibule entry and security glazing into areas where direct monitoring by Central Control staff is anticipated. The security glazing is typically designed to withstand a 45-minute or greater attack. Pass-through openings should be provided for keys, packages, and paperwork, and heating, ventilating, and air-conditioning (HVAC) systems should be secured. All power, data, and telecommunication service to and from Central Control should be secured.

◀ *Control station, Milwaukee County Jail and Criminal Justice Facility, Milwaukee, Wisconsin. Venture Architects. Photo: Howard Kaplan, HNK Architectural Photography, Inc.*

Intake/Transfer/Release Area

The ACA standards for the intake/transfer/release (ITR) functions of a detention facility address numerous issues related to policy, procedures, operations, and spaces. The ITR area must accommodate five critical functions:

1. Reception and short-term holding of persons arrested by law enforcement personnel or at court.

2. Short-term holding and custody supervision pending notification of a decision to release (on bond, recognizance, transfer to other detention facility, or other terms). Holding areas within the ITR area may be used for 2 to 12 hours or more.

3. Admission processing of detainees (if a decision is made to hold a detainee) and movement to special or standard jail housing areas.

4. Handling court and other transfers (preparation, movement out of the jail, processing at return).

5. Processing of inmates released from the jail.

The ITR area of the facility must be designed to handle prisoners with a wide variety of classifications, needs, and attitudes, including males, females, and (at some times and in some locations) juveniles. These people may be passive or violent, first or repeat offenders, mentally disturbed, intoxicated, or a danger to themselves or others.

In addition, there are many nonsecurity staff and visitors who will be involved in various aspects of the ITR process, including attorneys, screening and interviewing staff, and medical and mental health staff. The key ITR spaces are described in the following paragraphs.

▶ ITR area, Milwaukee County Jail and Criminal Justice Facility, Milwaukee, Wisconsin. Venture Architects. Photo: Howard Kaplan, HNK Architectural Photography, Inc.

▲ ITR area, St. Louis County Justice Center, Clayton, Missouri. Sverdrup/Hellmuth Obata Kassabaum Architects. Photo: Timothy Hursley.

Vehicle sally port

The vehicle sally port is typically enclosed and provides a secure environment from which prisoners can be safely moved from transport vehicles into the ITR receiving area. This area should be designed to permit transport vehicles to drive through the space, rather than pull in and back out, and should be sized to accommodate one or more transport buses in larger detention facilities.

Testing areas

Sobriety and controlled substance testing areas may be provided; they should be related to the arrest and report writing area of the jail. These areas may be located outside the primary security perimeter of the reception area of the jail but adjacent to or within the VSP area. The area should be sized to accommodate testing equipment, storage of supplies and forms, and seating for the detainee and the arresting officer(s).

Booking area

In the booking area, detention/supervision staff conduct a brief examination of the detainee and make a decision regarding admission into the facility. After a decision is made to admit an arrestee, the booking process involves receiving and inventorying personal property, interviewing and recording personal information related to arrest data, criminal history, medical history, and other required information. Recent booking areas are being designed as open work areas with computer terminals and equipment, forms and file storage, writing surfaces, property receipt equipment, and required electronic control equipment.

Arrest writing area

A visitation area with individual rooms or booths may be provided, where detainees can be placed to permit staff to complete interviews and arrest reports. These rooms typically have security glazing and are situated to provide a direct line of sight from the booking desk.

Identification processing

Spaces in the admissions area are required for photographing and fingerprinting. In some facilities, a separate area is required for this function and the equipment required; in others, the equipment may be located at the booking counter. The specific technology and equipment used will influence the appropriate design of the area. Storage space is needed for equipment, supplies, and forms.

Holding areas

Temporary holding areas are needed in the ITR area. Typically, several types of holding areas may be provided:

Good-behavior casual seating areas may be provided for cooperative and low-custody-risk detainees, typically in open spaces directly observed from the booking desk.

Single-occupancy holding areas for special-custody detainees, including those who are violent or uncooperative, those who require medical isolation, and those who should be separated for their own protection or the protection of others.

Multiple-occupancy or multipurpose waiting space for temporary holding during movement of jail defendants for court transfers, or for temporary holding of groups arrested during mass arrests.

In large facilities, separate areas may be provided for males and females; in smaller facilities, shared/multipurpose areas may be provided. Holding and processing areas should be able to serve both male and female detainees.

Visiting areas

Both contact and noncontact visiting areas may be provided in the ITR area. These areas are used for attorney-client interviews, release interviews (with pretrial release staff), bond interviews (with bondspersons), and visits with family and friends as permitted by state statute or federal regulations. These areas should be visible from a staff position.

Telephones

Access to telephones with outside lines should be provided in the ITR area. Telephone access is provided in some facilities within the holding areas; in other facilities, telephone access may be provided only outside the waiting/holding areas. Some privacy should be provided for phone calls.

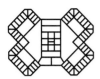

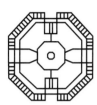

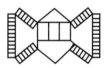

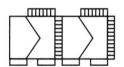

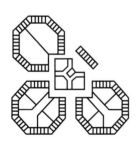

Admissions processing

After a decision is made to admit an individual, additional processing takes place as the prisoner showers, changes clothing, and undergoes a medical examination prior to entering the general population of the facility. Showering and clothing change areas should be private, but should allow communication and surveillance by appropriate staff.

Medical screening

The ITR area should include space for medical screening. Alternatively, medical screening for intake can be handled in a medical examination room if the medical area for the entire facility is located immediately adjacent to the ITR area.

Supplies and property storage

Storage space should be provided for standard jail uniforms and bedding supplies, and the prisoners' personal clothing and valuables should be stored in lockable cabinets, vaults, or drawers.

Housing

Housing areas typically comprise half of the total square footage of the facility. They support inmate sleeping, passive activities, and personal hygiene. Depending on the nature of the facility and the supervision plan, the housing areas may include eating, laundry/cleaning, physical and general recreation, as well as educational, library, and visitation spaces.

In many facilities, the variety of different housing environments provided for

◀ *Six of the many variations in detention housing units. Each of these units is characterized by exterior cells around dayroom spaces, typically with program and other support areas (recreation, multipurpose, and visitation) at the housing units. From top: butterfly, octagon, bow tie, nested "L" units, linked octagons, and quad "L" units.*

groups of prisoners affects the basic organization of the units; the amount of access to natural light and views; the selection of fixtures, furnishings, and equipment; and the materials used in constructing the units.

Housing unit flexibility

To accommodate changes and small populations, some or all housing units may be designed as swing units that can serve more than one inmate classification group and handle special populations on an as-needed basis. Flexibility is also achieved by having housing units or pods with physical, sight, and sound separation from each other. Each unit typically consists of single-occupancy cells and the required dayrooms, showers, and support spaces.

General housing

General housing areas are designed for prisoners who do not have special needs. In most facilities, general population housing is designed to accommodate adult males (ages 18 and above) and, in large facilities, may include adult females (housed together but separate from adult males). General population status may include both pretrial detainees and sentenced inmates, and housing of more than one security classification may be provided.

The units typically consist of dayroom space, with single-occupancy cells facing the dayroom. This configuration permits a clear view of the dayroom interiors and cell fronts from the staff surveillance station. Each cell includes a sleeping area with a bunk, desk and stool, toilet, sink, mirror, shelf, and clothing hook.

Each cell has access to natural light, either directly from the outside or "borrowed" from another space through a

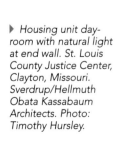

▲ Housing unit dayroom with direct supervision station. Milwaukee County Jail and Criminal Justice Facility, Milwaukee, Wisconsin. Venture Architects. Photo: Howard Kaplan, HNK Architectural Photography, Inc.

▶ Housing unit dayroom with natural light at end wall. St. Louis County Justice Center, Clayton, Missouri. Sverdrup/Hellmuth Obata Kassabaum Architects. Photo: Timothy Hursley.

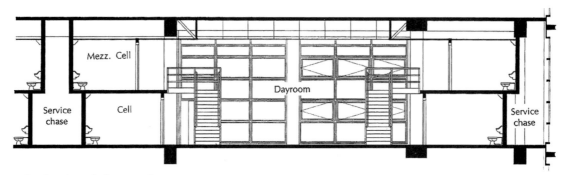

▲ Section through dayroom, St. Louis County Justice Center, Clayton, Missouri. Sverdrup/Hellmuth Obata Kassabaum Architects.

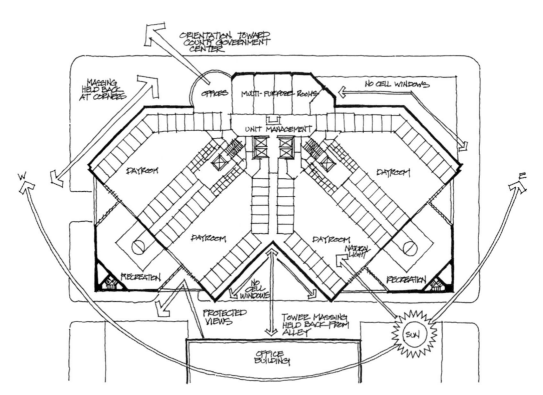

▲ Concept drawing of dayroom relationship to natural light. St. Louis County Justice Center, Clayton, Missouri. Sverdrup/Hellmuth Obata Kassabaum Architects.

security window in the cell door. Security windows and frames are used where windows are positioned within the reach of inmates. Windows out of the view of security staff should be out of the reach of inmates. Translucent glazing is frequently used in facilities where views must be controlled.

Dayrooms should be visually and acoustically separated from each other. Furnishings in each dayroom include tables and seats, one or more television sets, telephones for inmate calls, and an intercom for staff communication when direct supervision is not provided. Showers and toilets are directly accessible from the dayroom.

Housing units frequently have cells stacked on two levels, with a mezzanine walkway that preserves a good line of sight or view angles for supervision staff. Open risers are provided to allow a view behind a staircase, and mezzanine-level railings are designed to allow views through the railing. Designing for sight lines may require a raised staff position. Windows should be positioned to reduce the potential for glare in the supervising officer's line of sight.

Single versus multiple-occupancy cells

In some facilities, prisoners are housed in multiple-occupancy settings (double-occupancy cells, dormitories, etc.). National standards, policy, and opinion agree that this practice must be carefully controlled, and that it may be inappropriate for many types of detainees.

Multiple-occupancy space is less flexible and reduces the ability to subdivide the population into distinct groups. It also limits the ability to reduce night shift staffing and can impede the ability of staff to lock down housing in response to

Typical single occupant cell, Dickerson detention facility, Hamtramck, Michigan. Hellmuth Obata Kassabaum Architects. Photo: Rick Birger.

Typical double-occupancy cell. St. Louis County Justice Center, Clayton, Missouri. Sverdrup/Hellmuth Obata Kassabaum Architects. Photo: Timothy Hursley.

emergencies. Single-occupancy cells increase flexibility and provide inmates freedom from assault by others during lockdown periods, when staff supervision and surveillance are normally reduced.

Special housing

Special housing areas are provided for prisoners who require special medical or psychiatric attention, prisoners who require unique or high levels of observation (detoxification holding, suicide watch, or holding for the mentally disturbed), prisoners who are in administrative or disciplinary segregation, prisoners in protective custody, work release prisoners, or juveniles bound over to adult court.

ACA standards require that special segregation housing approximate the same living conditions as general housing. In addition, segregation cells/rooms are required to permit the inmates assigned to them to converse with and be observed by staff members.

Inmate Services

Food service

ACA and other standards and codes address food service operations in detention facilities. Food preparation and delivery can occur in various ways. Some facilities rely on outside food service providers. The use of outside vendors does not eliminate the need for a backup kitchen that can prepare meals on-site.

Food preparation activities are generally centralized. There are a range of options for dining. In centralized facilities, prisoners are moved to a central cafeteria(s) with food service lines. More frequently, food is moved from the central preparation area to dining or dayroom areas in or near housing units.

Laundry

ACA and state standards throughout the United States provide for regular laundering and exchange of bedding, clothing, linens, and towels. Laundry services in many facilities are staffed by prisoners working under staff supervision and control. Laundry areas should be sized for the basic functions and equipment involved in collection of soiled items, sorting, washing, drying, folding, and redistribution. Laundry service areas may be centralized or distributed in the housing units.

Medical/mental health services

ACA standards outline requirements for health care services in detention facilities, noting that spaces should be provided where inmates can be treated in private. The National Commission on Correctional Health Care also outlines standards in its *Standards for Health Care Services in Jails.*

Health care spaces can range from a small medical area with an examination room, medications storage area, and physician office, to a large area designed for outpatient and infirmary care. Staff offices and space for medical records and equipment storage are also necessary.

Customary services include the following:

Alcohol and drug detoxification

Initial and detailed medical screening at intake and admission to the facility

Routine physical examinations and testing for infectious diseases

Dispensing medicine

Medical isolation and inpatient care, when required

Emergency dental care

Medical diets

Mental health examinations, counseling, and short-term care for disturbed individuals

Inmate Programs

The design of detention facilities involves planning for the full day of both structured and unstructured time for all prisoners. Necessary daily activities (sleeping, eating, personal hygiene) take approximately 10 hours a day, leaving each prisoner 14 hours of nonprogrammed time to fill.

The challenge of providing meaningful out-of-cell activity is complicated by the short length of stay on average. This limits structured education programs to only a few days in many cases.

The courts have ruled that prisoners must be provided access to certain programs and services, including access to law library resources and religious services. ACA standards go further, calling for programs that include social services, religious services, recreation, and leisure-time activities.

Programs frequently provided in U.S. detention facilities include the following:

Religious programs and services

Educational programs

Access to law library resources

Recreational library access

Individual and group counseling

Passive recreational activities

▼ Medical unit, Milwaukee County Jail and Criminal Justice Facility, Milwaukee, Wisconsin. Venture Architects. Photo: Howard Kaplan, HNK Architectural Photography, Inc.

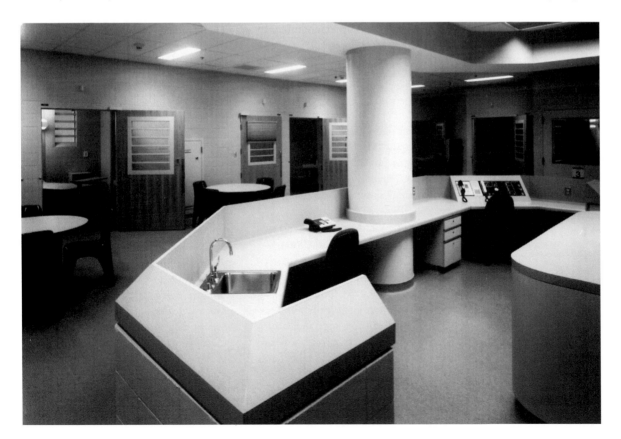

These programs typically take place in flexible, multipurpose, small and large group assembly spaces that are under continuous observation from a staff post.

Many facilities tap community resources to provide programs and services cost-effectively. Where outside professionals are involved in programs, the facility design should direct them through secure vestibule entries and metal detectors with X-ray units for packages prior to entry inside the secure perimeter. It is essential to provide safety for public participants in the programs and services of a detention facility.

To improve staffing efficiency and permit variation in the schedule for inmates sentenced to serve time, some jails bring inmates of different classifications together for various programs and services. In some facilities, adult males of minimum or medium security classification participate in religious or group counseling programs with adult female prisoners.

Recreation/exercise

National standards and guidelines call for the provision of recreational opportunities and equipment, including physical exercise for all inmates. Outdoor exercise is often required when weather permits. Minimum standards specify that 15 sq ft per inmate should be provided for outdoor exercise areas, and not less than 1,000 sq ft of unencumbered space.

Typical outdoor activities include walking, calisthenics, weight lifting, basketball, and volleyball. In large facilities, indoor spaces may accommodate these activities and others, such as table tennis, pool, and fusball.

Indoor and outdoor activity areas may be located adjacent to housing units. This approach allows inmates to exercise under the supervision of housing unit staff, thereby reducing the need for additional staff to supervise recreation. Areas of this type can also provide opportunities for natural light and ventilation into the dayrooms. This arrangement limits the number of inmates who are allowed to mix together during recreation.

In facilities that choose to centralize recreational and exercise activity areas, the areas can be sized for larger groups.

Visitation

The courts have upheld the importance of providing access to a wide range of visitors, including family, friends, religious counselors, and the news media staff. This activity involves bringing inmates to the edge of a security zone, requiring that visiting areas be designed to provide security, clear visibility and lines of sight for supervising staff, and yet appropriate privacy.

Noncontact visiting areas are generally provided for visits with family and friends. The areas designed for such visits provide visibility but are acoustically separated. Communication from the public side to the inmate side is allowed by means of through-window or through-wall sound ports or by the use of telephone-type handsets and wiring. In recent years, a system of noncontact visiting has been developed that uses CCVE equipment for video visitation.

Limited-contact visiting areas utilize welded wire screens or meshes and are generally reserved for attorney-client or similar visits.

Full-contact visiting, whereby prisoners are allowed direct and full contact with visitors, is generally reserved for attorney-client and official visits (with investigators, professional counseling staff, etc.). Visits involving nonofficial visitors may require

screening of the visitor prior to the visit (weapons or contraband screening) and screening of the prisoner after the visit.

Commissary
Many state standards require that prisoners be allowed to purchase discretionary items not provided by the facility. There may be a commissary that provides personal items over and above those required for personal hygiene.

Administrative and Support Areas
See Chapter 2, "Law Enforcement. Facilities."

SITE SELECTION
The selection of a site for a detention facility can be a complicated and often political process, but it is critical to the success of a project. The criteria include soil conditions, topography, and the avail-

ability of utilities. Issues of accessibility, size and capacity for expansion, context, and relationship to co-located or other justice facilities are also key.

Site Access
The site must be capable of handling food service/supply deliveries; staff access and parking; visitor access (public and/or official); in-custody transport access and delivery; provisions for work release/periodic inmates; emergencies; service (mechanical repair, equipment replacement); and access for other agencies in the facility.

Site Size and Expansion
More building area is required today than in the past because of increases in space per bed, larger program and support areas, and increased parking.

▲ Noncontact visitation booths. St. Louis County Justice Center, Clayton, Missouri. Sverdrup/Hellmuth Obata Kassabaum Architects. Photo: Timothy Hursley.

▶ Aerial view, St. Louis County Justice Center, Clayton, Missouri. Sverdrup/Hellmuth Obata Kassabaum Architects. Photo: Timothy Hursley.

▼ Aerial view, Milwaukee County Jail and Criminal Justice Facility, Milwaukee, Wisconsin. Venture Architects. Photo: Robert McCoy.

Exterior surface or structured parking can be calculated at 325–400 sq ft per car. Parking should be provided for staff, family/personal visitors, volunteers, service people, officials, and arresting officers. Multiple parking areas with separate circulation, access, and security are typically necessary.

The site must be able to accommodate building expansion. Options for expanding the facility itself include internal modification (fitting out shell areas that are built-in to the original building in anticipation of future growth), new additions (horizontal expansion onto adjacent site areas, already owned or acquired in future), and vertical expansion. Outdoor spaces can also grow to require more ground area if exercise yards or emergency egress/places of refuge, for example, are enlarged in the future.

Relationship to Surroundings

The fitness of a site is also determined in part by the appropriateness of its location relative to the other buildings nearby. Governmental, commercial, or industrial zones, or semirural areas, often provide the best sites. The facility should not be sited near a school, a church, or a residential or public recreational area such as a park or playground.

Relationship to Other Justice Facilities

A distinguishing feature of jails is often their proximity to court and/or law enforcement facilities. Detention can be co-located with these other functions, and there may be a mix of old and new construction on sites that were selected

and developed many years ago. The site selection process can therefore entail decisions about the continued use or demolition of other buildings.

When the detention facility is remote from the courts and the sheriff's department, the transport of prisoners and their supervision en route must be anticipated. The site selection process must consider the distances involved in prisoner transport, as well as the area required to ensure safe handling at destination points.

Site Design

The control of all sight lines and possibilities for physical contact within the facility, or across its perimeter to adjoining areas, is a priority of site design. Outdoor recreation spaces at ground level and higher must be secure against potential escape and screened from off-site views by solid walls, berms, fencing, or other visual buffers.

Walled site perimeter systems that are designed with aesthetics in mind are especially important when the facility is next to other public buildings or community areas. Where fences are used and visible to the community, single-arched fences and nonclimbable mesh systems are often chosen as an alternative to the razor-ribbon systems.

Other undesirable views between the facility and areas outside it, or internally between inmates of different classifications, are handled by architectural elements working in concert with site conditions. Windows may be eliminated, for example, in favor of overhead skylights in designs that provide natural light without views. Or windows may be provided, but with reflective glass.

UNIQUE DESIGN CONCERNS

Detention facility design today supports the idea that the purpose of the facility is to hold, not punish, and that holding should occur only under humane conditions.

For the most part, detention facilities are located in communities and, historically, they have been located in or near the courthouse at the center of a community's activities. Many facilities continue to function in these places, providing a centralized point for intake and release, convenient access to courts and local attorneys, and an identifiable image for county law enforcement.

A large number of facilities have been built on the outskirts of communities where there is ample space for low- or mid-rise detention projects, as well as sufficient area for future expansion and added functions. Increased reliance on prisoner-transport vehicles is a feature of these facilities.

The funding source for a detention facility is typically the local community. There is thus great emphasis on what the community regards as appropriate design. Many of the professionals and volunteers involved in daily operations are local residents. In the past, some facilities have appeared hard and inaccessible and have expressed the idea of punishment. That image has changed. The role of detention today is to stimulate normal behavior and to create a positive presence in the community.

Design for Staff

Staff represent the single most expensive component of detention budgets. Studies indicate that construction costs for a new standards-compliant facility are approximately 10 percent of the total combined cost of operations and construction over a 30-year life cycle. Of the 90 percent for nonconstruction costs, more than two-thirds will be the cost of staff.

Staff work in the facility an average of more than 200 days a year, as compared with an average length of stay of 11 days for prisoners. Operations are conducted on a 24-hour, 7 days-per-week, 365-days-per-year basis. Same-sex staffing, whereby female staff supervise female prisoners and male staff supervise male prisoners, is customary. A 24-hour post requires approximately five staff members to operate the position over the course of the year.

In some cases, detention officer positions may involve low pay and high job stress. Prisoner supervision and handling are demanding. Job satisfaction is an important consideration. Detention facilities design should therefore pay special attention to good working environments for staff, including:

Private offices, well-designed workstations, and support areas, including break areas, lockers, showers, toilets, and training areas

Appropriate provisions for personal safety and security, through good support space and communications systems for backup

Appropriate environments and environmental controls, including access to windows and natural light in administrative and break areas, and the ability to adjust sound, light, heating/air-conditioning, and ventilation levels

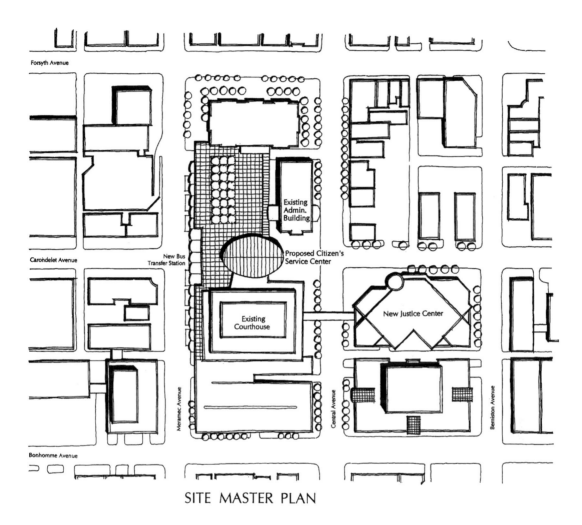

Forsyth Avenue

Carondelet Avenue

New Bus
Transfer Station

Existing
Admin.
Building

Proposed Citizen's
Service Center

Existing
Courthouse

New Justice Center

Meramec Avenue

Central Avenue

Bemiston Avenue

Bonhomme Avenue

SITE MASTER PLAN

Special attention should be given to the design of the Central Control post, because it is easy to overload this area. To support alertness, reduce stress and fatigue, and promote effective operations, workstations in Central Control should be ergonomically designed, with individual controls of environmental conditions (lighting, acoustics, temperature, and ventilation). A staff toilet and service unit should be provided.

Building Organization

Layout of major elements

The design of most detention facilities is driven by the relationship of housing to services, programs, and the intake/transfer/release (ITR) areas, as well as by the layout of the housing units themselves. Housing alternatives involving interior versus exterior cells, for example, have a major impact.

▲ Site plan showing relationship to existing court and administration buildings, St. Louis County Justice Center, Clayton, Missouri. Sverdrup/ Hellmuth Obata Kassabaum Architects.

61

Section and plans, St. Louis County Justice Center, Clayton, Missouri. Sverdrup/ Hellmuth Obata Kassabaum Architects.

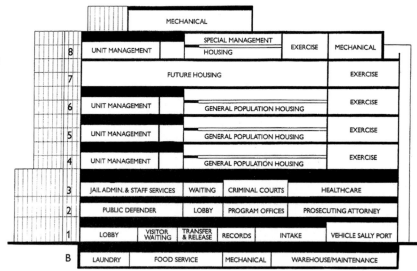

		MECHANICAL		
8	UNIT MANAGEMENT	SPECIAL MANAGEMENT HOUSING	EXERCISE	MECHANICAL
7	FUTURE HOUSING			EXERCISE
6	UNIT MANAGEMENT	GENERAL POPULATION HOUSING		EXERCISE
5	UNIT MANAGEMENT	GENERAL POPULATION HOUSING		EXERCISE
4	UNIT MANAGEMENT	GENERAL POPULATION HOUSING		EXERCISE
3	JAIL ADMIN. & STAFF SERVICES	WAITING	CRIMINAL COURTS	HEALTHCARE
2	PUBLIC DEFENDER	LOBBY	PROGRAM OFFICES	PROSECUTING ATTORNEY
1	LOBBY / VISITOR WAITING	TRANSFER & RELEASE / RECORDS	INTAKE	VEHICLE SALLY PORT
B	LAUNDRY	FOOD SERVICE	MECHANICAL	WAREHOUSE/MAINTENANCE

BUILDING SECTION

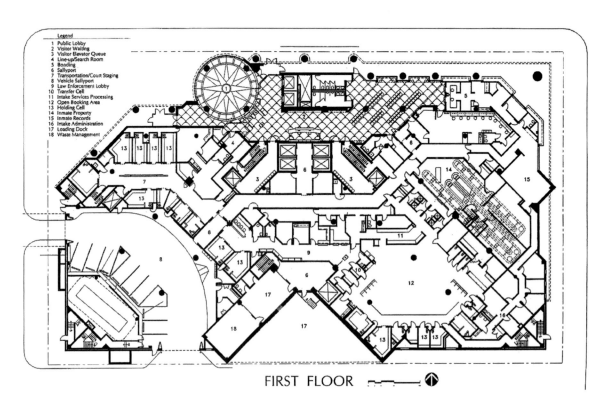

Legend
1 Public Lobby
2 Visitor Waiting
3 Visitor Elevator Queue
4 Line-up/Search Room
5 Bonding
6 Sallyport
7 Transportation/Court Staging
8 Vehicle Sallyport
9 Law Enforcement Lobby
10 Transfer Cell
11 Intake Services Processing
12 Open Booking Area
13 Holding Cell
14 Inmate Property
15 Inmate Records
16 Intake Administration
17 Loading Dock
18 Waste Management

FIRST FLOOR

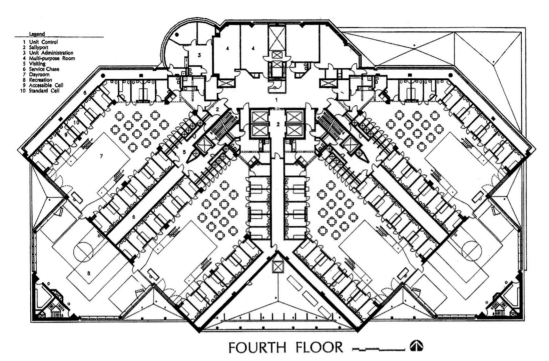

Legend
1 Unit Control
2 Sallyport
3 Unit Administration
4 Multi-purpose Room
5 Visiting
6 Service Chase
7 Dayroom
8 Recreation
9 Accessible Cell
10 Standard Cell

FOURTH FLOOR

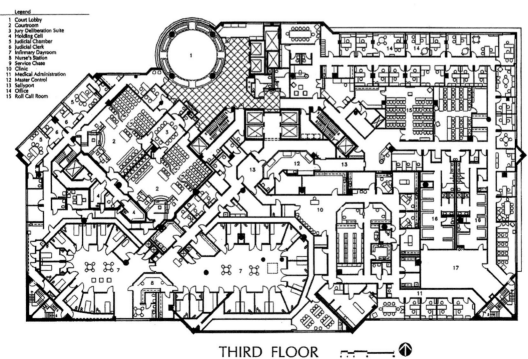

Legend
1 Court Lobby
2 Courtroom
3 Jury Deliberation Suite
4 Holding Cell
5 Judicial Chamber
6 Judicial Clerk
7 Infirmary Dayroom
8 Nurse's Station
9 Service Chase
10 Clinic
11 Medical Administration
12 Master Control
13 Sallyport
14 Office
15 Roll Call Room

THIRD FLOOR

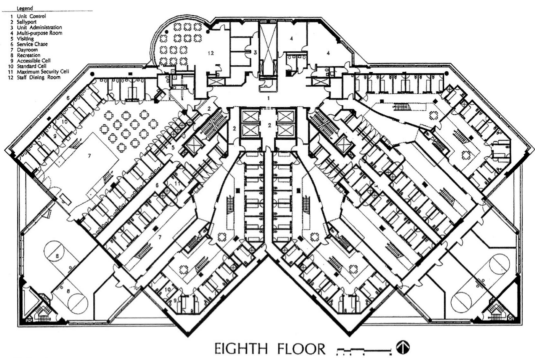

Legend
1 Unit Control
2 Sallyport
3 Unit Administration
4 Multi-purpose Room
5 Visiting
6 Service Chase
7 Dayroom
8 Recreation
9 Accessible Cell
10 Standard Cell
11 Maximum Security Cell
12 Staff Dining Room

EIGHTH FLOOR

▲ Plan, St. Louis County Justice Center, Clayton, Missouri. Sverdrup/ Hellmuth Obata Kassabaum Architects.

In urban areas and on tight sites, the administration and public areas of the facility are often located on an entry level, with the ITR functions on the same level or within one level above or below the public entry. Centralized support services may be located on these levels or on an intermediate level (Level 2 or 3). Inmate housing areas are typically stacked above these support functions. Critical relationships are maintained through the use of elevators and/or stairs. The ability to monitor movement on the elevators and stairs is a major design issue.

In suburban or more rural facilities, the housing areas and the administration, support, and ITR areas are located on the same level, but are distributed across a

site. They are linked horizontally, rather than vertically. Designs of this type for detention facilities may resemble correctional facility solutions, but their housing, visitation, and services/programs spaces are different.

Security

The organization of a detention facility is also driven by principles of design for security. A wide range of threats must be addressed, including the risk of assaults against staff or other prisoners, suicides, vandalism, the passage of contraband, and unauthorized intrusion or escape.

Security plans involve the integration of architecture, operations, and technology. Physical barriers are designed to complement specific staffing levels and supervision methods, and both are supported by technology-based security systems that are tailored to the individual project.

A number of standards address security design features and procedures. The American Correctional Association requires that:

The facility perimeter is controlled by appropriate means to provide that inmates remain within the perimeter and to prevent access by the general public without authorization (3-ALDF-2G-02).

Pedestrians and vehicles enter and leave at designated points in the perimeter. Safety vestibules and sally ports constitute the only breaches in the perimeter (3-ALDF-2G-03).

Establishing the security area

A three-dimensional barrier that encloses the security area, including all walls, ceilings, floors, and roofs contained in it, must be established. Every point of entry or access between the security perimeter and other areas should require movement through a vestibule—a sally port—consisting of interlocked doors that are opened one at a time.

Outside the perimeter of the security area, most facilities have the public entrance and lobby and administrative offices. Areas that are accessible to the public are at least partially controlled. All visitation areas are fully controlled, requiring screening and authorized admittance.

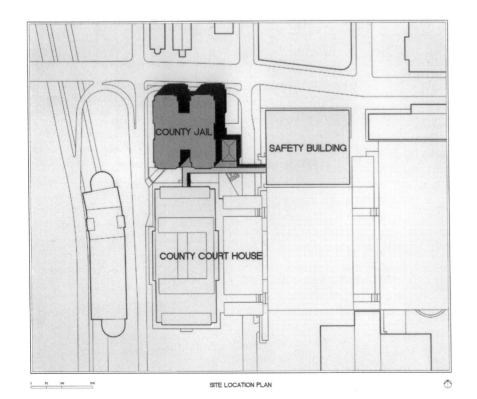

COUNTY JAIL

SAFETY BUILDING

COUNTY COURT HOUSE

◀ Site plan showing relationship to existing court and safety buildings. Milwaukee County Jail and Criminal Justice Facility, Milwaukee, Wisconsin. Venture Architects.

SITE LOCATION PLAN

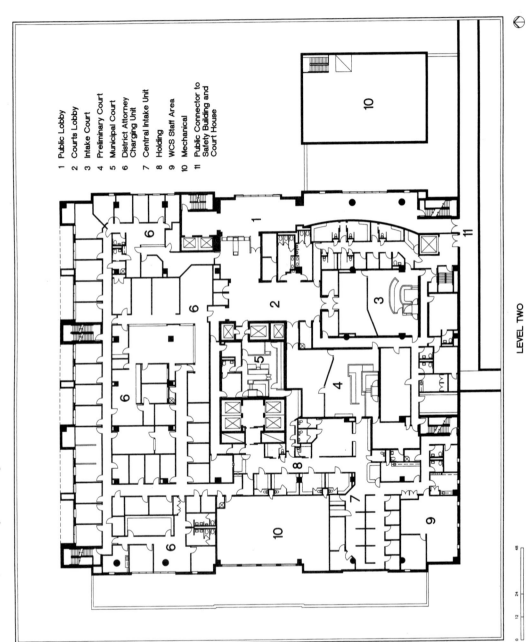

(Through page 69) Plans, Milwaukee County Jail and Criminal Justice Facility, Milwaukee, Wisconsin. Note sally port and intake areas on Level One, staff areas on Level Three, and variety of housing above. Venture Architects.

1 Public Lobby
2 Courts Lobby
3 Intake Court
4 Preliminary Court
5 Municipal Court
6 District Attorney Charging Unit
7 Central Intake Unit
8 Holding
9 WCS Staff Area
10 Mechanical
11 Public Connector to Safety Building and Court House

LEVEL TWO

MILWAUKEE COUNTY JAIL AND CRIMINAL JUSTICE FACILITY
MILWAUKEE, WISCONSIN

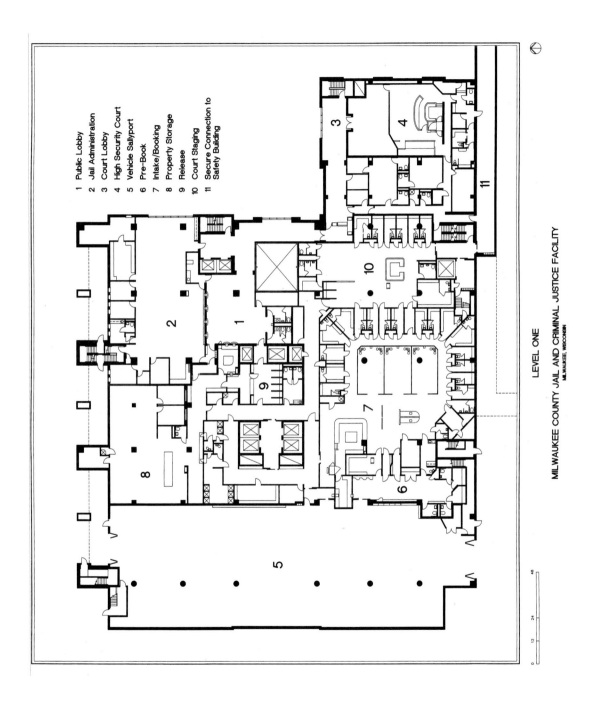

1 Public Lobby
2 Jail Administration
3 Court Lobby
4 High Security Court
5 Vehicle Sallyport
6 Pre-Book
7 Intake/Booking
8 Property Storage
9 Release
10 Court Staging
11 Secure Connection to Safety Building

LEVEL ONE

MILWAUKEE COUNTY JAIL AND CRIMINAL JUSTICE FACILITY

MILWAUKEE, WISCONSIN

0   12   24   48

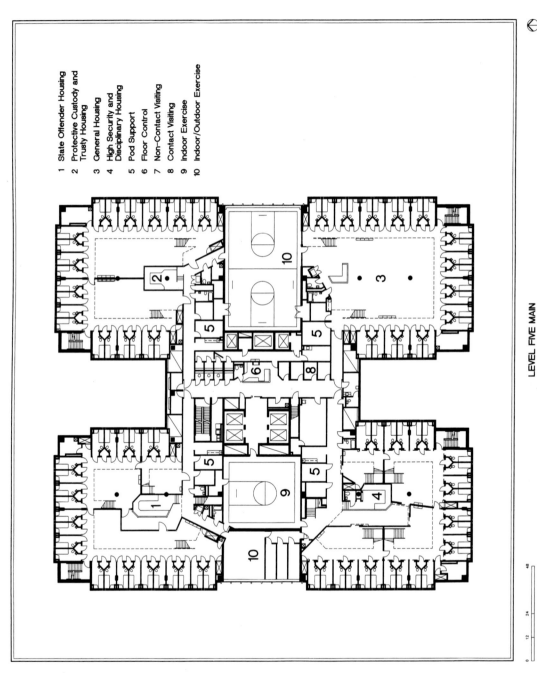

1 State Offender Housing
2 Protective Custody and Trusty Housing
3 General Housing
4 High Security and Disciplinary Housing
5 Pod Support
6 Floor Control
7 Non-Contact Visiting
8 Contact Visiting
9 Indoor Exercise
10 Indoor/Outdoor Exercise

LEVEL FIVE MAIN

MILWAUKEE COUNTY JAIL AND CRIMINAL JUSTICE FACILITY
MILWAUKEE, WISCONSIN
MARCH 1, 1990

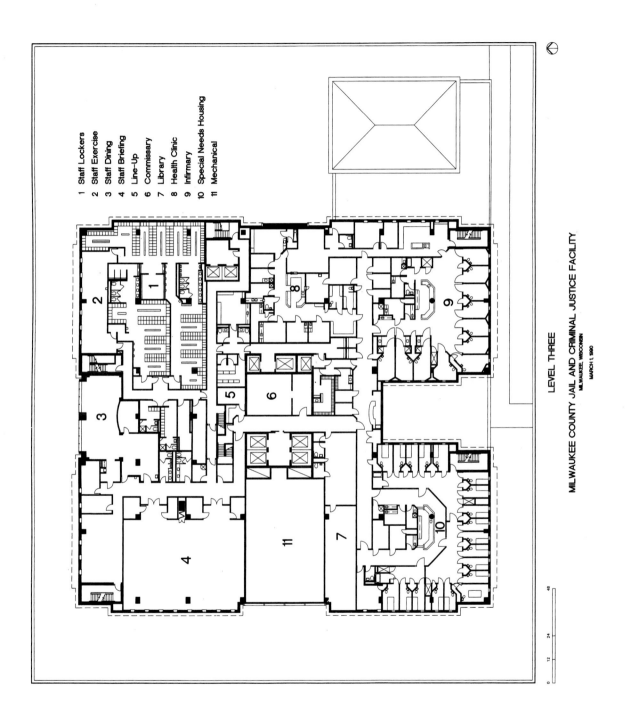

1 Staff Lockers
2 Staff Exercise
3 Staff Dining
4 Staff Briefing
5 Line-Up
6 Commissary
7 Library
8 Health Clinic
9 Infirmary
10 Special Needs Housing
11 Mechanical

LEVEL THREE

MILWAUKEE COUNTY JAIL AND CRIMINAL JUSTICE FACILITY

MILWAUKEE, WISCONSIN

MARCH 1, 1990

0   12   24   48

Inside the security perimeter are several security zones. Each zone exists within the overall security envelope, but is treated as a separate area. These internal zones may coincide with fire and smoke containment zones, and they typically correspond to specific separation and segregation requirements in the facility. The following are examples of these internal security zones:

Central Control

Each separate designated housing area

Special and female housing areas

Program areas and support service areas

Visiting areas

Where these zones are adjacent or overlap, the most stringent standards for design and construction should be applied to preserve the integrity of each zone's security.

The Building Exterior

Detention facilities are designed either as freestanding or as part of a governmental complex. When part of a complex, they are associated with courts, sheriff's department administration buildings or other law enforcement facilities, or other government functions on a shared site.

The location of the facility has a major impact on its aesthetics and design features. When it is developed as a stand-alone facility, the image conveyed is often one of function and economy. If it is part of a larger complex, the facility may be less likely to have an independent architectural identity. If co-located with other justice operations, the detention component may be designed to be as visually integral or subordinate to other buildings as possible. Similar materials, colors, and forms are used to match other facilities.

Mid- or high-rise facilities in downtown urban areas are generally designed to blend with the particular context, matching materials, colors, and massing insofar as possible. Where inmate cells are located on the exterior of housing units, narrow (5 in. or less) security windows or paired windows are frequently used. The integration of these windows on each level with the exterior material provides a distinctive design pattern that is typical of many projects. Several recent projects have incorporated larger openings into dayrooms, creating exterior designs that more closely resemble other urban and civic buildings.

Many detention facilities rely on the exterior walls, rather than fences, to serve as the security perimeter for the facility and site. Greater attention to aesthetics is necessary in these cases. There may be political pressure to develop designs that are unobtrusive and that do not detract from the surrounding neighborhood or urban area. The aesthetic goal is to achieve a normal appearance while ensuring that all openings along the security perimeter are locked, monitored, and fastened with security-type fasteners.

Regardless of the exterior design, detention facilities should be treated as restricted-access facilities. They should limit, control, and monitor access on all sides, including the walls, the site perimeter within 50 ft, and all roof areas.

Exterior cladding materials include masonry, stone, and concrete, designed for durability and permanence. Use of metal panels is typically limited. Exterior wall designs should incorporate planning for wind, water, and sunlight protection.

Exterior doors and windows should be

▶ *Entrance elevation, St. Louis County Justice Center, Clayton, Missouri. Sverdrup/Hellmuth Obata Kassabaum Architects. Photo: Timothy Hursley.*

▼ *Entrance elevation, Federal Detention Center, Sea Tac, Washington. NBBJ Group. Photo: Assassi Productions.*

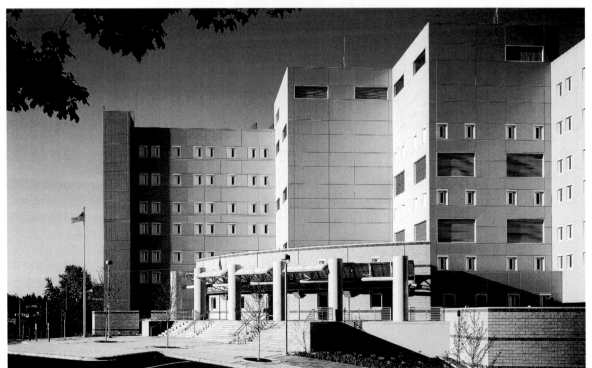

▲ *Secure exterior cladding, Federal Detention Center, Sea Tac, Washington. NBBJ Group. Photo: Assassi Productions.*

clear glazing at entrance lobby walls and entrance doors. Although public areas not within the security perimeter may be designed with insulated, shatter-resistant glazing, security attack–rated glazing is typically provided at control centers, in accordance with good security practice.

Roofing designs and materials should be developed to reduce access points, present an appropriate appearance, provide low maintenance, and minimize areas that can be used for concealment or that block visibility. Various roofing materials may be used, but any roofing system should have designated walkways for required routine maintenance of the roof and items located on the roof.

Interior Design

The major goals of interior design are to establish physical, sight, and sound separation and to ensure that circulation paths within the facility are clear, efficient, and safe.

Physical separation

Cell and dayroom layouts in housing units are designed to separate males and females, as well as different classifications of prisoners of the same gender. See Chapter 11, "Security Systems," for a discussion of construction materials and methods used to provide security.

Maintaining separation can be more complicated in areas where programs and services are provided, however. Although various classifications of prisoners are separated in housing units, they may participate jointly in counseling or educational programs or may wait in common areas for medical examinations, for example. The design of these areas must preserve unobstructed lines of sight for supervisory staff without allowing crowding or concealment.

designed to be compatible with the security and functional requirements of the interior spaces. Main entry areas and doors must be durable, of high quality, and secure in all seasons and weather conditions. Doors must be designed to comply with building code and fire egress requirements. All pathways from the exterior to public areas of the interior must comply with accessibility code requirements.

The need for a clear line of sight from interior Control Centers to public spaces and parking areas frequently requires

Ensuring separation in the ITR area is critical, because this area serves as the focus of all short-term holds (all classifications of males, females, and juveniles), daily transfers to other facilities and court, and all releases. This center of activity also involves processes that require privacy and confidentiality, including attorney-client and release program interviews, telephone conversations, identification checks, showers, and clothing exchanges.

In large facilities, there is often complete physical separation of ITR areas for males and females. In smaller facilities, separation may be accomplished through scheduling different groups at different times and by separating the intake/short-term holding areas from the related processing.

The ITR area should be open and businesslike. Secure spaces should be provided for prisoners who are uncooperative, but the design of the area overall should attempt to reduce tension and establish a calm, orderly and secure environment that reinforces good behavior.

Sight and sound separation

Interior design for security also requires control of sight lines and sound to ensure privacy, prevent harassment, reduce undesirable communication, and cut the risk of disturbances between groups. Attention to the sight and sound problem is central to detention facility design. See Chapter 8, "Lighting and Acoustics."

Sounds to be controlled include speech (conversation or shouting), impact sounds (banging or tapping), and sounds created by television sets and radios. Sound transmission between cells or housing pods should be controlled through the use of solid construction

instead of bars. In some cases, total sound separation may be achieved only by isolating particular areas.

Sound separation for most airborne sounds (shouting, conversation, and equipment-generated sounds) can be controlled by acoustically absorbing as much sound as possible within an area and by providing solid, insulated partitions between adjacent areas. This type of design requires heavy partitions and careful detailing of door and other openings where sound can be transmitted directly between housing areas or through shared spaces (such as corridors or shared security vestibules). Sound separation for structure-borne sounds (banging, tapping, etc.) should be reduced through elimination of common ductwork, plenums, electrical outlets, and structural members between areas.

Views afforded to prisoners should be controlled by placing units over each other and/or by designing dayroom and cell groupings to create visual barriers. The prisoners' views of staff can be controlled to some extent by using reflective glass in control stations (although reflective glass can also limit the view of the supervising officer), in cases where the supervision strategy calls for such stations.

Designing for the physical, sight, and sound separation of prisoners must not interfere with the sight lines required by detention officers for supervision or communication with each other.

Circulation

Designing for separation and control during movement by staff, prisoners, and visitors within the facility is crucial. There are many ongoing instances of movement within the security perimeter. Staff move to and from assignments and in response to the needs of the prisoners, who in turn circulate to and from activities and services. Members of the public and attorneys who come to the facility may also move within the secure perimeter for visiting, interviews, programs, and services.

Movement of prisoners poses one of the greatest risks. Official policies and procedures outline the best practices for moving prisoners individually and in groups. Every time prisoners move, there is a chance for passing contraband, for intimidation, or for improper communication (talking, flashing signals, etc.). Prisoners on their way to program and service areas should not pass by the housing units of inmates from whom they should be totally separated.

Circulation routes should be simple, straight, and wide. Corridors should not be less than 6 ft wide anywhere, and in prisoner areas, corridors designed for prisoner movement and for carts and mobile service equipment should not be less than 8 ft wide. Movement in corridors between housing units and other areas is controlled by direct staff observation or is supervised by staff through the use of CCVE equipment and audio communication. The ability to lock down and isolate circulation corridors and adjoining areas during troublesome incidents or emergencies is critical.

The circulation system should allow visitors to mix with staff and inmates at controlled access points along the edge of the security perimeter. Such points include the locations for supervised visitation rooms and program areas. Visitors and program staff go to these points from the public side; prisoners go to them from the secure side. After a meeting, interface areas are searched and cleaned, and each group returns to its respective public or secure zone.

CHAPTER 4
COURTHOUSE FACILITIES

The nation's courts are the centerpiece of the third branch of government, the judiciary. The courts have a twofold role. They are the instrument for administering the rule of law, and they are the check on the state in cases where the executive or legislative branches may have overstepped their bounds.

The courts are continually adapting to new challenges and using new tools. The challenges include more complex litigation proceedings involving numerous parties, and disputes that increasingly cut across jurisdictional lines. The new tools range from technology-based systems to new ways of working with court-related professionals and public and private resources.

It is said that there are 51 systems of law in the United States—the federal system and one each for the 50 states. This characterization acknowledges the differences between one jurisdiction (and its local legal culture) and another. The origins, age, size, and traditions of a particular jurisdiction, as well as its current leadership, will inevitably influence the way the role of the courts is understood and carried out in specific instances.

PROGRAM REQUIREMENTS
For planning and design purposes, one must consider adjudication, work processing, customer service, and court support services.

Adjudication
Adjudication is the process whereby judicial fact-finding takes place and judgments are rendered according to the law. Adjudication operations are basic to the courthouse facility's reason for being. It brings together judges, litigants, legal counsel, jurors, other involved parties and witnesses, and spectators. These people meet in courtrooms and deliberation rooms where the fact-finding and decision-making processes are carried out. When one includes alternative dispute resolution (ADR) processes, adjudication involves courtrooms, deliberation rooms, and various conferencing or small meeting spaces.

Work Processing
Work processing operations provide the clerical and related support required by adjudication. The management of case files is a major and complicated task involving various staff and information-handling systems. The great majority of files in courts continue to be paper-based. Their movement through the judicial process goes from initial filing with the clerk, to review by the judge, to final disposition. Storage and retrieval of both active and inactive records are part of the work processing operation.

Customer Service
Customer service operations encompass a range of activities, many of which involve general information dissemination to citizens who come to the courthouse for guidance. Some citizens may come seeking assistance in regard to incidents of domestic violence, child custody questions, landlord-tenant disputes, and "barking dog" disturbances. Others may wish to register a will or to be married by the Clerk of the Court in a civil ceremony.

Some customer services are provided by staff in a face-to-face and over-the-counter transaction; others, such as the processing of fees or fines, may be handled by an automatic teller machine (ATM) or similar device.

Court Support Services

Court support services include those provided by security personnel trained to ensure a safe environment for court staff and visitors. U.S. marshals play the lead role in security in federal facilities. Sheriff's departments typically control security in state and county facilities. A major element of court support is the handling and escorted movement of prisoners who are brought to the courthouse for trial. Court support also involves prosecuting attorneys, public defenders, probation officers, and others.

KEY OPERATIONAL AND ORGANIZATIONAL CONCEPTS

The physical organization of courthouse facilities may be about to change significantly. The next generation of facilities must handle a growing variety of operations under one roof or, alternately, must unbundle some operations. Unbundling options may involve networks of buildings that are widely dispersed or those that are grouped closely together in campus plans.

The boldest agents of change are emerging information technologies. The pace of such change is outrunning the ability of many institutions to adjust quickly. In the case of courts, changes are forcing design decision makers to think about individual facility projects as elements in a network of facilities connected by information systems. The freestanding courthouse is now part of a larger system-wide web of facilities and processes.

One fact is constant, however. It is that many different types of people come to a courthouse, and they do so for different reasons. There are citizens with routine business, citizens in distress, and citizens who are participating in the judicial process as jurors. There are justice system professionals, from judges to probation officers, as well as court staff, attorneys representing litigants, and others.

TYPICAL STATE COURT ORGANIZATION (UNIFIED SYSTEM)*

SUPREME COURT

COURT OF APPEALS

GENERAL JURISDICTION COURT

Civil/Criminal

		Family/Probate
Small Claims	General Civil	Domestic Relations Cases
Landlord Tenant	Negligence	Neglect/Abuse/Delinquency
Misdemeanors	Felonies	Custody/Support
Civil Infractions/Traffic	Administrative Agencies	Estates/Guardianship
Ordinance Violations	Other Appeals	Mental Health
Felony Preliminary Exams		Personal Protection
		Adoptions

COURT ADMINISTRATION AND SUPPORT AGENCIES

Budget/Facilities	Case Assignment/Scheduling	Mediation/Alernative Dispute Resolution
Jury Management	Court Services	Probation Services

*For a state with a single-tier court system.

◀ Mark O. Hatfield U.S. Courthouse, Portland, Oregon. BOORA Architects, Inc., and Kohn Pedersen Fox & Associates. Photo: Timothy Hursley.

Separation and Zones in the Courthouse

Managing the flow of people in a courthouse, and supporting the smooth conduct of operations generally, requires the development of distinct zones. The zones are in turn knit together by a three-way circulation system that separates public, private, and prisoner paths of movement from each other. The need for zones and proper circulation is a central organizing element in the planning and design of courthouses—as is the need for accessibility and security.

There are four primary zones in a courthouse: the public zone, the private zone,

▼ Section through courthouse showing public, interface, and private zones, with prisoner holding below grade.

the secure (prisoner) zone, and the "interface" zone. These are supported by service delivery areas, which include a loading dock and freight elevators.

Public zone

The public zone begins at the main point of entry into the courthouse. Citizens approach the building, step inside, and pass through a security screening checkpoint. They then enter a lobby, from which they move to various reception areas, counters, or rooms to conduct their business.

Court operations that involve a high volume of incoming citizens are typical-

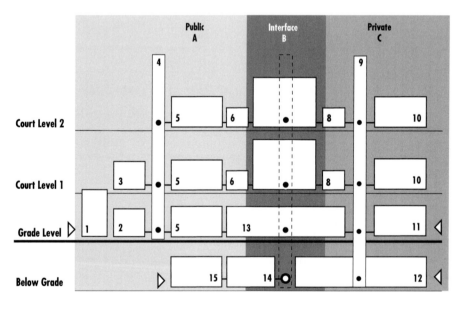

LEGEND
1. Public
2. Security Screening/Checkpoint
3. Jury Assembly
4. Public Elevator/Stairs
5. Public Corridor
6. Sound Lock Vestibule
7. Courtroom
8. Private/Judicial Corridor
9. Private Elevator/Stairs
10. Judicial Chambers
    Jury Deliberation Facilities
    Senior Court Staff Offices
11. Staff and Services Entry
12. Secure Parking
13. Central Court Office Area
    (Clerk, Court-related Offices)
14. Prisoner Holding

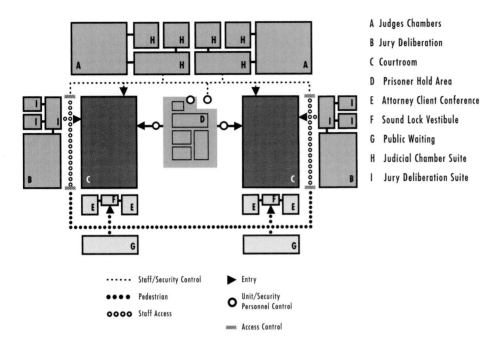

A Judges Chambers

B Jury Deliberation

C Courtroom

D Prisoner Hold Area

E Attorney Client Conference

F Sound Lock Vestibule

G Public Waiting

H Judicial Chamber Suite

I Jury Deliberation Suite

◄ Plan of pair of courtrooms (court set) with jury deliberation rooms, nearby judges' chambers, and prisoner holding cells in between.

· · · · · · Staff/Security Control

● ● ● ● Pedestrian

○○○○ Staff Access

▶ Entry

○ Unit/Security Personnel Control

▨ Access Control

ly located at grade and as close to the main entry area as possible. Although the public zone extends through the building to courtrooms and departmental reception areas on various floors, good planning and design seeks to avoid drawing citizens deeply into the building, which can be unnecessary and unsafe.

Private zone
The private zone is where judges, court staff, and authorized personnel are located and where invited visitors may come. The chambers of the judges and their support staff are typically located on upper floors and away from the hustle and bustle of public activity. The private zone also includes the departmental offices where court staff do their work. Some of the departmental offices may

interact with the public on an over-the-counter basis, but the "back of the house" administrative and support operations are in the private zone.

Prisoner zone
The prisoner zone is developed for the short-term detention and handling of persons in custody. It begins with secure sally port access to the building, generally at or below grade. It includes a central holding and prisoner distribution area to receive in-custody defendants. The prisoner zone extends to the holding cells next to courtrooms where prisoners are taken during their trial proceedings.

Interface zone
The interface zone is where the public, private, and prisoner zones converge. Its focal point is the courtroom, where all

the participants in the adjudication process come together. Here, the public and attorneys meet judges, court staff, jurors and those in custody. As destinations for each of the zones within the building that are otherwise separate, these places where the interface occurs require great care in location and design. They tend to be located on the upper floors of a building, and to be designed with issues of both safety and decorum in mind.

Circulation in the Courthouse

Well-conceived circulation supports the various zones independently and integrates them as needed. An effective system provides separate and distinct paths for the public, judges and staff, and in-custody defendants. The paths intersect only under highly controlled conditions, notably at the courtroom.

Public circulation

Public circulation within the courthouse is limited to main entrance and lobby areas, public service areas, and public hallways. It should be clear, easy to comprehend, and direct. It should be capable of being monitored by direct supervision or closed circuit television (CCVE) surveillance. One or more information centers may be provided, either at the entry (upstream from the security checkpoint) or on the main level in or near the public service areas.

Vertical movement is made possible by elevators or escalators. Public circulation on courtroom floors is limited to a corridor system that leads to the courtrooms and waiting areas. On floors with court support and office functions, the volume of public traffic is significantly less and is more controlled.

Private circulation

Private circulation paths are provided through the private zone for judges, jurors, staff, other authorized personnel, and invited visitors. These paths allow judges and staff to move along safe routes, through restricted entrance points, and to proceed to chambers and judicial work areas, all courtrooms, and all hearing rooms without encountering the general public or prisoners.

This private circulation system includes dedicated elevators to allow the vertical movement of judicial officers and court staff from the lowest level to all floors above. The system overall must ensure the desired levels of safety and separation without creating bottlenecks or blockage in circulation. Its effectiveness also depends, in part, on the proper screening of individuals allowed into it.

Prisoner movement

Prisoner movement in courthouses requires a circulation system that goes from the vehicular sally port and central holding areas in the lower level of the facility to a dedicated prisoner elevator(s) and stair(s) that leads directly to the smaller holding cells located between pairs of courtrooms. From these smaller cells adjoining the courtrooms, prisoners are escorted directly into the litigation area or "well" of the court.

Accessibility

Accessibility is a broad concept. It reaches beyond accommodations for physically disabled persons to include elderly, poor, and non-English-speaking people, and the law-abiding citizenry in general. *Accessibility* refers to a person's ability to gain physical entrance to and use of a facility. It also involves the ability of citi-

System A:
Basement prisoner access sallyports and central holding, with additional holdling at court floors.

System B:
Basement prisoner access mid-floor middle level central holding with additionbal holding and the court levels.

System C:
Basement prisoner access and mezzanine level holding areas directly serving courtrooms.

◄ *Alternative prisoner delivery systems.*

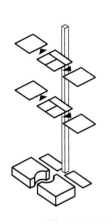
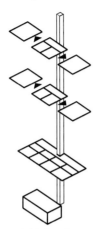
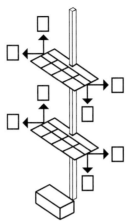

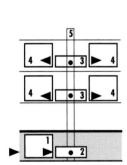
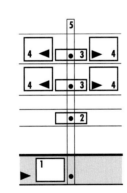
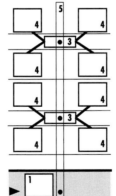

1 Sallyport
2 Central holding
3 Court holdling
4 Courtroom
5 Prisoner elevator

zens to obtain information about the workings of the justice system, especially within the jurisdiction where they reside.

Modern courthouses can make it possible to gain this information more readily by dedicating space and computer terminals for public use, and even staff to operate information centers. Designing lobbies or other public areas to anticipate the growth of such centers in the future is essential.

The degree of accessibility is also, in part, a function of how approachable or inviting a building is perceived to be. A building can be regarded by the public as user-friendly or not, depending on how its main entrance point is oriented relative to a bus stop or parking lot. An initial approach that is perceived to be awkward, or an intimidating entrance, discourages access.

According to the Americans with Disabilities Act (ADA), a courthouse must be designed to be as barrier-free as possible. Title II of the ADA requires an accessible interior path from the point of building entry to all public services in the building.

There are a number of specific requirements for specific spaces. Some of the issues and areas addressed involve vestibules, door widths and pressure of operations, corridors, elevator access and control, toilets, telephones, drinking fountains, visual and audible alarms, and signage. The location and quantity of accessible seating, including ramps and lifts allowing access to all areas of raised seating, such as the judge's bench, the witness box, and jury boxes, are also addressed by Title II.

Techniques for providing access for physically disabled persons have evolved in recent years. Individuals in wheelchairs are accommodated through the use of ramps, lifts, and other modifications. Hearing- and vision-impaired persons can be assisted with electronic transcription services, telephone handset amplifiers, text telephones (TTYs) or those compatible with hearing aids, open and closed captioning, video text displays, and other devices. The design of the facility must anticipate the support systems and space configurations that will be required.

Security

Like accessibility, security is a broad and many-faceted concern. Organizing a courthouse so as to provide security requires an awareness of the zoning and circulation issues discussed earlier. It also requires an awareness of the many different kinds of security threats that courthouse planning and design must consider.

For a more detailed discussion of security issues, see Chapter 11.

Variety of threats

A variety of circumstances may pose threats to the security of people, facilities, and processes. Such threats may occur inside a building, outside in an adjoining parking lot, or off-site altogether. Some kinds of threats involve random, spontaneous outbursts in courtrooms, in corridors, in waiting areas, or outdoors by litigants or family members and friends. Some threats may take the form of wrongdoing that is planned beforehand by an individual with a personal grievance, and some may be politically motivated. Terrorist assaults can have horrific consequences for both people and buildings, as evidenced by the bombing of the Federal Building in Oklahoma City in April 1995.

Spontaneous violence may not include weapons; or it may involve someone picking up and wielding a piece of furniture that is not anchored to the floor. Premeditated threats can involve explosive devices, chemical agents such as anthrax, and cyber-terrorism that can strike at electronics-based records and communication systems. An assailant may regard a facility's critical assets to be its building controls or work processing systems, rather than its occupants.

Integrated solutions

Effective design for security integrates physical form with security technology and trained security personnel. The integrated system should protect the courthouse occupants, its functions and operations, and its stored contents. The system should have the ability to deter actual or potential threats, detect breaches of security, and minimize the damage caused by disruptive incidents. The exact mix of architecture, technology, and personnel is determined by the unique characteristics of each project.

The orientation of the building on the site and the design of entrance drives, landscape elements, and setbacks should reflect security considerations. The primary security perimeter of a courthouse is its exterior enclosure system. Exterior walls and all required doors, windows, and other penetrations should be designed to restrict and delay unauthorized access and to notify security personnel if entry is attempted.

Inside, the organization of the facility in plan should emphasize clear, easy-to-navigate and easy-to-monitor circulation for the public, who enter through a controlled checkpoint where everyone is screened. Interior public spaces should not permit concealment or create excessive crowding. Departments or areas with the greatest influx of people, and the greatest need for access in the evenings and on weekends, should be located near the public entry and in such a way that other portions of the facility may be closed after normal operating hours.

The vertical organization of the facility should place the operations requiring most control below grade, in the case of central holding areas for in-custody defendants, and on upper levels, in the case of courtrooms and judicial chambers. As a facility is developed vertically, the risk of threats originating from outside at the sidewalk level may diminish, thereby making it easier to design some spaces to take advantage of natural light

and views. The amount of transparency in the exterior wall system may increase as a building rises.

The basic building systems may be influenced directly by security concerns, depending on the findings of the initial risk assessment for the project. Blast resistance or controlled collapse requirements will influence the selection and design of a structural system.

Distributed, rather than centralized, service cores for heating, ventilating, and air-conditioning (HVAC) may be considered if the risk of airborne biochemical threats is deemed significant and if the security plan calls for the ability to quarantine a portion of the building. Similarly, the power and data/telecom backbone of the courthouse should be designed with security in mind. Sophisticated information technologies and similar systems can be vulnerable.

Unobtrusive solutions

Security should be provided in a manner that is not unduly obtrusive or so overt that it creates a fortress-like atmosphere. This philosophy is best expressed by the American Bar Association Commission on Standards of Judicial Administration:

The business of the courts should be conducted in a dignified and secure environment. A courthouse should be designed and operated to limit the opportunities and occasions for disruption, violence, theft, and tampering, and to deal quickly and effectively with emergencies. Security programs, however, should not dominate the judicial process at the expense of such other important objectives as maintenance of courtroom dignity and respect for the rights of individuals (Standards Relating to Trial Courts, S.2.46 (1976), ABA Commission on Standards of Judicial Administration).

SITE SELECTION AND DESIGN

Selecting a site for a new courthouse involves weighing the availability of utilities, room for future expansion, civic presence, community interest, and many other concerns.

Site Selection

Courts are typically located close to other governmental entities, as well as clusters of professional offices and services, including lawyers, bail bond agencies, and so on. A supporting community infrastructure that provides food service, and allows both staff and court visitors to transact other business during workdays, is necessary. Of vital importance is a good public transportation system for the many court users who have no car, as well as roadways for access by private car.

The choice of a site may reinforce the positive features of a neighborhood. Courthouse facilities can contribute to the stability of an area, or they may help to initiate a revitalization process. Courthouse facilities inevitably convey a message; they have the ability to confer special importance on a location.

Courthouse facilities have traditionally served as anchor points in community development. The courthouse square at the center of many nineteenth-century county seat communities has long been seen as a physical reference point around which people have organized their patterns of living and working.

Changes in the built environment in the future may put greater burdens on civic buildings than ever before. As commercial and retail activity becomes more physically dispersed, civic buildings may become more important to the creation of a sense of place. The selection of a courthouse site is increasingly intertwined with the larger issues of community development.

Site Design

Accessibility and security are key considerations in site design. Tight urban sites that make it difficult to design comfortable setbacks, public entrance drives, and secure sally ports often call for vertical solutions in which the floor plates of a courthouse are stacked. Larger sites in suburban areas may allow a bigger footprint and fewer stacked floors.

When the courthouse shares a site with jail or detention facilities, issues of massing, scale, and overall character become more complicated. Jail and detention facilities tend to be low-rise structures, whereas larger courthouses often rise higher than the adjacent buildings. Site design that accommodates the necessary massing and scale should ensure paths of approach that are direct and free of obstacles or features that allow concealment.

AREAS AND SPACES

Courthouses are highly programmed facilities and require an array of spaces developed specifically for different operations. Key spaces are the courtroom and related areas associated with adjudication, and the work processing areas housing a variety of clerical operations. There are also spaces designed specifically for customer service activity, for the accommodation of court support operations and related agencies, and for the needs of routine building maintenance.

Adjudication Spaces

Courtrooms vary in size and number, depending on the types of proceedings

that take place in them, the volume of caseload activity, and the scale of the facility overall.

Courtrooms

A generic trial courtroom capable of handling criminal proceedings includes space for a jury. The courtroom is generally a column-free, high-volume rectangular space, deeper than it is wide, organized around the litigation area, or "well," of the court. It also includes spectator seating. As the interface zone where all parties involved in a dispute come together with the judge, legal counsel, witnesses, and others, the courtroom must have separate entrances that ensure separation and safety as people circulate in and out.

There can be considerable variety in the size of courtrooms, depending on the types of cases and the judicial proceedings that take place within them. The basic geometry of a generic trial courtroom, however—the arrangement of its main elements relative to each other and to the litigation area, or well, of the court—is governed by principles involving sight lines, acoustics, and proper distances, or proxemics, that have remained remarkably constant for centuries. The ability to hear, to see, and to articulate a point in a normal tone of voice is essential. The distance between a defendant and a victim

▲ Historic renovation courtroom, U.S. Courthouse, Portland, Maine. Leers Weinzapfel Associates. Photo: Brian Vanden Brink.

85

▶ Courtroom, Harold J. Donohue Federal Building and U.S. Courthouse, Worcester, Massachusetts. Leers Weinzapfel Associates. Photo: Steve Rosenthal.

▼ Courtroom, New Queens Civil Court, New York, New York. Perkins Eastman Architects. Photo: Chuck Choi.

or witness should not be so close that it risks causing fear. Nor should it be so far that it compromises a defendant's constitutional right to confront an accuser.

The key courtroom elements are as follows:

- Judge's bench
- Witness box
- Jury box
- Tables for legal counsel
- Spectator seating

There are also positions for a court reporter or recorder and a clerk and, often, a movable lectern.

The location of the judge's bench can vary from a central position on the long axis of the courtroom space to a diagonal location in a corner of the room. The symbolic power of the bench is easier to preserve with a central location and sym-

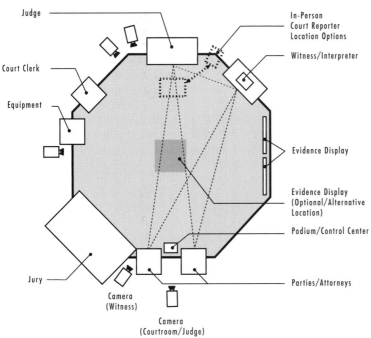

Judge

Court Clerk

Equipment

In-Person
Court Reporter
Location Options

Witness/Interpreter

Evidence Display

Evidence Display
(Optional/Alternative
Location)

Podium/Control Center

Parties/Attorneys

Jury

Camera
(Witness)

Camera
(Courtroom/Judge)

▲ *Courtroom featuring natural light. U.S. Courthouse, Seattle, Washington. NBBJ Group. Delineator: William Hook.*

◀ *Diagram of relationships between courtroom elements and sight lines for display technology. This configuration shows the jury box opposite the witness box.*

▲ *Judge's chamber, Harold J. Donohue Federal Building and U.S. Courthouse, Worcester, Massachusetts. Leers Weinzapfel Associates. Photo: Steve Rosenthal.*

▲ *Judicial library, Harold J. Donohue Federal Building and U.S. Courthouse, Worcester, Massachusetts. Leers Weinzapfel Associates. Photo: Steve Rosenthal.*

metry. On the other hand, corner bench configurations sometimes work better. Some designs call for the witness box to be located on the same side of the bench as the jury box, thereby placing the person who is testifying closer to the jurors. Other designs position the witness box directly opposite the jurors and across the room. Judges and attorneys differ over optimal arrangement, but all agree that it should be possible for all parties to have direct eye contact with each other throughout the proceeding.

Electronics-based information and display technologies have entered courtrooms rapidly in recent years. They are used for the presentation of evidence and argument, for taking the record, and for assisting disabled persons. As the courtroom has become more technology intensive—supported by an infrastructure that can accommodate changing equipment and furniture arrangements, as well as more sophisticated environmental controls—there has been considerable discussion about the desirability of preserving the traditional attributes of dignified courtroom space. The increasing use of display technology has also underscored the importance of proper sight lines and lighting.

Courtrooms are not video arcades. Technology should be as unobtrusive and transparent as possible. To this end, designers have welcomed improvements in the quality and costs of flat screen technology that is easier to integrate discreetly into millwork or within walls and ceilings.

Judge's chambers

Chambers are generously sized spaces in which work involving mental concentration can take place without visual or acoustic distraction. Small meetings or conferences can also be held in chambers with colleagues, staff, and attorneys. Chambers typically include space for the judge's personal library, as well as furniture and equipment required to review the law, study case files, and prepare written opinions.

Adjoining the judge's chambers is a suite of rooms for the judicial support staff, consisting of a receptionist, a secretary, a law clerk, and, in some facilities, a scheduling clerk and a bailiff or court officer. A waiting area for visitors and an additional conference room may also be part of the support area.

Jury assembly room

Jury operations generally involve a large assembly and waiting area. Citizens who are summoned to serve as jurors come to the courthouse for orientation. If they are selected to serve, they may then wait in a lounge or casual seating area until called. This area is designed to provide as much comfort and amenity as possible.

▼ Jury assembly room and waiting area, New Queens Civil Court, New York City. Perkins Eastman Architects. Photo: Chuck Choi.

Jury deliberation room

Smaller spaces that are able to accommodate as many as 14 persons are provided for jury deliberation. There is ideally one deliberation room per courtroom. Access is controlled. The confidential and potentially impassioned nature of the discussions that take place in these rooms requires careful attention to acoustics. Such rooms should be at least 280 sq ft in size and have access to natural light as long as security and the integrity of the deliberative process are not compromised. Adjacent rest rooms for the jurors are also necessary.

Grand jury room

A room of approximately 800 sq ft should be provided for processes in which juries of as many as two dozen people hear arguments and evaluate evidence to determine whether the prosecuting attorney can carry a case forward to indictment. Determining the adequacy of the evidence can take many weeks or months. It may involve testimony by many persons whose safety and confidentiality must be ensured. Circulation in and out of the hearing room must be controlled. Adjoining waiting areas and rest rooms, attorney conference rooms, and a jurors' lounge are arranged as an integrated cluster of spaces.

Conference areas

Flexible conferencing space for mediation, or the nonadversarial resolution of disputes without resorting to a trial, are increasingly necessary and desired as an increasing number of cases are handled through alternative dispute resolution (ADR) processes. In many jurisdictions, the overwhelming majority of civil cases are handled through ADR. The terms of a settlement can be hammered out in a corridor, a parking lot, or an attorney's office off-site, but a dignified setting in the courthouse, with its reminder of the trial that may ensue if settlement is not reached, is considered to be best. Such settings, like the courtrooms, are likely in the future to include more conferencing technology that can reach other parties in distant locations.

Work Processing Spaces

Work processing and court administration operations involve large areas of what should be designed as high-performance office space. Office areas may be private, semiprivate, or open. The largest concentration of office space is often in the Clerk of the Court's department. The Clerk's office is a vital program element. The number of staff can range from a few people to many dozens, or in the case of large courthouses, hundreds.

Office areas in courthouses are increasingly subject to dramatic change. New work processing technologies are being introduced. They are affecting operations, staffing patterns, and space requirements. Office areas may be where the greatest innovation lies in courthouse design in coming years.

There are ongoing changes in the amount of space allocated to individual workers as the proliferation of PCs, printers, modems, drives, scanners, and other equipment consumes more desktop surface. Future changes in equipment and new office arrangements for teamwork or multitasking will continue to challenge traditional assumptions about space requirements.

Individual workstation design must support desktop technology, ergonomically safe and comfortable furniture, visual and acoustical privacy, and control over light, air, temperature, and humidity. Acoustics, especially, can be a major problem in open office environments. Lighting design has also acquired greater importance as the introduction of more display technology has raised awareness of glare and brightness-contrast ratios.

The provision of daylight and views to office workers, required by law in much of Europe, is now recognized as a hallmark of good office design generally. Office layouts that ignore natural light, and floor plates that are so deep that they deprive office workers of visual access to the outdoors, should be avoided.

Office design also requires greater attention to whole-building and systems integration issues. For example, the exterior enclosure system for those portions of a courthouse that contain offices may seek to optimize natural conditioning and the quality of the indoor space through the handling of daylight with shading devices, light shelves, and the like.

The use of raised flooring for both cabling and air handling is becoming widespread in supporting workstations that can be relocated quickly and economically on a plug-and-play basis. Flexible, reconfigurable lighting systems overhead and at task heights should be developed to ensure adequate illumination as workstations are moved. Sensors that monitor the environmental conditions in functional areas, and that can operate in conjunction with personal environmental controls at a workstation, should also be considered.

Clerk of the court

The Clerk's office has responsibility for files, documents, records, and evidence handling, for preparing court calendars and scheduling trials, for processing the payment of fees and fines, for managing jury selection and for producing reports. One aspect of the Clerk's operation involves interacting with citizens who come to the courthouse to transact business at a counter position with court staff or to review public records in a viewing room equipped with tables, chairs, and, often, microfilm reading machines and copiers. The volume of foot traffic is generally great enough to require locating these areas close to the main entrance.

The Clerk's operation also requires significant amounts of space for the storage of active and inactive records. The advent of new forms of records that do not depend on paper and may not require as much storage space on site has been anticipated for several years. The transition to an entirely paperless court will be very gradual.

The size of the courthouse, the types of civil and/or criminal cases it handles, and the case management system used by the Clerk determine the layout of workstations, offices, and storage space. Some Clerks work in specialized teams to deal with all of the procedural steps involved in cases of a certain type or for an individual judge. Other work processes have Clerks dealing with only a limited number of procedural steps as the cases are conveyed along a path from station to station. A large open-plan area fitted out with systems furniture is a familiar feature of many Clerk of the Court operations.

Customer Service Spaces

Public spaces in the courthouse require corridor, queuing, and waiting areas that must be sized to accommodate the num-

▶ Entrance lobby, New
Queens Civil Court,
New York City. Perkins
Eastman Architects.
Photo: Chuck Choi.

ber of citizens using the facility. It is not
uncommon for some courts, such as a
general traffic court in a large municipality, to have to handle several thousand
people per hour. These people must pass
through the entry screening point and
make their way to destinations that are
often unfamiliar.

The architectural treatment of the public
spaces must enable them to handle large
numbers of people while, at the same time,
conveying a feeling of dignity and order.
Undersized or ambiguous spaces that cause
congestion or confusion can compromise
operations and undermine respect.

Architecture that conveys a sense of
dignity can contribute to greater securi-

ty. People may be less likely to misbe-
have in spaces that are comfortable and
easy to comprehend and where evident
care has been taken in the design and
construction.

Navigating through public circulation
areas to a destination point—whether a
courtroom, a transaction counter, or a
cafeteria—requires simple circulation
paths and complementary signage, often
in several languages. Signage and related
information systems may include video
monitors that resemble the "arrival" and
"departure" screens in airports, as well as
touch-screen kiosks in lobby areas.

Privacy in public space is an issue wherever two or more people want to converse

▶ Central atrium, Edward W. Brooke Courthouse, Suffolk County, Boston, Massachusetts. Kallman McKinnell Wood Architects. Photo: Steve Rosenthal.

▲ Public corridor area, New Queens Civil Court, New York City. Perkins Eastman Architects. Photo: Chuck Choi.

◀ Public corridor area, Edward W. Brooke Courthouse, Suffolk County, Boston, Massachusetts. Kallman McKinnell Wood Architects. Photo: Steve Rosenthal.

without being overheard. Counter areas where individual citizens meet with court staff deserve special attention. The counter itself should be deep enough to enable a person to spread out papers or fill out court forms. There should also be some side-to-side partitioning at each counter station. It should be possible for individuals to pose a question or to reference a personal matter to a court clerk without feeling a need to whisper or cover up the documents they may have brought with them. Nor should they feel as if they are being crowded from behind by other people queuing in a cramped space.

The clerk's side of the counter must accommodate the technology, communications equipment, and paper materials such as the forms and brochures required to provide effective customer service. The citizen's side of the counter should be designed as an attractive and durable piece of furniture that many people will touch or lean against. Optimal counter heights are 36" to 42", with a lower height for wheelchair-bound persons.

Waiting areas

Public waiting areas should be generously sized. Litigants and their friends and family members, attorneys, court-related or public agency professionals, police officers, members of the news media—all need to be able to move through the facility and to wait in designated areas without disturbance and dangerous congestion.

It is all too easy to undersize these public spaces. They are often vulnerable to last-minute cost-cutting measures as planning and design nears completion. Value engineering processes can wreak havoc with them.

Separate waiting rooms for victims and witnesses, as well as small conferencing rooms where attorneys and clients can meet in private while waiting to be called to the courtroom, should be provided.

Pressroom

The growing importance of public information programs conducted by the courts and the occasional high-profile or celebrity trials that attract news media in large numbers necessitate a pressroom where interviews and briefings can be held with reporters. Office and clerical support space for the court's public information officer should also be provided.

Court Support Spaces

Administrative office space for the court administrator or manager and staff will vary according to the size of the facility and the way it handles maintenance operations, budgeting processes, equipment and supplies purchasing, human resources affairs, and so on. Some administrators in older facilities occupy the space that is left over after remodeling and relocation of departments in the building have occurred several times.

New design should anticipate a large private office for the administrator or manager of approximately 250–350 sq ft. It should be able to accommodate small group meetings with attorneys or citizens and should be located in a portion of the building with easy access to both public and restricted areas. The administrator works closely with the judges and the clerks.

Prosecutors and defenders

Office and related support space for the operations of the prosecuting attorney can involve dozens or hundreds of people in a courthouse. It is a major program element. The attorneys typically have private offices of 120–150 sq ft. There are numerous adjoining spaces for use by investigators and paralegal staff, as well as interview and conference rooms, storage and copier areas, and a reception point that provides controlled access. Separate access for investigators working undercover may also be required.

There is no consensus among justice professionals on how prominent a prosecuting attorney's presence in a courthouse should be. Some judges believe that it is better for prosecutors to have a limited presence within the building, with the bulk of their operations located off-site.

Adjacency with and cross-circulation between the prosecutors and the operations of the public defender is undesirable. Like the prosecutor, the defender requires office and support spaces that allow confidentiality, concentration, study of documentation in various forms, and decision making about trials and sentencing-related issues. Prosecutors and defenders, and the people whom they serve, should not cross paths in uncontrolled circumstances in the courthouse.

Probation

Adult probation may be a major component of a courthouse, both in terms of the variety of its operations as well as its location in the building. This function should be located in an area with easy access during evening and weekend hours when the rest of the building is secured. Probation officers work with individuals on both a pretrial and postadjudication basis. Activities that can take place after sentencing and release on probation or parole include counseling and substance abuse treatment programs, periodic testing, and various kinds of supervision and monitoring.

The emphasis on rehabilitation inherent in probation and parole work means that ties to the community and its resources are important. The offices and support spaces should therefore include a waiting area that can comfortably accommodate family members, social service professionals, and others.

Other offices and agencies

The mix of occupants in a courthouse may include local government employees and elected officials who are not related to the courts. There may even be commercial rental space. More often, there are court-related professionals who are providing information, such as pro bono legal advice and contacts with public and private assistance. These activities generally relate to legal matters and the social services with which the courts have ties. There may be an office for the representative of a nonprofit, community-based organization that provides shelter, for example. The amount of space devoted to these activities may or may not be large, depending in part on whether the facility is intended to serve as a multioccupant complex where citizens can go with many different issues.

Prisoner holding

All general jurisdiction courts in which criminal trials take place require the ability to handle in-custody defendants. Central holding areas that can accommodate prisoners who are transported to and from the courthouse must be designed for complete security and for the ability to separate different types of prisoners according to gender and other factors.

Group holding cells should provide at least 12–15 sq ft per prisoner to reduce the risk of dangerous crowding. Control areas and equipment for security person-

▶ *Exterior elevation, U.S. Courthouse, Seattle, Washington. NBBJ Group.*

nel should be close by. Interview booths, where attorneys can confer with prisoners, are also necessary. Smaller holding cells for individual prisoners being brought into the litigation areas of individual courtrooms are typically provided between pairs of courtrooms and are accessed directly through vertical circulation dedicated solely to escorted prisoner movement.

Building control center

A control center, where alarm annunciator panels, closed-circuit video equipment (CCVE) monitors, a public address system, and other security equipment are housed, is necessary. This area serves as the primary security control center and as a headquarters during an emergency. It is the central reporting station to which police and fire agencies will come when summoned. If the control center is located near the main entry screening checkpoint, placement of the equipment and the counter design should enable security staff to monitor cameras and equipment while screening visitors.

UNIQUE DESIGN CONCERNS

Designing a good courthouse is difficult. Such projects have complex programs and are technically demanding. The user groups range from judges and professional staff to citizens walking in. Courthouses are also more accountable to the public interest and civic values than other buildings.

Image and identity are primary issues. "Lacking the power of the purse or the sword, the court's authority rests upon a moral plane. So the court's reason for being — to provide places where justice is administered and affirmed — must be architecturally legible."[1] Courthouses belong to the people and should be capable of instilling public trust and confidence.

Some design priorities have the potential to compete with each other. This is especially true for accessibility and security — two key mandates that must be made to work together without compromising either one.

Permanence and flexibility must also be reconciled. The structures must be durable enough to serve for several decades, at least, and to exhibit in their materials and form some authentic permanence. But many changes in the ways that courts do their work, and in the demographics of the population to be served, can occur over the course of a building's life cycle. A courthouse will probably be altered many times.

Courthouse architecture also addresses, in varying ways, the relationships between the past, the present and the future. The design may strive intentionally to serve as an element of continuity through time and across generations.

A traditional style for courthouses is the classical, with temple-of-justice forms that refer to the founding ideals of a democratic republic. Other courthouse architecture has taken its cues from other sources, ranging from the surrounding physical context — natural or man-made — to attitudes toward the best representation of the

> The frankest statement of guidelines for the aesthetic attributes of a courthouse appears in the U.S. Courts Design Guide (USCDG) developed for federal facilities:
>
> *A courthouse facility must express solemnity, stability, integrity, rigor, and fairness. The facility must also provide a civic presence and contribute to the architecture of the local community.*
>
> *To achieve these goals, massing must be strong and direct with a sense of repose, and the scale of design should reflect a national judicial enterprise. All architectural elements must be proportional and arranged hierarchically to signify orderliness. The materials employed must be consistently applied, natural and regional in origin, durable, and invoke a sense of permanence. Colors should be subdued and complement the natural materials used in the design.*[2]

law in a diverse society. Some courthouses are explicitly didactic, with inscriptions on their walls; others express their purpose in ways that are more abstract.

Complicating the question of an appropriate image is the growing importance of green design. The federal courts are now taking a serious look at sustainability, or how to design a facility that is as environmentally sound as a reasonable budget will allow.

Organization of the Building

The organization of the court floor, and its relationship to the office and support areas, drives the overall design of the building.

1. Todd S. Phillips, "Courthouses: Designing Justice for All," *Architectural Record*, March 1999, p. 105.

2. Judicial Conference of the U.S., *U.S. Courts Design Guide* (Washington, D.C.: Administrative Office of the U.S. Courts, 1997), chap. 3, p. 9.

▶ *Front entrance, Edward W. Brooke Courthouse, Suffolk County, Boston, Massachusetts. Kallman McKinnell Wood Architects. Photo: Steve Rosenthal.*

▲ *Front entrance, New Queens Civil Court, New York, New York. Perkins Eastman Architects. Photo: Chuck Choi.*

Court floors

The court floor comprises one or more court sets. A court set, in turn, consists of the courtroom and its adjacent support areas: judicial chambers, jury deliberation room, prisoner access/holding cells, clerical support area, and visitor waiting space. The circulation pattern within the court set must support its operational needs.

When the courts are in session, movement of prisoners from the central holding area in the lower portion of the facility may be required. For simplicity and cost-effectiveness, two court sets are frequently grouped together, as they can be served by a single prisoner circulation system consisting of an elevator and a small holding cell. Entire court floors in large facilities may consist of two or more pairs of court sets.

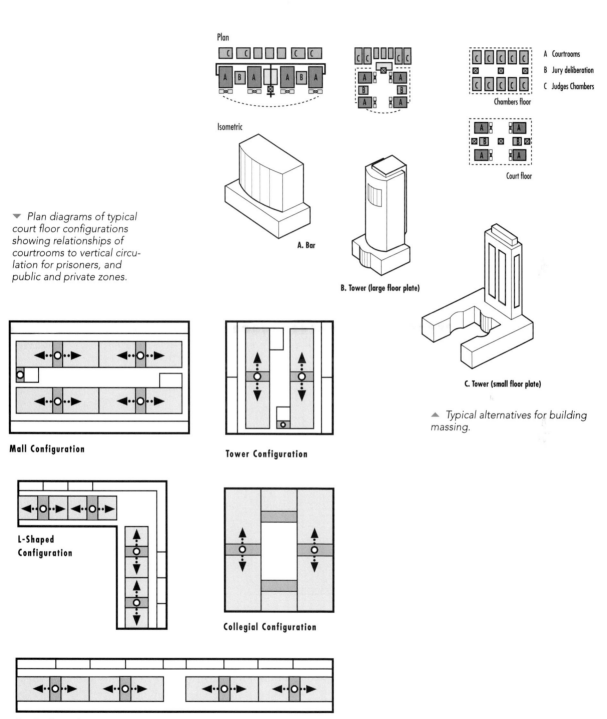

Plan

Isometric

A. Bar

A Courtrooms

B Jury deliberation

C Judges Chambers

Chambers floor

Court floor

B. Tower (large floor plate)

C. Tower (small floor plate)

▼ *Plan diagrams of typical court floor configurations showing relationships of courtrooms to vertical circulation for prisoners, and public and private zones.*

▲ *Typical alternatives for building massing.*

Mall Configuration

Tower Configuration

L-Shaped Configuration

Collegial Configuration

Bar Configuration

99

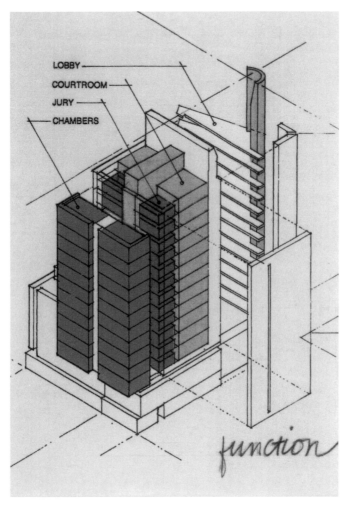

LOBBY
COURTROOM
JURY
CHAMBERS

function

▲ *Concept sketch showing relationships of key court elements. Mark O. Hatfield U.S. Courthouse, Portland, Oregon. BOORA Architects, Inc. and Kohn Pedersen Fox & Associates.*

The layout of court floors, with their column spacing and floor-to-floor height requirements, should anticipate the potential for change to accommodate different courtrooms and court sets within the same structural module. Future changes may entail different seating capacities in the courtroom, different jury (versus nonjury) requirements, different ratios of attorney-client consultation spaces and witness rooms, more space dedicated to alternative dispute resolution (ADR), and other court support spaces. It is not uncommon for several alternative plans for the future to be predesigned so that they will fit within the general architectural and engineering systems of the building at a later time.

Familiar court floor layouts often have the courtroom itself located entirely inboard from any perimeter wall, a design decision that prompts some observers to characterize the courtroom as "entombed." The value of natural light in the courtroom is weighed against other issues, notably security, and different courthouse projects reflect different attitudes.

Natural daylight and views should be provided for judicial chambers and support areas. Public circulation and waiting areas outside courtrooms are also given views of the outdoors. The primary role of public, private, and secure (prisoner) circulation in court floor design is evident in the diagrams.

An important variant of these design strategies for a court floor involves a different development of the facility in section. A "collegial floor" approach locates the judges' chambers and support areas on a different level from the courtrooms, matching the high floor-to-floor heights of the courtroom volumes in a favorable relationship to the lower floor-to-floor heights of the chambers.

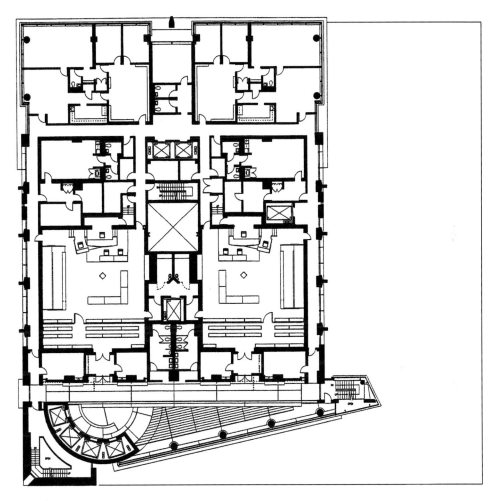

▲ *Typical court floor, Mark O. Hatfield U.S. Courthouse, Portland, Oregon. BOORA Architects, Inc. and Kohn Pedersen Fox & Associates.*

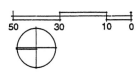

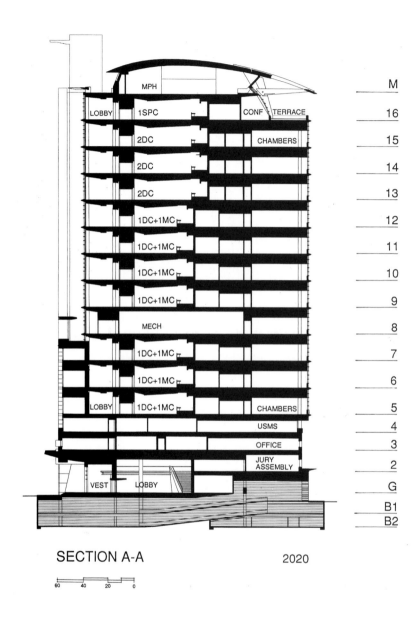

		M
MPH		
LOBBY 1SPC	CONF TERRACE	16
2DC	CHAMBERS	15
2DC		14
2DC		13
1DC+1MC		12
1DC+1MC		11
1DC+1MC		10
1DC+1MC		9
MECH		8
1DC+1MC		7
1DC+1MC		6
LOBBY 1DC+1MC	CHAMBERS	5
	USMS	4
	OFFICE	3
	JURY ASSEMBLY	2
VEST LOBBY		G
		B1
		B2

SECTION A-A   2020

60   40   20   0

▲ Section, Mark O. Hatfield U.S. Courthouse, Portland, Oregon. BOORA Architects, Inc. and Kohn Pedersen Fox & Associates.

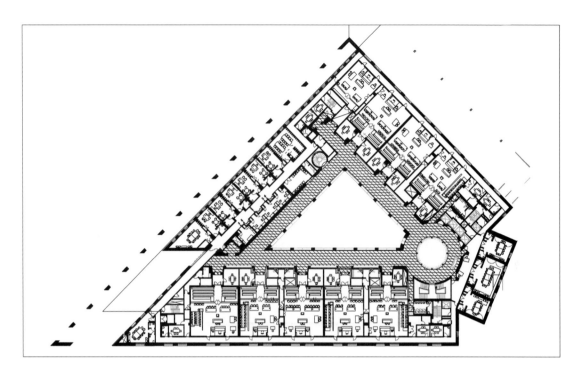

▲ Typical court floor, Edward W. Brooke Courthouse, Suffolk County, Boston, Massachusetts. Kallman McKinnell Wood Architects.

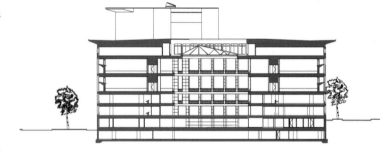

▶ Section through atrium and courtrooms, Edward W. Brooke Courthouse, Suffolk County, Boston, Massachusetts. Kallman McKinnell Wood Architects.

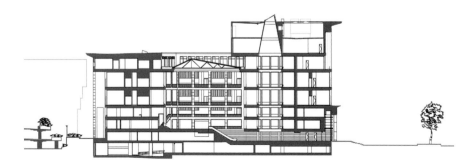

Typical court floor with three judge's chambers per two courtrooms. Level 8 plan shows "office bar" for Clerk of Court and administrative operations. U.S. Courthouse, Seattle, Washington. NBBJ Group.

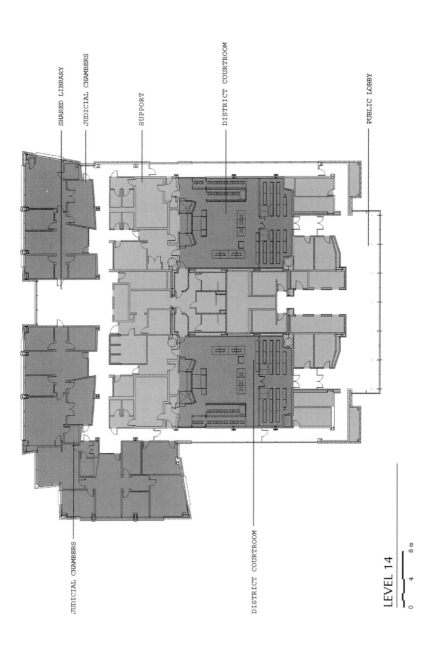

SHARED LIBRARY

JUDICIAL CHAMBERS

SUPPORT

DISTRICT COURTROOM

PUBLIC LOBBY

JUDICIAL CHAMBERS

DISTRICT COURTROOM

LEVEL 14

0   4   8 m

JUDICIAL CHAMBERS

ATRIUM

JUDICIAL CHAMBERS

BANKRUPTCY COURTROOM

PUBLIC LOBBY

LEVEL 8

0   4   8 m

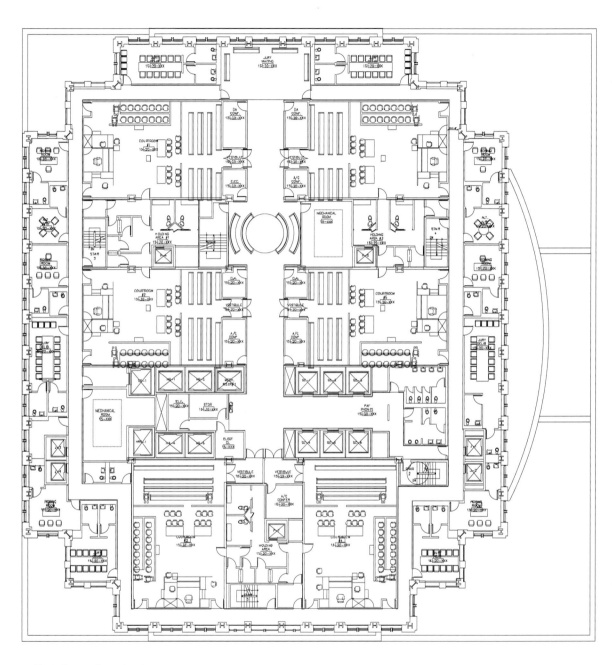

▲ *Typical court floor showing "four and two" configuration. Brooklyn Family and Supreme Court, Brooklyn, New York. Perkins Eastman Architects.*

▶ *Typical court floor of four courtrooms at the perimeter with natural light. Daniel P. Moynihan U.S. Courthouse, Foley Square, New York City. Kohn Pedersen Fox & Associates.*

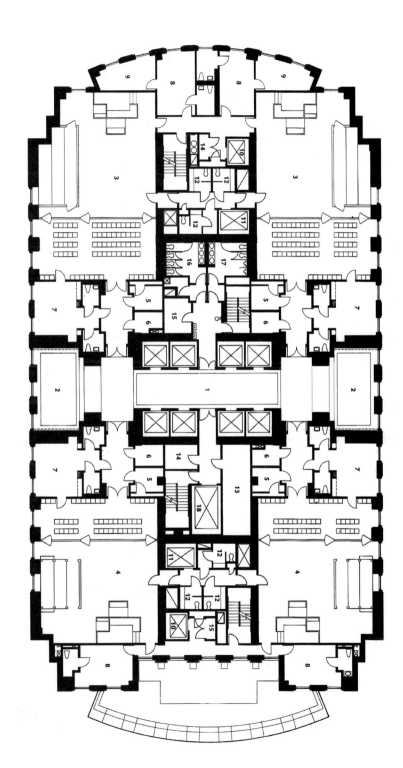

1 HIGH RISE ELEVATOR LOBBY
2 PUBLIC WAITING
3 STANDARD DISTRICT COURTROOM
4 MAGISTRATE COURTROOM
5 WITNESS ROOM
6 ATTORNEY CONSULTATION ROOM
7 JURY DELIBERATION ROOM
8 CONFERENCE/ROBING
9 COURT CLERK
10 JUDGES ELEVATOR
11 PRISONER ELEVATOR
12 PRISONER HOLDING
13 MECHANICAL ROOM
14 TELEPHONE CLOSET
15 ELECTRICAL CLOSET
16 WOMEN'S TOILET
17 MEN'S TOILET
18 FREIGHT ELEVATOR

The Building Exterior

Exterior wall designs should consider wind, sun, and water. Suitable cladding materials include limestone, granite, pre-cast concrete, and face brick. The use of curtain wall or other all-glass glazing systems is appropriate for entrance areas or other feature areas such as public waiting and jury assembly spaces. The use of metal panels is generally limited to accessory applications, but is not used for cladding or penthouse equipment enclosures.

Exterior windows and doors should be distributed to maximize views and minimize negative heat gains, with appropriate shading systems for sun angles, shadows, and glare from nearby buildings. Main entry doors should be designed for heavy use and be of excellent quality and appearance. Balanced-type doors or doors with concealed automatic swing-type closers should be provided on the handicapped accessible route into the building. Clear glazing should be provided at entrance lobby glass wall and

▼ *Rendering of pedestrian approach to entrance, U.S. Courthouse, Seattle, Washington. NBBJ Group. Delineator: William Hook.*

entrance doors, with windows and entrance doors designed of insulated glazing (shatter-resistant and/or special security) in accordance with good design and security practice.

Roofing materials should provide an excellent appearance and low maintenance. An area of the roof should be planned for current and future placement of antennae and microwave dishes. Various roofing materials may be used, but any roofing system should have designated walkways for the required routine maintenance of the roof and items located on the roof.

Interior Design

Entry areas and all other public spaces should convey an image of dignity through the use of materials, detailing, and proportioning. Hierarchies of space and function can be signaled subtly through the handling of different materials, colors, and volumes. The transition from a hard surface underfoot to carpeting, for example, can serve as a cue that a certain destination has been reached.

Interior construction should meet specific functional requirements for acoustical performance and fire code or resistance ratings. See Chapter 8, "Lighting and

▲ Rendering of entrance lobby featuring transparency and natural light, U.S. Courthouse, Seattle, Washington. NBBJ Group. Delineator: William Hook.

Acoustics." Partitions typically should be designed. Special construction and finishes are required in areas heavily contacted by the public, such as lobby and entrances, to ensure durability and ease of maintenance. Particular attention must be provided at corners, where abuse can be substantial and appearance is crucial.

Ceilings

Accessible suspended acoustical ceilings and appropriate acoustical performance are provided in most areas of the court facility, but smooth, hard ceilings and specially designed ceilings are featured in major public areas, courtrooms, chambers, and special areas (jury assembly rooms, grand jury spaces, and the like).

Walls

An appropriate hierarchy of materials is typically provided in court facilities, ranging in order from most public to least public spaces. Surfaces in public areas may include stone. Entry areas and doors into courtrooms may feature stained hardwood paneling, with hardwood millwork and finishes provided in courtrooms and judges' chambers. Painted woodwork and wallcovering may be provided in special office and support areas. Painted gypsum wallboard is provided in most office and general support areas. Materials and construction for prisoner holding areas are described in Chapter 11, "Security Systems."

Flooring

Carpeting with a wood or rubber base is provided in approximately 75 percent of a courthouse, with special flooring provided in entrance and elevator lobbies, rest rooms, department storage and workrooms, food service and vending areas, and prisoner holding and detention areas.

Special finishes

In general, special finishes are required in the following areas:

- *Public areas.* These should feature the use of stone or terrazzo flooring, with seamless wall coating or vinyl wall covering on walls, and drywall ceilings with appropriate design for lighting. Ceiling heights should as high as possible. Directional and locational graphics, directories, departmental emblems, and display cases should be incorporated into the design.

- *Courtrooms and chambers.* The materials and finishes selected for courtrooms must be durable enough to withstand heavy use. They should also be of high quality and appropriate to the gravity of the proceedings. Dignified spaces entail an extra emphasis on craftsmanship. Issues of real consequence to people should not be handled in a shabby space. Courtrooms should therefore feature the use of carpet, wood and wood wainscot, wall coverings with acoustic panels/treatment, as required, and drywall and acoustical ceilings with appropriate lighting.

- *Conference rooms.* The materials and finishes selected for conference rooms should be of high quality and provide acoustic control, including for meetings in which confidentiality is required. Carpet is typically used along with drywall, acoustical ceilings, and recessed lighting. Lighting design should anticipate the presence of video or other display systems in the space. Wood and other more expensive materials may be used when the gravity or formality of the conferencing warrants it.

- *Rest rooms.* These should be designed with ceramic wall tile on wet walls and vinyl wall covering on other wall surfaces. All finishes and materials should be selected for durability, ease of maintenance, and water and chemical resistance.
- *Storage and utility areas.* These areas should be designed for low maintenance and high durability.
- *Prisoner holding, detention, and processing areas.* See Chapter 11, "Security Systems."

Furniture and other appurtenances should be selected to meet the specific functional requirements of the various departments and agencies. Built-in furniture, casework, and architectural woodwork are provided in prominent areas of a courthouse, including the public and elevator lobbies (security stations, entry and counter areas, directional and location signage), courtrooms and chambers, grand jury area, jury assembly area, conference rooms, and general staff work areas.

The design and specification of all special casework and woodwork should comply with the Architectural Woodwork Institute (AWI) and other industry specifications. The design and detailing of custom-designed counters and millwork should meet specific functional and user requirements.

RENOVATION, RETROFIT, AND ADAPTIVE REUSE

Many courthouses are old. Some are venerable and have historic, if not architectural, significance. Many design issues therefore arise during improvement projects. Such projects may involve the restoration and upgrade of historic structures, renovation or refurbishment of an entire building or a portion of it, or adaptive reuse for new purposes.

Facilities age, and the functional demands on them change over time. Periodic upgrade or retrofit work can often ensure that a facility continues to perform at the levels required by current standards and best practice. In some cases, however, it is not possible to modify an existing facility to meet current standards or practice in every respect, and only strong compensating features or issues make its continued use desirable.

Historic Courthouses

Historic courthouses almost never provide for controlled, three-way circulation systems that today's facilities require for public-private separation and prisoner movement. In many nineteenth-century county courthouses, public areas are above grade in ways that create accessibility problems for physically disabled persons. Nonetheless, correcting the accessibility problems and making operational adjustments may be the best course if civic presence, budget constraints, or other factors argue for such alterations.

An alternative way of preserving historic courthouses as vital elements of a forward-looking justice system is to reprogram them to perform administrative or other court-related functions that they can still accommodate.

The use of historic courthouses for modern court or court-related operations involves preservation of those portions or features of a building that are deemed to be historically, architecturally, and/or culturally important. In these projects, there should be a preservation plan to identify zones of architectural importance and areas in which character-giving elements of the building are to be preserved. Standards developed by a trained preservationist should guide the work.

▲ Exterior elevation showing addition to Grant County
Courthouse, Lancaster, Wisconsin. The community
made a deliberate decision to build related space on a
nearby site, and to renovate and enlarge its historic
courthouse, in order to preserve a valued landmark.
Ayres Associates Architects. Photo: Franz Halls.

▲ *Renovated interior showing dome that is a com-munity landmark. Grant County Courthouse, Lancaster, Wisconsin. Ayres Associates Architects. Photo: Franz Halls.*

COURTHOUSE FACILITIES

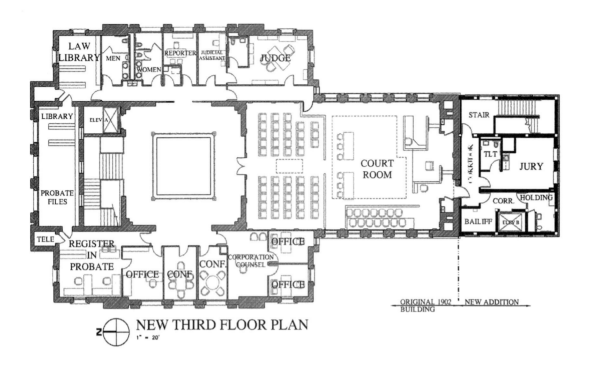

LAW LIBRARY | MEN | WOMEN | REPORTER | JUDICIAL ASSISTANT | JUDGE

LIBRARY | ELEV. A

PROBATE FILES

TELE | REGISTER IN PROBATE | OFFICE | CONF. | CONF. | CORPORATION COUNSEL | OFFICE | OFFICE

COURT ROOM

STAIR | TLT | JURY | CORR. | HOLDING | BAILIFF | ELEV. B

ORIGINAL 1902 BUILDING | NEW ADDITION

NEW THIRD FLOOR PLAN
1" = 20'

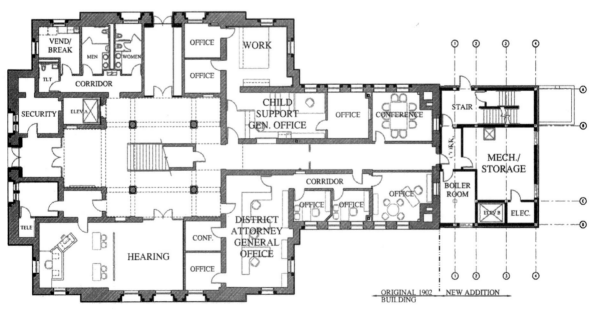

VEND/ BREAK | MEN | WOMEN | OFFICE | OFFICE | WORK

TLT | CORRIDOR

SECURITY | ELEV. A

CHILD SUPPORT GEN. OFFICE | OFFICE | CONFERENCE

STAIR | MECH./ STORAGE | BOILER ROOM | ELEV. B | ELEC.

CORRIDOR | OFFICE | OFFICE | OFFICE

TELE | HEARING | CONF. | DISTRICT ATTORNEY GENERAL OFFICE | OFFICE

ORIGINAL 1902 BUILDING | NEW ADDITION

NEW FIRST FLOOR PLAN
1" = 20'

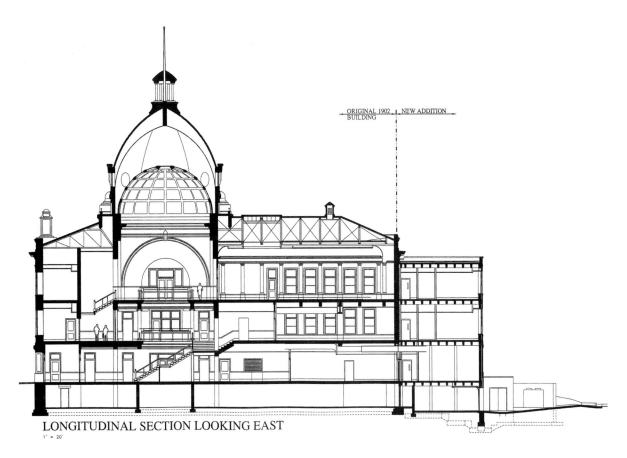

ORIGINAL 1902 | NEW ADDITION
BUILDING

LONGITUDINAL SECTION LOOKING EAST

1" = 20'

Retrofit Systems

Finding appropriate space for air-conditioning, power, and data/telecommunication cabling is a major design challenge in historic buildings. Existing shafts or ceiling spaces are often too small or shallow for today's systems. In these cases, options for conditioning the indoor environment may include decentralized air-conditioning units with little or no ductwork.

Power for desktop equipment may be routed partially through prewired systems furniture. New wireless technologies may ease the problem of bringing communications to some spaces without affecting their historic fabric.

"Loose fit" buildings are those older structures that may not be historic, but often have high floor-to-floor clearances, as well as smaller floor plates that can reduce the distance from a workstation to a perimeter wall with a window. The loose fit clearances allow several options for distributing ductwork, electrical service, or data/telecommunication cabling. The use of a raised access floor or distribution through very deep ceiling spaces can be possible with generous clearances.

The installation of raised access flooring can be a good choice in large projects. Raised flooring can be provided that is lower than the 6–8 in. typically

▲ *Section, showing new addition , Grant County Courthouse, Lancaster, Wisconsin. Ayres Associates Architects.*

◄◄ *Plan showing addition, reconfigured and renovated space, Grant County Courthouse, Lancaster, Wisconsin. Ayres Associates Architects.*

installed in new construction. Another option involves creating a deep ceiling space for all utilities, but keeping ceilings above the level of window heads. In narrow buildings, furred horizontal spaces can be created adjacent to exterior and core walls and used as raceways for utilities. Vertical furring on columns and walls for receptacles is another technique used in these projects. Space for new shafts can sometimes be found in new or existing stairwells.

If elevator systems must be replaced, existing elevator shafts can be used as duct shafts or can provide areas for electrical and data/telecommunication system risers. Vertical risers may be integrated with facade designs and upgrades if façade work is anticipated.

Adaptive Reuse

Adaptive reuse projects that seek to use standard office buildings for adjudication functions—as distinct from using older courthouses for office functions—can be challenging. Rarely does any existing office building meet the structural requirements for bay sizes or floor-to-floor heights required by the large and high-volume spaces of courts (courtrooms, jury assembly spaces, and the like). Most existing office buildings also fail to meet circulation requirements, such as elevators and egress stairs.

Many existing buildings require extensive structural modifications which can prove to be economically unfeasible. The modification of structural bays and floor-loading capacities involves alteration of the total structure from floor framing to column sizes to footings and foundations. Frequently, buildings with concrete frames are not suitable for such structural modifications.

For projects that contemplate the reuse of existing buildings, a building engineering report should be developed to document existing conditions and system capacities. The report should evaluate the existing building for code deficiencies and functional limitations. If, for historic or other compelling reasons, an existing structure is used for court functions but current court design standards cannot be met, it is especially important that planning and design teams review all design information and issues with the courts.

CHAPTER 5
ADULT CORRECTIONAL FACILITIES

The role of correctional facilities is to protect society from unruly or dangerous persons who have broken the law and have been sentenced by the courts to incarceration. The confinement of offenders in secure facilities is the first level of protection. Another level is provided when facilities deter potential offenders through awareness programs either for young people at risk or for the public in general.

Underlying the role of these facilities is the belief that protection results from modifying the behavior of offenders in ways that enable them to return to society as law-abiding and productive citizens. Incarceration therefore includes an emphasis on rehabilitation. It is recognized that most offenders will return to society at some point after having served their sentences and that their chances of becoming productive citizens are increased when they have literacy, vocational, and life management skills. Modern correctional facilities provide offenders opportunities to acquire these skills.

There are different points of view about what kinds of rehabilitative programs are most effective. Corrections professionals agree, however, that the role of their facilities is multifaceted—they confine the offender in a secure setting while providing opportunities for self-improvement. They also have links with the community to develop reentry programs for discharged persons. Correctional programs often have a community-based component.

Administrative standards have been developed by the American Correctional Association (ACA). Most of the ACA standards address administrative, organizational, and procedural subjects, but they are directly relevant to facility design.[1]

The standards set the base-level threshold for facilities that are safe and humane and in which essential human and civil rights are respected. They also inform the decision maker about the scope of many services and programs, from food and medical care to educational and vocational training.

PROGRAM REQUIREMENTS

The key operations of a correctional facility involve the housing of the inmate population and the provision of basic support services and programs for that population. Housing is central to the facility's reason for being, and the amount of space devoted to it far exceeds that assigned to any other operation.

Core support services for the housing include food, laundry, and medical care. Typical programs for inmates include education (general and vocational), industrial work, recreation, religion, and, in some facilities, treatment for substance abuse or other special problems.

1. Excellent complementary information can be found in the compilation of essays on specialized subjects by leading planning and design experts in Leonard R. Witke, ed., *Planning and Design Guide for Secure Adult and Juvenile Facilities* (Lanham, Md.: American Correctional Association, 1998). Peter C. Krasnow, *Correctional Facilities Design and Detailing* (New York: McGraw-Hill, 1998), provides the most exhaustive architectural guidance.

Federal correctional institution, Estill, South Carolina. LS3P Architects. Photo: Gordon Shenk.

The scale and complexity of inmate services and programs are greater in correctional environments than in detention facilities. Correctional facilities contain inmates who are sentenced to serve long terms. Daytime hours must be filled with purposeful activity. The facility must also be able to handle medical and other conditions that arise among inmates who are housed for many years.

The administration of the operations entails numerous other responsibilities, such as the reception, orientation, and transfer of inmates and the management of visitation. The administration component itself is a major operation. It involves significant numbers of highly trained and multidisciplinary staff, as well as the maintenance of a large and complicated physical plant.

KEY OPERATIONAL AND ORGANIZATIONAL CONCEPTS

The planning and design of correctional facilities have been increasingly influenced by concepts that involve the classification and separation of inmates, various supervision methods, and centralized versus decentralized strategies for the delivery of inmate services and programs.

Classification and Separation of Inmates

Like detention facilities, correctional facilities classify and separate inmates according to their gender, physical and mental capabilities, degree of security risk, criminal history, and special needs. Classification systems recognize that not all inmates are the same. The separation of inmates according to their classification is based on the need to prevent them from being a danger to each other and, in some cases, to themselves.

Classification and separation in a correctional setting is especially important because of the long length of stay. Inmates who are incarcerated for long periods can form dangerous subcultures within the prisoner population if they are not separated by classification. Large, undifferentiated populations are more difficult to manage.

It is not uncommon for large facilities to have inmate populations that involve minimum-, medium-, and maximum-security housing requirements. When the population reflects the full range of security levels, the types of housing vary accordingly.

Direct Versus Indirect Supervision

Several supervision concepts have emerged since the late 1960s. They complement principles of classification and reflect the idea that it is desirable to subdivide large inmate populations into smaller groups of like individuals. These smaller groups are housed in housing modules or pods. Each pod may contain two dozen or more inmates. Two or more pods are typically combined to form a housing unit.

Direct supervision places the corrections officer outside a control room and at an open officer's station inside the pod. There is no barrier between the officer and the inmates. The officer is positioned to monitor the behavior of the inmates, to engage them directly, and to intervene in situations in which it is necessary and possible to modify behavior positively.

This approach argues that a corrections officer who is trained in direct supervision can instill trust and advance the goals of rehabilitation. Direct supervision can also reduce costs through the improved staffing and other efficiencies that result when potential problems are intercepted before they erupt into serious incidents.

Indirect supervision, in contrast, involves a corrections officer monitoring the inmates in a unit from inside an enclosed control room. The officer has a clear line of sight to the common space in each pod and can observe the inmates' behavior. If necessary, the officer can summon a response team quickly to enter the pod and handle a disturbance. Enclosed control rooms are designed to monitor two or more pods at the same time.

Intermittent supervision involves periodic observation of the inmates by corrections officers who patrol through, or are stationed in, the housing units at intervals.

Correctional facilities with inmates that represent the full spectrum of security classifications employ a combination of supervision methods, from direct engagement by staff to remote surveillance by closed-circuit video equipment (CCVE) and audio systems.

▲ Indirect supervision station seen from inmate housing area. Jackson Correctional Facility, Black River Falls, Wisconsin. Venture Architects. Photo: James Morrill, JJ Images.

▶ Officer's view from indirect supervision station. Jackson Correctional Facility, Black River Falls, Wisconsin. Venture Architects. Photo: James Morrill, JJ Images.

Centralized Versus Decentralized Operations

The relationship of a facility's housing to its services and programs is the key adjacency question. The solution is generally more complicated in corrections than in detention because the size of the inmate population is much larger, and the extent of the supporting services and programs is greater. See the set of diagrams on page 122 for examples of different approaches to the overall layout of a facility.

One approach calls for centralizing the services and programs in a manner that requires the inmate population to be moved back and forth from housing. At a mealtime, for example, the inmates go to a dining area that is generally adjacent to a food preparation area and some distance away from housing. This approach is required when the support services and programs themselves are large and depend on other spaces and equipment.

▲ Aerial view showing support buildings opposite inmate housing units. Note staff parking, administration, and other support facilities outside the secure perimeter. Jackson Correctional Facility, Black River Falls, Wisconsin. Venture Architects. Photo: James Morrill, JJ Images.

◀ View from central control tower across outdoor recreation fields to housing units. Jackson Correctional Facility, Black River Falls, Wisconsin. Venture Architects. Photo: James Morrill, JJ Images.

Other approaches take the opposite tack. Services and programs are brought to the inmates, who remain in a housing unit all or most of the time.

AREAS AND SPACES

Housing—General

The housing of inmate populations can take various forms. In low- or minimum-security institutions, dormitory housing can be a satisfactory and cost-effective approach. The inmates require comparatively little supervision, and shared spaces for toilets and showers, for example, are sufficient.

In maximum-security institutions, inmates are confined in individual cells that typically have a lavatory and toilet. The cells are often arranged in a linear cell block fashion and are monitored by

security staff. Services, including daily medical checks and visits by counselors and others, are brought to the cells.

In recent years the majority of medium-security institutions housing general inmate populations have adopted a podular housing approach. Single- and double-occupancy rooms for inmates are clustered together around a shared open area, the "dayroom" space. The inmate rooms are often stacked in two tiers with a mezzanine. The pod is managed by correctional staff via direct or indirect supervision.

Inmate rooms

Individual rooms for inmates should be at least 75–80 sq ft in size and equipped with a bed(s), writing surface, and clothes storage cabinet. Some inmate rooms contain a lavatory and toilet. A security window to the outdoors should be provided

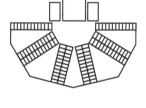

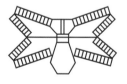

◀ Six of the many variations in prison housing units. Each of these units is characterized by exterior-facing cells, although the relationship of the cells to the dayroom and unit support spaces differs. From top: three-part triangular units, side-by-side "L" units, bisected "L" unit, radial layout of linear housing units (double-loaded corridor), modified bow tie, and back-to-back triangular units.

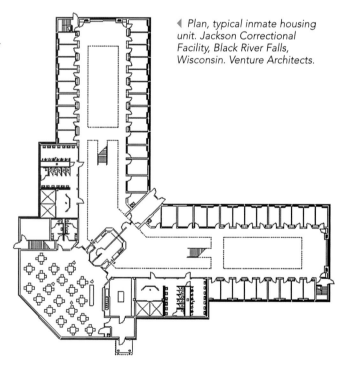

◀ Plan, typical inmate housing unit. Jackson Correctional Facility, Black River Falls, Wisconsin. Venture Architects.

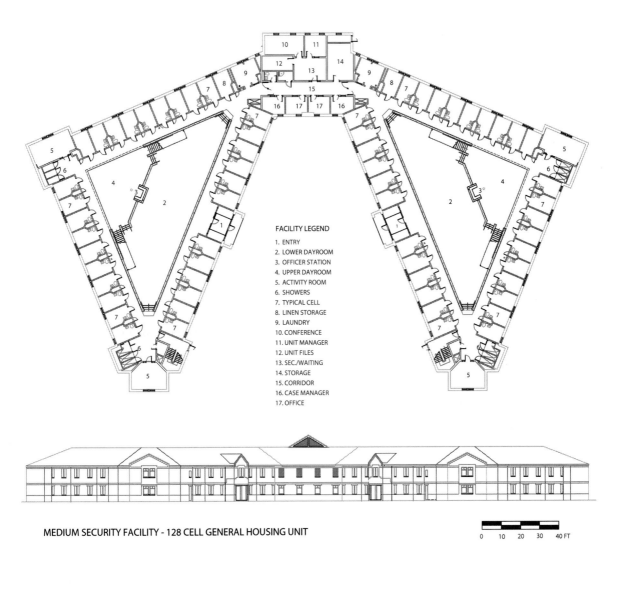

FACILITY LEGEND

1. ENTRY
2. LOWER DAYROOM
3. OFFICER STATION
4. UPPER DAYROOM
5. ACTIVITY ROOM
6. SHOWERS
7. TYPICAL CELL
8. LINEN STORAGE
9. LAUNDRY
10. CONFERENCE
11. UNIT MANAGER
12. UNIT FILES
13. SEC./WAITING
14. STORAGE
15. CORRIDOR
16. CASE MANAGER
17. OFFICE

MEDIUM SECURITY FACILITY - 128 CELL GENERAL HOUSING UNIT

0   10   20   30   40 FT

▲ Plan, typical medium-security
housing unit. Federal correctional institution, Estill, South
Carolina. LS3P Architects

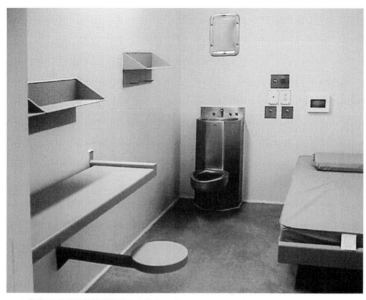

▲ *Typical single-occupant cell. Two Rivers correctional institution, Umatilla, Oregon. Hellmuth Obata Kassabaum Architects. Photo: Charles Smith.*

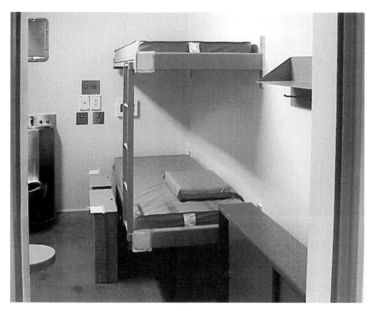

▲ *Typical double-occupancy cell. Two Rivers correctional institution, Umatilla, Oregon. Hellmuth Obata Kassabaum Architects. Photo: Charles Smith.*

for natural light or, alternately, natural light should be borrowed from the day-lighted dayroom through a glass panel in or next to the door.

Single-occupancy inmate rooms are judged to be most desirable for several reasons. The privacy they afford to inmates can contribute to a more normative environment. They also enable the institution to maintain greater control. Single-occupancy rooms provide greater flexibility for changing inmates of different classifications over the course of the facility's life cycle.

Dayroom

The dimensions of the dayroom should provide a minimum of 35 sq ft per inmate in the space and, as a high-ceiling volume, should ideally have skylights overhead or clerestory windows for natural light. In correctional facilities, the dayroom is used for a limited range of activities, chiefly passive recreation (e.g., conversation, television viewing, etc.). In detention facilities or those employing a decentralized services approach, the dayroom is where dining and many program activities occur. Tables and chairs in the dayroom can be either stationary or movable.

Where direct supervision is provided, the dayroom includes an officer's station, approximately 40 sq ft in size, that is equipped with communications and control technology. The location of the station in the dayroom space is determined by the sight line requirement that all areas be visible to the officer.

Showers

Each level of the housing pod should contain a shower area—typically, one shower per eight inmates—with space for drying. Some privacy screening

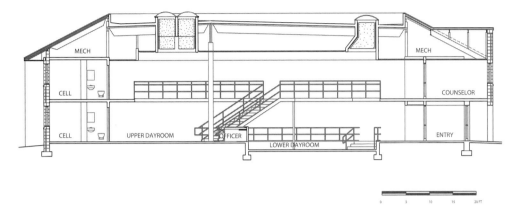

Section, typical medium-security housing unit. Federal correctional institution, Estill, South Carolina. LS3P Architects.

should be provided, both as a consideration to the inmates and in anticipation of possible gender differences between the inmate population and the staff.

Offices and program spaces

When two or more pods are grouped together and managed as a unit, offices and program spaces are provided for the unit management team. The team may include a unit manager, a caseworker, two or more counselors, clerical support, and the correctional staff. The caseworker and a counselor should have offices of approximately 100 sq ft each. Additional offices should be provided for professionals who come to the unit periodically. Flexible, multiuse rooms should also be provided next to the dayroom, with a clear glass panel in the separating wall to facilitate supervision, for passive recreation, training, and program activities.

Housing—Special Inmate Populations

Planning and design must anticipate the issues that are raised by the presence of inmates whose gender, health, physical or mental capabilities, and cultural characteristics may pose special challenges. In many cases, the challenges can be met through a modification of familiar approaches, rather than a major rethinking of facility design. In other cases, however, such as the housing and treatment of violent sex offenders, new strategies and facility types may have to be developed.

Inmate housing unit with open, direct-supervision station at right. Federal correctional institution, Estill, South Carolina. LS3P Architects. Photo: Gordon Shenk.

125

Three categories of inmates that need to be anticipated in almost every instance are physically disabled inmates, geriatric inmates, and female offenders.

Physically disabled inmates

Correctional facilities must comply with the provisions of the Americans with Disabilities Act of 1990 (ADA), specifically Section 12 of the Accessibility Guidelines developed by the Architectural and Transportation Barriers Compliance Board. All public and common-use areas throughout an institution—from the parking lot and entrance points to special cells for medical isolation—are subject to the requirement that inmates with serious mobility, hearing, or vision impairments be accommodated.

The barrier-free requirements for inmate housing units call for at least 2 percent of the facility's general inmate rooms or cells to be designed for disabled persons. If there are special-purpose rooms or cells (e.g., for medical treatment, discipline, etc.), at least one cell for each special purpose must be accessible.

Space for a wheelchair turning radius must be provided in the accessible inmate room, and there must be grab bars at the toilet fixture. At least 36 in. must be provided next to the bed for the wheelchair. Inmate rooms that are equipped for disabled persons must be located in areas and along paths of travel that are barrier free, except as controlled by the facility's security staff.

Geriatric inmates

Not every inmate who enters an institution is subsequently freed, and not all remain able-bodied through various stages of life. An increasing number of institutions are having to handle elderly and infirm individuals. The reduction in physical capabilities that comes with the aging process includes reduced hearing and vision, cardiovascular changes, increased susceptibility to falling and breaking bones, and a greater likelihood of urological problems. Depression and other mental health issues among older inmates, including Alzheimer's disease, may also become significant problems.

Housing design for geriatric inmates can involve segregated rooms or entire wings where the living is on one level, with toilet and bathing facilities that are modified to provide adequate space, fixtures, and hardware. Floor materials, wall and ceiling finishes, colors, and lighting levels can also be modified to minimize problems of glare, slipping, or the inability to easily hear a normal speaking voice. Assisted living or skilled nursing and medical care for seriously ill inmates must also be provided.

Female offenders

The number of female inmates in correctional institutions has grown with the more widespread use of hard drugs and related crime since the early 1980s, and with tougher sentencing policies generally. Full security and the ability to segregate dangerous or unruly female inmates must be provided in the same manner as required for males, but there should also be some design differences that acknowledge the privacy issues associated with females.

Housing design for females should preclude sexual misconduct between the inmates and the correctional staff. The ability of staff to observe sleeping rooms, showers, and toilets for security purposes must take inmate privacy into account. Showers should be designed with divid-

◀ Minimum-security food services building. Federal correctional institution, Estill, South Carolina. LS3P Architects. Photo: Gordon Shenk.

ing walls and equipped with doors that provide partial screening. Some measure of privacy should also be provided between inmates when an inmate room includes a toilet and a lavatory.

Multiple-occupancy rooms of two to six inmates may be desirable when the classifications permit and when the corrections program encourages self-discipline in a small-group setting. Multiple-occupancy rooms that include a shower area can provide added security because of the reduced movement of inmates to other spaces. The size of open dayroom areas and their seating options should support smaller-group interaction.

Inmate Services

Essential inmate services involve food, laundry, and medical/mental health. These services require spaces in which operational, architectural, and engineering systems are well integrated. Food and laundry operations include equipment that must be supported by mechanical, electrical, and plumbing systems design. Special air handling can also be a concern in the medical area.

Decisions about the size and layout of spaces for these services should include an analysis of possible growth and change in the future to ensure adequate capacity over the full life of the facility. Food, laundry, and medical/mental health services are easy to miscalculate.

Food service

Food production methods can vary, requiring different amounts of freezer and other storage space to be located inside or outside the institution's security perimeter. Bulk storage can be in a central warehouse, with delivery of items through a loading dock. The movement of items to and through the food preparation and serving areas requires adequate circulation space and proper sight lines for supervision by staff.

Food production is generally done by inmate labor. The process can provide opportunities for the introduction of contraband or for tampering with equipment. The designer should configure the space and its equipment so as to avoid crowding and obstructions that compromise security.

127

▶ *Serving area, minimum-security food services. Federal correctional institution, Estill, South Carolina. LS3P Architects. Photo: Gordon Shenk.*

▼ *Dining area, minimum-security food services. Federal correctional institution, Estill, South Carolina. LS3P Architects. Photo: Gordon Shenk.*

Laundry service

Like food production, laundry services are generally performed by inmates, both as a matter of economy and as a management technique for keeping the inmate population busy. The movement of cleaned and soiled clothing and linen in carts, from housing areas to washing and drying equipment elsewhere, requires continuous monitoring by staff. Occasionally, a washer and dryer may be provided in a dayroom, especially where female offenders are housed. A centralized laundry area is preferred.

Medical/mental health services

Some incarcerated populations can be time bombs in terms of their potential to overwhelm the health care delivery capabilities of an institution. Undersized or poorly equipped infirmaries in crowded institutions may face serious problems if the numbers of geriatric or ill patients grow beyond initial projections.

Medical services areas should include a waiting room that can separate different classifications of patients, interview rooms, examination and treatment rooms with running water and medical gas, and an infirmary with beds in an appropriate ratio to the entire population.

The ability of the institution's medical services to operate as both an outpatient clinic and an inpatient unit is important. The need for at least one infectious isolation room with the ability to control airborne contaminants should be anticipated for patients with communicable diseases. A laboratory, a pharmacy, and storage areas for both clean and dirty medical supplies are also necessary.

Medical service areas are likely to include more audio- and video-conferencing capabilities in the future, making it possible for staff to link with diagnostic and treatment expertise located off-site.

The health care staff itself must be supported with adequate space to do its job without undue constraints or stress. Offices and conferencing space for resident and contracted physicians, nurses, and mental health professionals should be generously sized and furnished for both functionality and amenity. The space should also be designed to accommodate display technology and appropriate lighting controls.

Inmate Programs

Correctional facilities provide a variety of inmate programs that address the goals of rehabilitation. Some programs, such as recreation and religion, focus on the quality of life afforded to the inmate on a day-to-day basis. Other programs, such as education and work training, are intended to support (aid) the inmate once released. Although some programs can be conducted in multipurpose areas, others require dedicated space and special equipment.

Education programs

The lack of literacy, to varying degrees, is often a problem among inmates, and general education programs may be provided in classrooms equipped with a teacher's desk, students' desks, and instructional equipment such as video and audio recorders and television. Computer training may also be provided in classrooms designed for computer stations.

The size and number of classrooms will be determined by regulations governing student-teacher ratios, as well as the institution's program objectives and resources. Classrooms should ideally have natural light and should be easy to monitor by correctional staff.

A general library that is located close to the classroom(s) area should be large enough to contain the books, magazines, newspapers, and audiovisual materials required to support inmate studies and to encourage recreational reading. In addition, a separate legal library containing standard legal reference materials is required by law. All library materials must be arranged in ways that preserve the ability of the staff to supervise the space. Adjacent rest rooms help to limit the movement of inmates in the education area.

If possible, a media center should be provided that can serve as a hub for broadcasting educational and informational material to all spaces, including to the inmate rooms. The use of broadcast media and distance learning programs is likely to grow in coming years.

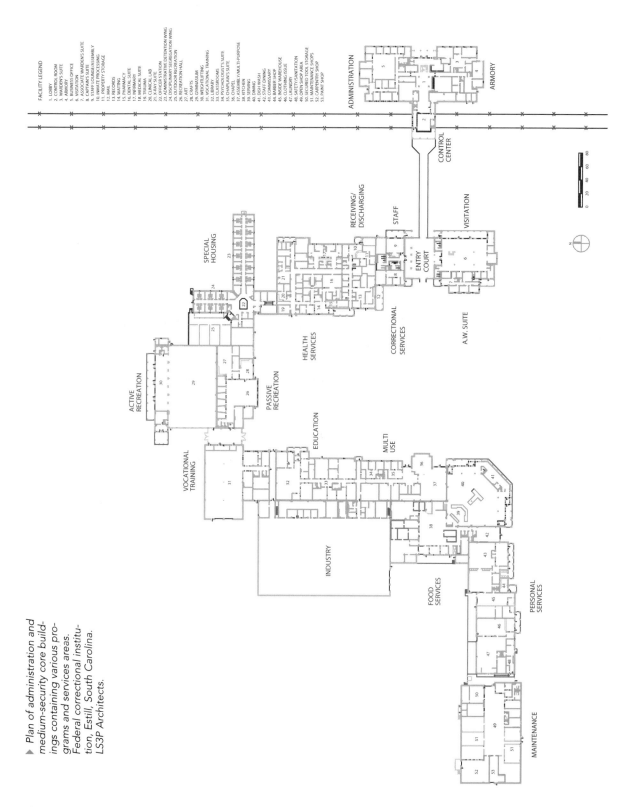

FACILITY LEGEND

1. LOBBY
2. CONTROL ROOM
3. WARDEN'S SUITE
4. ARMORY
5. BUSINESS OFFICE
6. VISITATION
7. ASSOCIATE WARDEN'S SUITE
8. CAPTAIN'S SUITE
9. STAFF LOUNGE/ASSEMBLY
10. INMATE PROCESSING
11. PROPERTY STORAGE
12. MAIL
13. RECORDS
14. WAITING
15. PHARMACY
16. DENTAL SUITE
17. INFIRMARY
18. MEDICAL SUITE
19. TRAUMA
20. CLINICAL LAB
21. X-RAY SUITE
22. OFFICER STATION
23. ADMINISTRATIVE DETENTION WING
24. DISCIPLINARY SEGREGATION WING
25. OUTDOOR RECREATION
26. RECREATION HALL
27. ART
28. CRAFTS
29. GYMNASIUM
30. WEIGHTLIFTING
31. VOCATIONAL TRAINING
32. LIBRARY
33. CLASSROOMS
34. PSYCHOLOGIST'S SUITE
35. CHAPLAIN'S SUITE
36. CHAPEL
37. ASSEMBLY/MULTI-PURPOSE
38. KITCHEN
39. SERVING
40. DINING
41. DISH WASH
42. STAFF DINING
43. COMMISSARY
44. BARBER SHOP
45. INSIDE WAREHOUSE
46. CLOTHING ISSUE
47. LAUNDRY
48. SAFETY/SANITATION
49. OPEN SHOP AREA
50. SECURED TOOL STORAGE
51. MAINTENANCE SHOPS
52. CARPENTRY SHOP
53. PAINT SHOP

ADMINISTRATION

ARMORY

CONTROL CENTER

SPECIAL HOUSING

RECEIVING/DISCHARGING

STAFF

ENTRY COURT

VISITATION

A.W. SUITE

HEALTH SERVICES

CORRECTIONAL SERVICES

ACTIVE RECREATION

PASSIVE RECREATION

VOCATIONAL TRAINING

EDUCATION

MULTI USE

INDUSTRY

FOOD SERVICES

PERSONAL SERVICES

MAINTENANCE

N

0   20   40   60   80

▲ Plan of administration and medium-security core buildings containing various programs and services areas. Federal correctional institution, Estill, South Carolina. LS3P Architects.

Instructional staff require separate offices, each accommodating a standard desk, chairs, desktop technology, shelving, and storage for records. A shared work area should be available, where equipment and supplies can also be stored.

Vocational training

Vocational training programs, designed to teach employment skills, have traditionally focused on such familiar trades as auto mechanics, welding, and carpentry. In recent years, additional skills involving computers and related technology have become part of vocational education curricula. The growing diversity of programs reflects the efforts of many institutions to provide training programs that are relevant to the realities of the job market.

The diverse spaces necessary to provide vocational programs range from large workshop areas (for mechanics, welding, etc.) to academic classroom settings (for computer-based office skills). When general and vocational education programs are integrated, some classroom spaces may be shared.

Vocational programs that involve heavy equipment, tools, and dirty processes may be located in a different building(s). Flexible, easy-to-modify spaces are necessary because the specific programs may change over time. Vocational staff, like their colleagues in the general education program, need enclosed office and support space.

Industrial programs

Corrections industries provide employment to inmates who work in the manufacturing of products. Many products are sold or distributed in the general market. The variety of people involved in administrative and supervisory roles, as well as

▲Training room. Two Rivers correctional institution, Umatilla, Oregon. Hellmuth Obata Kassabaum Architects. Photo: Charles Smith.

▲Building trades vocational education classroom. Women's Eastern Reception, Diagnostic and Correctional Center, Vandalia, Missouri. Hellmuth Obata Kassabaum Architects. Photo: Rick Birger.

▶ Industries technology classroom. Women's Eastern Reception, Diagnostic and Correctional Center, Vandalia, Missouri. Hellmuth Obata Kassabaum Architects. Photo: Rick Birger.

▼ Multipurpose room. Women's Eastern Reception, Diagnostic and Correctional Center, Vandalia, Missouri. Hellmuth Obata Kassabaum Architects. Photo: Rick Birger.

Production may require high-volume factory space that can be easily observed by staff on the production floor and in adjacent offices that look onto the space through glazed panels. Separate toilets should be available for inmate workers and staff.

Treatment programs

Many inmates have a background of alcohol and substance abuse. This is often accompanied by other mental and behavioral problems. Providing intensive, long-term treatment programs for these inmates requires the creation of therapeutic environments segregated from the facility's general population. The treatment goals are to enable an inmate to identify and modify his or her negative behavior on a self-governing basis. The design of the space should reinforce the goals of the program.

the amount of interaction with other parties outside the security perimeter, is generally greater in industrial programs than in other programs. Spaces for shipping, receiving, and materials storage must be planned for considerable back-and-forth movement.

Maintaining a regimen of individual counseling and group meetings of various size entails more staff and staff office space, and a greater variety of multipurpose rooms, than are normally provided.

▲ *Nondenominational chapel building. Federal correctional institution, Estill, South Carolina. LS3P Architects. Photo: Gordon Shenk.*

Recreation

The spaces required for recreation programs range from dayrooms and multipurpose rooms indoors to outdoor recreation yards that are large enough to support several field sports and a running track. The indoor spaces may be used for passive recreation (e.g., television viewing, reading), tabletop games (e.g. chess, checkers, Ping-Pong), or arts and crafts programs in large rooms with storage areas for materials and tools.

The most extensive indoor space for recreation is a full-size gymnasium for full-court basketball, spectator seating, and locker rooms with toilets and showers for competing teams. Sports and group assembly activities can take place inside the gymnasium regardless of weather conditions outside. There should be adequate storage space for sports equipment and folding chairs. Staff offices should be adjacent to the court area for observation.

Outdoor recreation can involve team sports, such as baseball, softball, basketball, volleyball, and soccer, or individual activities, such as walking, jogging, or weight lifting. The size and location of an outdoor recreation space must be considered carefully in relation to other parts of the facility and the area beyond the security perimeter. No portion of the recreation yard should be hidden from view; staff should have sight lines of the entire area.

Religious programs

Inmates have the right to freedom of religious worship. A flexible, nondenominational space for religious services should be provided, with adjoining offices for a chaplain or visiting clergy. Inmates should be able to confer with clergy in private, in a manner that preserves confidentiality. The worship space or chapel should, ideally, have natural light. It should be located in an area that can accommodate visitors from the outside, such as community-based professionals and volunteers who may conduct seminars or other activities related to the institution's overall religious program. Storage space is necessary for religious materials used in services.

▲ *Visitation area. Snake River Correctional Institution Phase II, Ontario, Oregon. Hellmuth Obata Kassabaum Architects. Photo: Phyllis King.*

Visitation

Visitation programs allow inmates to meet with family members, friends, and legal or other professionals. Contact or noncontact visitation occurs in secure spaces that are specifically designed for such programs. The location of the spaces is important, because all visitors must be carefully screened and their movement inside the security perimeter must be continuously monitored.

Contact visitation typically occurs in a room, furnished with tables and chairs, that is large enough to accommodate several inmates and their visitors at the same time. The size of the space and the number of occupants are determined by the facility's operational policies and security resources. Separate rest rooms for inmates and visitors should be provided, as well as an adjacent holding area(s) where inmates can be searched for contraband after their visits.

Some institutions may provide separate visiting rooms for added privacy, as well as apartment space for overnight visits by spouses or other family members. An apartment should have a residential character and be suitable for children, if they are allowed.

Noncontact visitation is typically used when an inmate poses a security risk or requires more control. Small visitation booths, each with a transparent separation barrier between the inmate and the visitor, are provided. The spaces behind the inmates and the visitors are often open to facilitate supervision by correctional staff. A completely enclosed booth or "interview room" makes it possible for inmates to confer with lawyers, clergy, or others in private. At least one booth must comply with the ADA and be accessible on both the visitor and the inmate sides when the visitation area itself is serving a portion of the facility that contains accessible inmate rooms.

Videoconferencing technology for televisiting has been adopted by some institutions as an enhancement of their visitation programs. Televisiting can have benefits in terms of security and reduced staffing costs. It can also facilitate visitation in situations in which family members might otherwise be kept from visiting by long travel distances. Televisiting sites that are more accessible for visitors can be located in places within, close to, or remote from the institution.

Admissions, Transfer, and Discharge

Admitting inmates to an institution for long terms entails a number of standards. It requires a highly programmed sequence of spaces designed specifically for the different steps. There are many variables to consider. Incoming inmates may reflect great diversity in terms of age, gender, physical or mental capabilities and health, security risk, literacy or language skills, degree of notoriety, and other characteristics.

Some inmates may be in an agitated or even suicidal state of mind as they enter a facility to serve a sentence. Some may be a threat to others. The ability to segregate inmates to avoid inappropriate or dangerous mixing is important. Single-occupancy cells designed for suicide prevention are preferred.

Unlike the comparatively quick intake processes of detention facilities, the admissions processes in corrections facilities can be time-consuming, often taking many days or weeks. Each incoming inmate is carefully checked for basic documentation as he or she is admitted through a controlled entry point to a temporary holding cell. From there, the inmate proceeds through a series of steps that include photographic and other identification, physical and mental health evaluations, and an orientation program as they prepare to serve a sentence.

Space and equipment for medical and dental examinations, including X-ray and laboratory work for which the institution may contract with a private service, must be provided. Similarly, mental health assessments require the ability to observe and interview the inmate in a secure room where confidentiality can be preserved. At least one room may have to be designed for videoconferencing technology that can be used for evaluations involving professional expertise that is located off-site.

Some admissions processes may include treatment for an extended period of time before the inmate is moved to the main housing area for which he or she is classified. All admissions areas should anticipate the provision of food, clothing issuance and laundry services, some general shared or dayroom space, and recreation. The space dedicated to admissions, transfer, and discharge should be configured to minimize the time and distance required to escort each inmate through the steps.

Administration

Space for the general administration of a correctional institution is typically located at the interface between the public zone, outside the security perimeter, and the secure zone, within it. The nature of the site (e.g., densely urban or remote and open, etc.) as well as the philosophy of the institution influence decisions about where to locate the administration area.

Some institutions have opted for the provision of administrative space in a separate building outside the security perimeter on the grounds that it is more secure and convenient for processes involving interaction with the public. Other institutions provide space inside the perimeter and close to the inmate population.

The public entrance point and reception area may or may not be integrated with the pedestrian and vehicular sally port used by staff and other authorized personnel. Adjacent to the reception area should be the suite of offices required for the warden; the deputy warden or others who manage the inmate services, programs, and other operations; public information personnel; and clerical support. At least one conference room should be provided.

Records management for the inmate population, current and historical, requires storage and workstation space, equipment, and staff adequate for the size of the facility. Inmate records are exceedingly important. Business office functions also require space to support procurement, contracting, and financial records management.

Institutions that engage private, out-of-house services extensively can anticipate frequent visits by representatives. All administrative spaces that are accessible to visitors from outside the institution should be designed to provide protection for staff, such as bullet-proof materials in counter areas.

The corrections professionals, senior officers who supervise and train the uniformed staff stationed throughout the facility, need full-size offices of approximately 120 sq ft each. A large, multipurpose space for staff briefing, and classrooms with storage for training equipment and materials, must also be provided, along with a break room, exercise room, and locker rooms with showers. The institution must conduct continuous training of its corrections staff, utilizing the latest instructional technology available. Staff relief area(s) to allow time away from the stresses of certain posts are also essential.

SITE SELECTION AND DESIGN

The site selection process can involve political action, formal and informal, as well as organized activity by civic associations to whom design proposals must be clear and persuasive.

Site Selection

The criteria used in selecting a site include access, soil characteristics, and the community-based resources in the vicinity.

Technical considerations include the ability to access the site easily from adjacent roads, the quality of the soils and types of construction they will support, topography and drainage, the presence of special ecological features or hazards that may entail costly site work, climatic conditions, and views to and from all directions. The capacity to expand in the future may also be a lead item.

In addition, the adequacy of existing utilities, or the potential for new ones, is a major issue. The facility will require a utilities infrastructure that enables it to feed and house a large population in both warm and dry conditions.

The availability of nearby resources for inmate services and programs is also a key consideration. The provision of medical and mental health services will almost certainly involve ties to a hospital or other health care providers outside the institution, as well as a cadre of professionals who reside within a daily commuting distance.

Similarly, the ability to mount education and vocational training programs may depend on nearby instructors and schools that can augment the in-house resources of the institution. Residential and community areas that are appealing to the administrative and correctional staff are also major factors in site selection.

Site Design

Two issues are especially important in site design: the function of the security perimeter and the various ways it can be developed architecturally, and the extensive back-and-forth movement through the perimeter that must be anticipated.

Security perimeters involve combinations of hard physical barriers—walls, berms, fences, and the like—and detection systems that use both technology and visual surveillance by posted or patrolling staff, and response systems that can terminate an escape attempt rapidly as soon as it is spotted. Perimeter security specialists can assist the design team with the task of determining the severity of the security risks on a given site and with the selection of the most cost-effective and reliable detection technology to deploy on the site. The technology ranges from cable-based or infrared and microwave systems to video motion detection systems.

The design must also anticipate night illumination of building rooftops, walls, buffer zones, setbacks, and no-man's-land areas. Whether the perimeter is a hard wall or a see-through fencing system, the presence of high-intensity lighting, typically on tall poles, is a prominent design element.

Back-and-forth movement through the security perimeter is extensive, and the design of the site must be able to manage it successfully. Correctional institutions interact with the world outside their perimeters much more than many people realize. Several kinds of entrance to the site should be provided: secure pedestrian and vehicular sally ports for the transport of prisoners and access by authorized personnel, service entrances that can handle large trucks moving to and from shipping and receiving docks, and the public entrance to which visitors—family members or others on professional business—must come.

The location, number, size, security level, layout, associated signage and image

▲ *Grand Valley Institution for Women, Kitchener, Ontario. Kuwabara Payne McKenna Blumberg Architects. Photo: Steven Evans.*

of these entry points must be designed to ensure that each works on its own and in support of the others. The design must make it possible to control the flow of people and vehicles within and through the perimeter.

UNIQUE DESIGN CONCERNS

The stereotype of a correctional facility is a grim, hulking presence—thick walls, sharp wire, high watchtowers. This is the Big House. The image has been reinforced by the reality of numerous older facilities, as well as by Hollywood and other popular culture. And at least one actual facility, Alcatraz, has found a permanent place in American folklore.

Today's design decision maker is faced with numerous questions about what kind of image to project. The facility is a symbol of the system. It sends messages about the rule of law. It also has links with the community, and its architecture may reflect that connection.

▶ Four general concepts for the organization of the housing, programs, services, and other support elements of a facility. A distinguishing feature among them is the varying relationship of the housing units to recreation areas and large open spaces. For a thorough and extensively illustrated discussion of different approaches, see Peter Krasnow, Correctional Facility Design and Detailing (New York: McGraw-Hill, 1998), pp. 117–179.

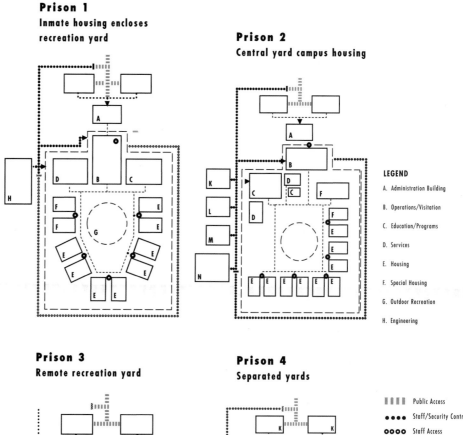

Prison 1
Inmate housing encloses recreation yard

Prison 2
Central yard campus housing

LEGEND

A. Administration Building

B. Operations/Visitation

C. Education/Programs

D. Services

E. Housing

F. Special Housing

G. Outdoor Recreation

H. Engineering

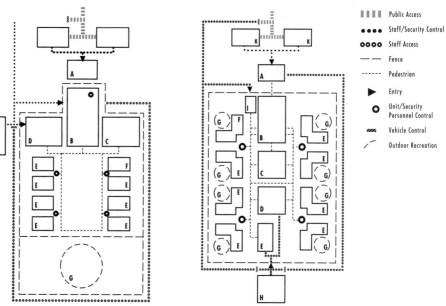

Prison 3
Remote recreation yard

Prison 4
Separated yards

▮▮▮▮ Public Access

●●●● Staff/Security Control

○○○○ Staff Access

——— Fence

------- Pedestrian

▶ Entry

○ Unit/Security Personnel Control

▨▨ Vehicle Control

⟋ Outdoor Recreation

In contrast to the design issues posed by other elements of the justice system, notably courts, the architecture of large-scale correctional facilities may seek to mask or camouflage the actual nature of the project.

The Building Organization

The physical organization of the facility overall is driven by the classifications and size of the inmate population, the super-vision methods used, and the relation-ships of the housing to the other pro-grams.

Most general population housing for medium-security inmates consists of block or podular units (pods). Inmates who are classified in low- or minimum-security categories may be housed in multiple-occupancy rooms or even in dormitory spaces. Inmates who are classi-fied as maximum-security risks may be

▲ *Aerial view showing inmate housing developed as cottages opposite pro-grams and services buildings in a residential campus plan. Grand Valley Institution for Women, Kitchener, Ontario. Kuwabara Payne McKenna Blumberg Architects. Photo: Peter Gill.*

◀ Multiple-occupancy inmate rooms in a minimum security building. Federal correctional institution, Estill, South Carolina. LS3P Architects. Photo: Gordon Shenk.

▲ Segregated housing for maximum-security-risk inmates. Jackson correctional institution, Black River Falls, Wisconsin. Venture Architects. Photo: James Morrill, JJ Images.

housed in single-occupancy rooms that are segregated from the rest of the population.

Circulation

Facilities that are organized around a centralized, inmates-to-services-and-programs concept often have housing units developed as discrete blocks or pods. The units are connected by circulation systems to service and program areas that are located in other portions of the building or in other buildings on a secure campus site. A low-rise facility that occupies a large site, often in a remote location, has an extensive horizontal circulation system.

The movement of the inmate population inside a facility must be via secure corridors and control points that are sized for the volume of persons they serve. In some cases, a dual or stacked corridor system is developed in which the lower level is for the use of inmates and staff exclusively, and the upper level is for staff and escorted public visitors.

If services are centralized in a high-rise facility, where the inmates are housed in stacked units on the upper levels, vertical circulation in dedicated elevator systems must be designed.

Alternative layouts based on a decentralized operations strategy also entail special circulation systems, but the primary movement is of authorized personnel and materiel, rather than large numbers of inmates. Corridor and elevator design must support the conveyance of food and supplies on large carts, for example.

Exterior Design

Numerous facilities are in remote locations on large sites that allow low-rise buildings in campus-like arrangements. In such settings, where the surrounding area is empty terrain, the primary elevation in the design of an institution may be its patrol road and electric fencing. The checkpoint for entry may involve an administrative building outside or at the security perimeter.

Tight, limited sites in populated areas may generate high-rise designs on small footprints. The scale and massing of the building forms change accordingly, and they may rely on walls, rather than fences, to establish the perimeter. The use of walls is also typical with minimum-security, women's, and other facilities of special classifications.

Aesthetically designed wall systems can be developed to control views to the site from neighboring buildings, roads, or communities. Where fences are visible to the public, single-arched and non-climbable mesh systems can provide alternatives to the double-fence with razor ribbon.

Outside the security perimeter

Administration buildings and visitor screening centers located outside or along the security perimeter should appear secure and safe. These buildings should be designed to look like straightforward office and visitors buildings. Clear glazing at entrance lobby walls and doors should provide an unobstructed line of sight from interior control centers to public and parking areas. Although public areas not within the security perimeter may be designed with insulated, shatter-resistant glazing, attack-rated security glazing is typically provided at control centers.

The aesthetic goal is to achieve a relatively normal look for the buildings outside the perimeter while also ensuring that they are designed for restricted access. The design should make it possible to monitor and control nonauthorized personnel on all sides of the facility, including the walls and all roof areas, and within a 50 ft zone outside the site perimeter. Other structures (such as shops, central plants, and support buildings) may be outside the security perimeter as well, and access to these buildings should be strictly limited and controlled.

Inside the security perimeter

In corrections buildings within the secure zone, windows are small and few. Building planes of hard material tend to be uniform and lacking in decorative detail. Typical exterior cladding materials include masonry, concrete, and stone, designed for permanence. The large expanses of hard material generally involve a bland color palette. Scale-giving features are not present to the extent they are in other building types.

▲ Skillful use of durable materials and detailing to establish scale and visual interest. Federal correctional institution, Estill, South Carolina. LS3P Architects. Photo: Gordon Shenk.

Exterior doors and windows should be designed to be consistent with the security and functional requirements of the interior spaces. Entry areas and doors must be durable and designed for heavy use in all seasons and weather conditions.

Roofing designs and materials should be developed to reduce access points, provide an appropriate appearance, and minimize areas for concealment. Various roofing materials may be used, but any roofing system should have designated walkways for the required routine maintenance of the roof and items located on it.

The resulting challenges for the designer include the need to manage transitions in scale, to relieve the monotony of a bland palette, and to develop entry

sequences and building-to-building circulation systems that are easy to understand, comfortable, and safe. The design challenges may be compounded when there is political sensitivity to spending taxpayer dollars on what some people perceive as frills.

Interior Design

The interiors of all functional areas inside correctional facilities are designed for both security and long-term living.

Design for security

Security is an overriding requirement. It entails the hard issues of providing physical barriers and the soft issues of how the look and feel of the physical environment may influence inmate behavior.

Physical barriers

To protect society from individuals who have been judged to pose a danger, as well as to protect those individuals from each other and, in cases of potential suicide, from themselves, the facility is designed and constructed as a series of static physical barriers inside a clearly defined perimeter. See Chapter 11, "Security Systems," for a discussion of appropriate materials and related systems.

The physical barriers work in concert with operations. In institutions that employ direct supervision methods, staff contact is a key part of any security design. The architecture of interior spaces should support this, reinforcing the methods and goals of the operations.

Some inmates are subject to virtually absolute control: 23 hours per day of lockdown time in a single-occupancy cell of a super-maximum-security facility, with 5 or more hours of time in the outdoors per week. Other inmates in a low-security facility, or at some stage in a program planned to result in their release, occupy different kinds of environments controlled in other ways.

Comprehensible space

Correctional interiors should be easy for the people in them to "understand." The physical extent or boundaries of a space should be clear and unambiguous.

Interiors in large facilities are characterized by repetitive forms and alternating combinations of large, high-ceiling volumes and small, cellular spaces. The length and width of corridors, and the rhythms of spatial sequencing from one area to the next, can include important transitions. The transitions may involve the movement of a person from one space to another, or the shifts from human scale to smaller or larger scales by the physical parts of the facility.

Circulation

Circulation systems and corridor space should be as uncomplicated and efficient as possible. Corridors for inmate movement are not less than 8 ft wide and are often developed in tree patterns—that is, without intersections that make it possible for an inmate to take a wrong turn. Alcoves, blind spots, or other features that obstruct sight lines and provide opportunities for congestion or concealment should not be designed. If inmate movement involves going from one building to another in a campus-like institution, clearly marked and covered walkways should be provided.

All corridors and similar spaces should be designed to enable staff to isolate and contain a disturbance in an emergency, as well as to carry out the routine securing of areas that are shut down after hours.

Design for living

The realities are stark. Many hundreds of people may be housed for many years in the same building(s). Interior conditions, like proper sanitation and a balanced diet, are facts of life that must meet the levels required for safe habitation.

Sound and light

Correctional facilities are notoriously hard-surface environments. Sound travels easily. If the design of a facility does not include good acoustical control, the reverberation of thuds and clanging metal and the sounds of human voices can be harsh to the point of undermining habitability. See Chapter 8, "Lighting and Acoustics."

▶ Residential cottage-style inmate housing. Grand Valley Institution for Women, Kitchener, Ontario. Kuwabara Payne McKenna Blumberg Architects. Photo: Steven Evans.

Controlling noise at its source, providing separation between areas that generate noise and those that are disturbed by it, insulating enclosure systems against noise, and installing sound-absorptive materials are important to the overall design for living. Each major area or occupancy will have its own acoustical design requirements, from inmate housing to the offices where staff confer or conduct confidential counseling.

The acoustics of program spaces, such as classrooms or multipurpose rooms, should be designed to support individual head-down concentration for studying or group gatherings that depend on normal speaking levels. It should be possible to participate in an instructional or treatment program without having to shout. Sound control materials that could be

vandalized should be applied only on ceilings and on high wall surfaces.

Light, like sound, goes far in determining the quality of a space. The ACA standards specify that each inmate room must have access to natural light from a source that is no farther than 20 ft from the room. A window from the inmate room directly to the outdoors may or may not be provided, but at least borrowed light from the dayroom adjacent to the inmate room is required. This access to the natural environment provided by the ability to observe sun angles is considered essential to both physical and psychological well-being.

Integrating natural light and artificial light during the day is an effective way to provide high-quality general illumination while also reducing energy con-

0 ——————— 30 feet

0 ——————— 10 metres

sumption. Direct artificial lighting is customary in high-volume spaces. In spaces with lower ceiling heights, indirect lighting, supplemented by task lighting, is generally regarded as preferable. Light fixtures—suspended, surface mounted, or recessed—that are within the reach of inmates must be durable and resistant to vandalism.

Designing to counteract gloom and darkness, depression and danger, includes decisions about the colors and reflectance values of finishes. Light colors in warm tones, with nonspecular surfaces for paint and dull finishes for metal, are preferable in general, and they can be

important for some inmates, particularly geriatric inmates, who may have impaired vision or may be suffering from depression. Light deprivation can be a serious problem.

Normative design

The term *normative design* applies to design that seeks to make the environment noninstitutional without sacrificing security. Although not typical for general-custody populations, normative design is associated with inmates who are classified as minimum-security risks and who may be nearing the end of a sentence. The techniques for "normalizing" an inmate housing unit include the introduction of

▲ Plan, inmate housing cottage. Note the mix of shared and private space. Grand Valley Institution for Women, Kitchener, Ontario. Kuwabara Payne McKenna Blumberg Architects.

145

Role of the Private Sector

Private sector services frequently focus on care for younger and less serious offenders. Private agencies in some states provide the majority of beds for young female offenders and help keep these youth out of the state systems. Most private sector organizations do not provide the most restrictive high-security beds. The more difficult youth are placed in state facilities.

Some Recent Trends

Throughout the 1970s and 1980s, the design of many juvenile detention and training school facilities reflected an emphasis on educational and training programs designed to teach the skills required to reenter society successfully. This goal remains. Since the early 1990s, however, older juveniles, 14–16 years of age, have often been considered to be more serious offenders. Some of these youth are more likely to have committed more serious offenses than those in earlier years. These trends, combined with stiffer "three-strikes" sentencing in some courts

and overcrowding in some places, have underscored security issues in the design of juvenile facilities.

JUVENILE AND FAMILY COURT SYSTEMS

Case jurisdiction in juvenile and family courts varies from state to state. The role of these courts is generally twofold: to intervene early and effectively to prevent children from returning into the justice system as victims or later offenders, and to intervene with the entire family unit.

Most juvenile and family courts across the United States handle divorce cases, child custody cases, visitation and support cases. Many also handle dependency and delinquency matters, truancy, and runaway youth problems. Some handle cases involving child abuse and neglect (both civil and criminal cases), children at risk, child in need of services (CHINS) cases, and civil domestic relations.

The jurisdiction may also include termination of parental rights and adoption proceedings, criminal matters (including

▼ Queens Family Court and Family Agency facility, Jamaica, New York. Approach from Rufus King Park to elevation featuring transparency at waiting areas inside. Pei Cobb Freed/Gruzen Samton Associated Architects.

◀ *Queens Family Court and Family Agency facility, Jamaica, New York. Aerial view of photomontage showing mixed nature of the site. Pei Cobb Freed/Gruzen Samton Associated Architects.*

criminal domestic violence), abortion waiver cases, guardianship cases, and cases involving children with mental illnesses and other disabilities.

The structure of these courts varies from location to location. In some systems, juvenile and family courts are separate and distinct from other courts. In others, juvenile and family cases are heard by judges within the same courts as other criminal and civil cases. In systems that have designated juvenile and/or family courts, the judges may be assigned to handle juvenile and family matters exclusively, or they may rotate from other judicial assignments according to a schedule.

The roles of the court-related state and county agencies also vary from place to place. The agencies work with the courts when judges apply their broad powers to correct situations by ordering commitments, rearranging families, and compelling adult cooperation. The courts also use probation officers to investigate facts and provide supervision of youth.

Differences from General Jurisdiction Courts

Juvenile and family justice facilities are distinguished from general jurisdiction civil and criminal courts in several important ways:

- The proceedings have traditionally been relatively "closed" (i.e., a high degree of confidentiality is maintained). Access to files and court records is restricted. In most states, there are significant restrictions governing the presence of parties to the dispute, victims, witnesses, and the public in the court.

- Security requirements are high. Family and juvenile court proceedings are emotionally charged, involving very personal issues and intense emotions, and thus increased risk. Often, a court hearing brings together people who have been separated by court order. Planning for security in public areas and during "precourtroom times" is of particular importance. Providing for adequate observation and control of public areas, often by staff, and appropriate separation of the parties in the public areas of the courthouse is crucial.

- Family court systems feature the presence of social service agencies and groups during court proceedings. It is not uncommon to have separate counsel present representing each parent, the child (or children), the state, and other agencies in family and juvenile cases.

- The volume of people involved in juvenile and family cases, and occupying the public spaces of a court, can be high. There are wide ranges in age (from very young children to elderly persons), and many people have little experience with the court system. Many are attempting to navigate through the system *pro se,* or by self-representation. This increases the need for self-help areas and centers in family courts, and staff are constantly involved in education of and assistance to the public.

- Juvenile and family courts may operate during evenings and on weekends. Certain activities and support services must be available throughout all periods (e.g., protective orders must be signed when needed).

Areas and Spaces

Courtrooms and hearing rooms

Courtrooms

Courtrooms are used for many different cases and matters, including detention hearings, trials, arraignments, divorce cases, child custody and support hearings, and mental health commitments.

A courtroom is typically designed for one judge or judicial hearing officer, a court reporter or reporting system, security personnel, a court clerk, and a prosecutor. In addition, there are often several attorneys, parents, advocates and guardian *ad litem* staff, protective service workers, and probation officers. Other family members, witnesses, interpreters, and sometimes members of the public and the media may also be present.

Courtrooms and hearing rooms of several sizes are provided in some facilities. Large courtrooms are used for matters involving more complex cases with a greater number of parties and counsel; smaller courtrooms and hearing rooms are used for hearings involving dependency, contested divorce cases, and more personal matters.

Courtrooms designed specifically for juvenile and family courts are different from general jurisdiction courtrooms in several ways:

Nonjury courtrooms. Most juvenile and many family court proceedings do not use juries. The size of the courtroom is therefore reduced inasmuch as the jury box is omitted and jury panels are not called to report to the room for selection.

Reduced spectator seating. Many juvenile and family proceedings are closed to all persons except the parties involved and representatives of agencies concerned with the interests of the state, the courts, or the general welfare of a child. In most states, there are higher standards of confidentiality for juvenile and family cases. Most courtrooms therefore have smaller spectator seating requirements.

Accommodation of additional parties.
Many proceedings in family court involve more parties than are traditionally represented in typical criminal or civil cases in general jurisdiction courts. It is not uncommon to have five or more distinct individuals or groups represented in some cases, such as the following:

- Each parent, with counsel
- Each child, with counsel
- Counsel for the intervening party
- Representatives of juvenile probation or court-related support agencies
- Social workers
- Others (investigators, detention officers/custody staff for the adult and/or juveniles in custody, court clerks, law clerks, etc.)

These parties should be provided separate and distinct accommodations in the courtroom, with the ability to have a private, confidential conversation without being overheard. Generally, the rule of thumb is that such accommodation requires approximately 8 ft of distance between parties or groups.

Separation of victims and witnesses. The right of the accused to face an accuser is a central tenet of U.S. law. In juvenile and family courts, however, discretion is allowed to reduce opportunities for intimidation in cases of violence and abuse. The courtroom should provide separation and control of victims and witnesses to promote a sense of safety, security, and fairness.

Hearing rooms

Juvenile and family courts lead the court systems of the United States in the use of alternative dispute resolution (ADR), mediation, conciliation, and settlement alternatives to trials. Conference and hearing rooms provide the appropriate areas for the negotiation, meeting, and resolution phases of these hearings. Users include all parties. Hearing and ADR/mediation rooms should be located with appropriate and separate access from public, staff, judicial, and prisoner areas.

Hearing and mediation rooms should include at least one additional breakout room to enable parties to move from the formal hearing to a separate space for consultation and discussion. Provisions should be made for appropriate technology and design to accommodate the full range of adult and juvenile users.

Court support elements

Judges' chambers

In most jurisdictions, judges' chambers serve as more than office and preparation areas for the judges. Acoustical privacy is essential. The chambers should be sized and located to permit their use as small conference rooms. There should be controlled access to permit parties to move from courtrooms to chambers, or to report directly to the chambers for hearings or conferences.

In-custody holding areas

Juvenile and family court facilities should provide separate holding areas for juveniles and adults, males and females. In facilities where a single secure circulation system is used for both adults and juveniles, operational procedures must ensure that they are kept separate from each other. All prisoner areas, including elevators and corridors for secure prisoner circulation, should be visually and acoustically separated from the public, judicial/staff, and courtroom areas of the building.

The prisoner circulation, access, and detention areas should be designed with appropriate security sally port access and control points and monitoring and control equipment. Easy access between these areas and the sheriff's office or other security personnel is important.

The holding cells should be designed to meet national and state standards for temporary holding facilities. They should be equipped with duress alarms, modern communications equipment, and closed-circuit television for monitoring defendants during trial. Holding areas for juveniles in particular should be designed to allow both separation and constant observation.

Courtroom waiting areas

Waiting areas outside courtrooms should be open, safe, and secure for children,

families, and other parties. Waiting periods may be long, because hearings can go on for extended periods, and there may be associated activities (filing papers, interviews, etc.) that take time. Adults and parents must be able to observe and supervise their children in these spaces, and room for changing diapers and breast-feeding is desirable.

Attorney-client conference rooms

Workstations and interview rooms should be provided for prehearing preparation and conferences between attorneys and parties to the dispute, witnesses, and victims, who should not be located in public circulation and waiting areas. These rooms should provide acoustic separation and accommodate a variety of changing groups. They should also be conveniently located close to

▼ ▶ Plans of Levels one, three, and five, Queens Family Court and Family Agency facility, Jamaica, New York. Note adjoining Family Agency facility, as well as generous waiting areas outside courtrooms and hearing rooms. Pei Cobb Freed/Gruzen Samton Associated Architects.

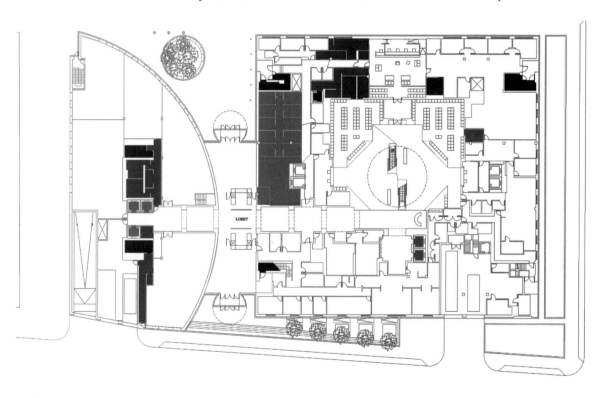

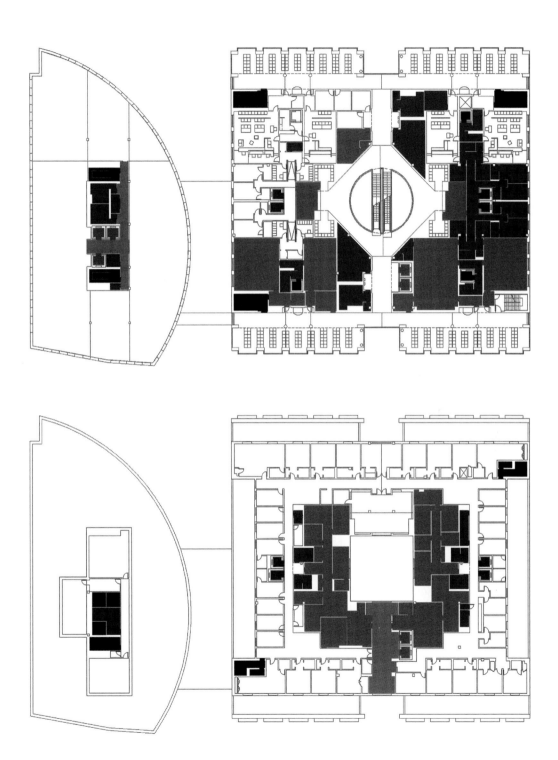

courtrooms. Two to four rooms should be provided per courtroom.

Court administration and Clerk of Court areas

Court administration

Court administrative staff may be involved in calendaring functions, providing administrative assistance to the judges, and serving as liaison with state, county, and other agencies. Court administrative areas for juvenile or family courts should be located close to public circulation areas.

Clerk of the Court

Office areas for clerical functions should support advanced records handling systems. There are specific requirements in juvenile and family courts for confidentiality and for the length of time records are kept. Most files do not go to archives. Records keep growing, and issues of access and control are critical. Various records-handling systems are used, which may entail various degrees of automation and integration with other court systems.

Public queuing and waiting areas

The design of the Court Clerk/juvenile and family staff areas should be open, professional, and businesslike. Office and workstation areas should be designed for comfort and efficiency. Clear separation and control of publicly accessible areas (e.g., counters, waiting/queuing areas, document viewing areas, and work rooms) should be provided.

Staff at workstations in most Court Clerk offices should be positioned to see and assist at counters as required. Public queuing and waiting areas should be designed to provide fast and convenient service and access. In places where public waiting can be anticipated, seating with "take-a-number" or other automated queuing systems should be provided.

Prose center

Juvenile and family courts tend to have a high percentage of self-represented, or *prose,* litigants. The large number of such litigants can have a dramatic impact on staff levels and court operations.

Prose and victim witness centers are often provided to assist the parties involved in cases. The design of a *prose* center should provide ready access to those who are familiar with legal requirements, processes, and documents, but the majority of users in *prose* centers will require personal assistance from lawyers (frequently pro bono) or other volunteers.

A *prose* center may be established in conjunction with or separate from a law library, and public access terminals and information distribution areas should be designed for easy access and use.

Victim/witness center

In some court facilities, separate reporting and waiting areas are provided for victims and witnesses, who should be separated prior to, during, and after hearings and appearances. Although these centers were originally designed to serve victims during criminal proceedings, today they serve victims and witnesses in a wide variety of cases, including civil domestic violence cases, child support hearings, and juvenile and other family matters.

This area should be accessible but not visible (to assist its protective value). It should accommodate children, elderly persons, disabled persons, and volunteer support activities. Separate rest room facilities should be provided to reduce opportunities for intimidation and inter-

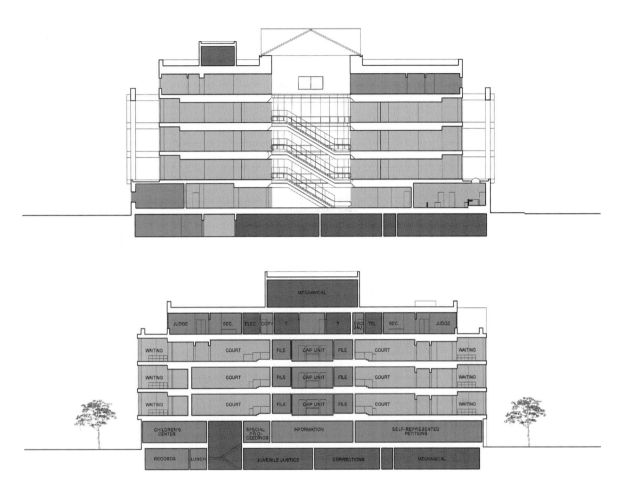

action with other parties. Victims and witnesses are escorted to court and the prosecutor's office as needed.

Court-related agencies

Prosecuting attorney's office

In many juvenile and family court facilities, space is provided for a branch office, typically housing the attorneys and support staff responsible for prosecution of misdemeanor and felony cases involving juveniles. The office is involved in confidential matters and requires clear separation and security from general public areas of the building.

Within the office, there should be private areas for confidential interviews, as well as open-office and flexible work areas for support staff, records, and shared equipment. Special spaces may include witness interview and deposition rooms, waiting areas for general visitors and law enforcement officers, and waiting areas for victims and witnesses. Typically, a receptionist controls access to the office.

Public defender's office

In some courts, a juvenile unit public defender's office may be provided for minors and adults who are unable to afford private counsel. Like those in the prosecuting attorney's office, staff in the public defender's office are involved in confidential matters requiring a secure environment that is acoustically and visually private. Typical spaces provided include private offices, workstations, shared open-office support areas, one or more interview and conference areas, and appropriate waiting areas.

Adult and juvenile probation, parole, pretrial, and community services

Juvenile and family courts frequently involve probation and other oversight services for supervision and monitoring. Probation offices may be open before and after court hours, and staff conduct both in-office and out-of-office supervision and reporting activities. Private offices, conference/interview rooms, open-office workstations, and appropriate office support spaces are typically provided for these functions.

Separate waiting areas with privacy from the general public should be provided. Intake interviews are an important function of probation offices when they are located in court facilities, and separate interview rooms capable of accommodating six to eight people are necessary.

Drug and alcohol testing is frequently required as a condition of probation. A small laboratory or other space for this testing is essential. It should be safe, confidential, and designed to support all necessary testing equipment.

Other agencies

Spaces may be provided for other public and private agencies involved in juvenile and family cases. Activities include advocacy programs, family court counseling programs, social services, and city or county counsel (prosecution in child support cases). These agencies are involved in confidential matters and require a secure environment. Their representatives may be involved at many stages before, during, and after proceedings.

These agencies are present in the facility to simplify access to services for families involved in juvenile or family court matters, and to enhance multidisciplinary solutions to family-related problems. The amount and type of space assigned to agency staff and programs will vary from location to location, but they constitute a critical and growing factor in juvenile and family court planning generally.

Evaluation and guidance centers (or child centers) have been recently established in some of the major juvenile and family court systems (e.g., Chicago and Los Angeles). These centers are responsible for the identification and, in some cases, treatment of emotionally disturbed minors as they and their families become involved with the court system. Observation, play, testing, treatment, interview, and counseling areas, plus adult/family and child waiting areas (separated and sometimes viewable) may be required, as well as staff support areas for offices, workstations, records, and equipment.

Public/building support functions

Lobby

A public entrance lobby creates an initial impression and can influence the expectations of the users significantly. It should be designed for the security screening function and should be open, inviting, and easily supervised. Security personnel should be able to monitor the space easily so as to reduce opportunities for parties to intimidate victims or witnesses.

In many juvenile and family court facilities, public access and movement of visitors in the facility is regulated, with only limited access permitted to court floors and courtroom waiting areas for specific proceedings. At times, parties are directed to specific waiting areas to reduce opportunities for intimidation and unplanned encounters with others.

Regardless of the level of intervention by staff, the lobby space should promote efficient movement and filtering of different groups entering the facility. The visitors may or may not be familiar with the building. Information graphics and monitors should be provided to help people know where to go and how to move through the building, and provisions should be made for multilingual aides and those who can help with accessibility for impaired individuals.

Associated spaces in or adjacent to the entrance lobby include a public desk, public counters and information areas, public waiting areas, public rest rooms, and children's waiting and/or day care areas.

Food services

Provisions should be made for food and drinks for visitors and staff at a court, particularly because children and extended families may be in the building for long periods and for multiple meetings. Large courts typically have full-service cafeterias capable of handling peak periods at breakfast and lunch. Seating and waiting areas should be open for use between meal periods. Vending machines should be provided for drinks and snacks.

JUVENILE DETENTION CENTERS

Juvenile detention facilities have a central role in the continuum of care services developed for young people. These facilities are used for short-term holding of

juveniles awaiting hearings, often for pretrial periods of a few days or one to two weeks. An important emphasis in short-term detention is managing the behavior of youth who may be in an anxious or dangerous condition. Long-term detention of juveniles sentenced to serve many weeks or months is handled in residential facilities, with programs aimed at modifying their behavior and skill levels over an extended period.

Some facilities are designed to accommodate both short-term detention and long-term residential programs for sentenced offenders, particularly in large urban areas. Facilities may be designed for both male and female populations. Program and treatment spaces can be designed for separated and/or mixed groups.

Standards

Planning and design for local and state residential facilities should comply with standards for secure juvenile facilities, including those of the American Bar Association (ABA), the National Advisory

▼ Exterior elevation, Crossroads Detention Center, Brooklyn, New York. Kaplan McLaughlin Diaz/Goncher-Sput Associated Architects. Photo: Bo Parker.

Committee for Juvenile Justice and Delinquency Prevention (NAC), the American Correctional Association (ACA), and the applicable state standards, codes, and licensure requirements.

The standards provide guidelines for the development of supportive, nonrepressive but security-based programs and services. State licensure standards focus on health and safety, staffing, and physical plant requirements. The ABA and NAC standards show a preference for unobtrusive, staff-oriented security measures. ACA standards focus on programs, policies, and procedures, and they also offer guidance on individual area requirements for indoor rooms, dayrooms, activity areas, and dining spaces. A facility may operate without ACA accreditation, but a license from the state or authority having jurisdiction is typically required.

Operational and Organizational Concepts

Facility size and location

There are only a few large juvenile detention facilities in the United States. Large, centralized institutions provide opportunities for a greater range of programs and specialty services, as well as some economies of scale.

Usually, however, facilities provide 100 or fewer beds, and housing units are designed in groups of 16 beds or fewer per unit. The widespread support for smaller, less institutional, but controllable, facilities is based on the need for local services and the desire to keep youth close to the community and family. Smaller environments are more effective for treatment and can be less intimidating to the youth they house.

Supervision and security

Juvenile detention facilities, in general, are designed for direct staff supervision and contact between residents and staff. In most cases, single-story facilities and single-occupancy resident rooms are desired. Individual rooms make it easier for staff to use confinement of residents to their respective rooms as a behavior management tool.

Separation and segregation

Housing areas may be designed to various security levels. However, the small populations served and the need for flexibility in assignment cause many juvenile detention facilities to be designed to high security levels in the resident rooms and housing units. This allows greater flexibility in using the beds and housing units to accommodate various levels of security and assignment as needs change. Within the security framework, the emphasis in design is on minimizing the harshness of the security environment, especially for lower-security-risk defendants.

Service-delivery options

A variety of service-delivery options are employed. In many cases, food service, educational, and recreational programs are provided in central locations within the facility, since the movement of the youth to the services is believed to promote a greater sense of normalcy. Provisions are often made for special-needs youth, however, for whom food and educational programs are brought to the dayrooms.

Areas and Spaces

Public lobby

The main public lobby should serve as the central entrance point during standard hours for all staff, resident visitors, and administrative visitors. It should also serve as a staging area for all visitors until they have been screened through a metal detector.

The lobby should be supervised by a receptionist, who screens and directs visitors to appropriate areas, with backup assistance from Central Control. After hours, the lobby should be secured and accessible only by staff. In larger facilities, parents coming to pick up youth after hours may enter the receiving/screening lobby (discussed in a later section) directly without going through the public lobby. The public lobby should accommodate phones, rest rooms, and comfortable seating.

Administration

The administrative staff area should accommodate offices, spaces for training and testing, and other staff support functions. This area should be restricted to staff only and is generally located outside the security perimeter.

Central Control

The Central Control station is staffed on a 24-hour basis. It is responsible for controlling access through the security perimeter, monitoring life safety and security systems, key control and staff check-in, conducting head counts in the facility, and serving as the communications center for the facility during emergencies.

In many facilities, the Central Control station is responsible for direct supervision and visual observation of the special holding/housing areas. It may also have direct supervision and control of visitation. In small facilities, Central Control may handle all incoming phone calls, particularly during evening or night shifts. A

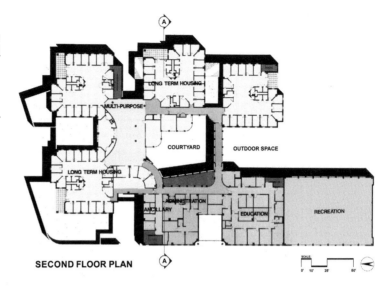

SECOND FLOOR PLAN

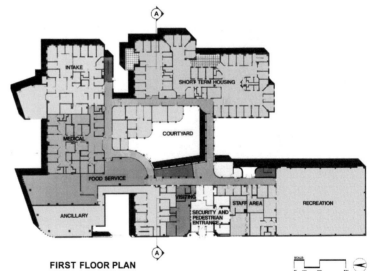

FIRST FLOOR PLAN

separate rest room and coffee area, accessible only from within Central Control, should be provided.

Receiving/screening/release

The receiving/screening/release area of a juvenile detention facility serves as its central intake point. Typically, law enforcement officers transport youth to

▲ Plans showing housing and related functions organized around open courtyard. Crossroads Detention Center, Brooklyn, New York. Kaplan McLaughlin Diaz/Goncher-Sput Associated Architects.

the facility, and staff handle the necessary paperwork. Initial contacts with the youth are aimed at producing a cooperative attitude and calming the youth by reducing confusion and anxiety.

All youth brought to this area are screened and assigned to appropriate placements, including placements in other facilities, or sent home after processing. Staff working in this area must have access to as much information as possible to make good decisions regarding placement, admission, or release. The atmosphere of the area should reduce the anxiety of the youth being processed.

The receiving/screening/release area should be located on the exterior of the facility, along the security perimeter, to limit movement inside. Direct access to the public lobby is provided for visitors, screening and medical staff, and parents/guardians. The entire receiving/screening/release area should be visible from staff work counter areas. Central Control should monitor and control movement into and out of the area.

The area should be designed to prevent cross circulation between youth being processed into the facility and youth going to or from the juvenile court or being released. The entire area should be secured when processing is not taking place.

Housing during intake/classification

Youth admitted to a juvenile detention facility are screened and evaluated by classification staff to determine the appropriate housing or placement assignment. Youth may reside initially in an intake/classification unit until detention hearings or classification assessments are complete and permanent housing assignments are made. In some locations, intake housing may constitute 5–15 percent of all beds,

and it should be separated from general housing. Because this housing is designed for youth in their initial hours at the facility, provisions are often made for constant staff supervision and observation.

General housing

After detention hearings and classification screening, residents are assigned to permanent housing units. These units are typically smaller than those in adult detention and correctional facilities. Unit sizes frequently respond to staffing levels promulgated in ACA or other standards. Units of 8–16 beds are common and are often designed to provide additional flexibility to accommodate subgroups of 8 beds or fewer. Housing units are often grouped together to permit expanded programming and achieve staffing efficiency.

Housing units are located within the security perimeter of the facility. They are supervised by youth managers, with back-up by staff both in Central Control and roaming through the facility. Most units are designed to include adjacent spaces for a variety of programs and services. This provides efficiencies for staff and encourages all residents to be involved. Dayrooms are provided at all housing units as common quiet-activity areas. Areas also are frequently designed with "time-out" or special needs rooms to allow staff to separate youth if and when required.

Residents of juvenile detention facilities typically participate in programs for 6 or 7 hours each weekday, and evening hours are used for visiting and special programs. Specialized programs can be provided at the housing units or may be offered in centralized program areas.

Educational/learning center

Most institutions require juvenile residents to participate in educational pro-

◀ *Housing unit dayroom, Crossroads Detention Center, Brooklyn, New York. Kaplan McLaughlin Diaz/Goncher-Sput Associated Architects. Photo: Bo Parker.*

▶ *Typical single-bed cell, Crossroads Detention Center, Brooklyn, New York. Kaplan McLaughlin Diaz/Goncher-Sput Associated Architects. Photo: Bo Parker.*

▼ *Classroom, Crossroads Detention Center, Brooklyn, New York. Kaplan McLaughlin Diaz/Goncher-Sput Associated Architects. Photo: Bo Parker.*

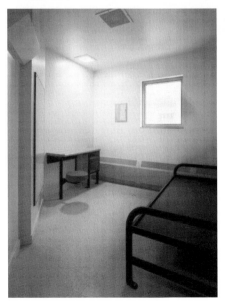

▲ Exterior elevation, Crossroads Detention Center, Brooklyn, New York. Kaplan McLaughlin Diaz/Goncher-Sput Associated Architects. Photo: Bo Parker.

grams. Programs may include academic, vocational, and life-skills subjects and recreation.

The academic programs are often tailored to work assignments from the children's public schools. Instructors may be part of the detention center staff or from the local school systems. The strong tie to community and school systems helps to focus youth attitudes and direction.

The spaces for these programs are often clustered to improve staff observation, supervision, and efficiency.

Recreation

With few exceptions, all youth in juvenile detention facilities are required to participate in recreational programs, both active (indoor or outdoor, weather permitting), and passive (including table and board games, arts and crafts). Access to recreation can be used as part of a behavior modification program.

Recreation generally takes place for two or three hours per weekday on an alternating schedule with academic programs. Active recreation spaces are provided at the housing units or in other gym or outdoor areas to which residents are moved, with youth managers or escort staff.

Social services

Juvenile detention programs provide access to counseling, social service, and mental health professionals. Social service staff conduct classification assessments

and evaluations (which may take place in reception and intake area conference and meeting rooms), treatment and training programs (in centralized or distributed program areas), and crisis management and response activities.

Visitation

Youth in juvenile detention centers are typically allowed to visit two or more times weekly with parents or guardians. Primary visiting hours are typically on weekday evenings and during the day on weekends, although attorney-client and probation officer visits can occur at any time of the day or evening.

In most facilities, group visiting (maximum of two visitors) and private visiting rooms are provided. The entire visiting area should be visible to the supervising staff and should be acoustically treated to provide a casual or classroom-type environment.

Food services

Food services provided in juvenile detention facilities typically consist of three full meals per day. In most facilities, a minimum of two of the meals must include hot entrées. A snack often is provided at night.

Food can be prepared on- or off-site. In many cases, meals are prepared in institutional or commercial kitchens and brought to preparation or reheat kitchens at the facility. In other

▲ Interior courtyard, Crossroads Detention Center, Brooklyn, New York. Kaplan McLaughlin Diaz/Goncher-Sput Architects. Photo: Bo Parker.

instances, food is prepared in a central kitchen and served in one or more central dining rooms.

Health services

All youth entering the screening/reception area are screened by medical staff for immediate and/or chronic health problems. In most juvenile detention facilities, spaces for medical and dental services are centralized and designed to permit easy access to the intake/screening, intake housing, and general housing areas. Waiting areas should be visually supervised by medical or security staff. Movement to examining areas should be controlled. Patient room doors should be glazed to allow patients to be visible at all times from a nursing or supervising station.

The health services provided in these facilities are consistent with community health standards. Policies and procedures govern situations in which medical care is provided on-site or by other communi-

ty or institutional care centers. All medical areas should be designed to support full handicapped access and the movement of patients on gurneys.

Medical beds often are provided in larger juvenile detention facilities and are used for limited, short-term care for isolation and treatment of contagious diseases, injuries, and diagnostic services. These areas are designed to comply with applicable standards for correctional health care. They require clean and soiled linen areas, cleaning and waste-handling areas, nursing and control stations with direct visual observation of beds, and access to examination and treatment areas.

JUVENILE TRAINING SCHOOLS

All states and some larger metropolitan centers operate one or more juvenile training schools/correctional centers. The training schools provide long-term housing for the most serious or chronic juvenile offenders. Although most juvenile programs emphasize alternatives to con-

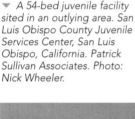

▼ A 54-bed juvenile facility sited in an outlying area. San Luis Obispo County Juvenile Services Center, San Luis Obispo, California. Patrick Sullivan Associates. Photo: Nick Wheeler.

finement, if possible, training schools are used for young offenders requiring higher levels of security and treatment. A training school serves 125–500 juveniles of various classifications. These facilities often look like adult detention or correctional institutions.

Inside, however, most residential juvenile training schools are focused on providing a secure and safe environment for education, skills development, and self-sufficiency. The primary mission of training schools is reintegration into society.

Standards

Planning and design for juvenile residential facilities should comply with standards for secure juvenile facilities, including those of the American Bar Association (ABA), the National Advisory Committee for Juvenile Justice and Delinquency Prevention (NAC), the American Correctional Association (ACA), and the applicable state standards, codes, and licensure requirements.[1]

ACA standards give specific guidance on individual area requirements, particularly as related to indoor rooms, dayrooms, activity areas, and dining spaces. Even the title of the publication *ACA Standards for Juvenile Training Schools* underscores the emphasis on training and education.

Operational and Organizational Concepts

Facility size and location
Even with larger populations, training schools rely on smaller housing unit sizes

[1]A facility may operate without ACA accreditation, but a license from the state or authority having jurisdiction is required.

▲ *A typical housing building, San Luis Obispo County Juvenile Services Center, San Luis Obispo, California. Patrick Sullivan Associates. Photo: Nick Wheeler.*

to promote better supervision and increased interaction with the youth. ACA standards support housing unit sizes of 25 residents or fewer. Many facilities are designed with smaller unit sizes.

Supervision and security
Juvenile training schools are designed to optimize direct staff supervision and contact between the residents and staff. The use of direct-supervision units, with the unit manager located directly in the housing unit, is common. The constant presence of the unit manager helps prevent conflict.

All housing and program areas should be designed with good sight lines from staff positions and should be visible from multiple adjacent spaces or hallways.

Housing areas may be designed for various levels of security. Housing is often designed to high security levels to provide greater flexibility as assignment needs change. Multi-occupancy housing is allowed in as much as 20 percent of a facility under ACA standards, but the use of single-occupancy resident rooms is preferred. Like detention facilities, training schools often utilize individual rooms because this arrangement makes it easier for staff to use confinement to rooms as a behavior management tool.

Within the security framework, the design emphasis is on minimizing the harshness of the environment, particularly for lower-security-risk detainees.

Programs

In training schools, programs for youthshould occupy residents throughout the day (from wakeup to lights out), with most activity on a group basis. All program areas are typically sized to fit the largest user groups and to allow efficient utilization of space during all periods.

Service delivery concepts

A variety of service delivery options may be employed. In many cases, food service and educational and recreational programs are provided in central locations. Like detention facilities, many training schools are organized to support the movement of residents to and from activities. Such movement is seen to contribute to an atmosphere of greater normalcy. Where necessary, provisions are made for special-needs youth, who are served at the housing unit.

Areas and Spaces

Reception/admissions

Admissions in a training school involves receiving youth through a secure vehicle sally port. The admissions area should be close to the perimeter of the facility and monitored through direct supervision or closed-circuit video equipment (CCVE).

Reception/orientation housing unit

Initial housing for juveniles should provide for separation and observation during a period of interviews, assessments, and program evaluations. Initial decisions on classification are made within several days of admission to training schools. Prior to final assignments, residents may be held in temporary housing consistent with their needs. There is variety among incoming populations. Units should be designed to serve more than one inmate classification group and to accommodate special populations on an as-needed basis. These "special management units" typically consist of a number of housing areas (pods) with physical, sight, and sound separation from each other. Each pod or unit consists of single-occupancy cells, required dayrooms, showers, and support spaces. It may incorporate other provisions for interview, program, and/or service spaces.

The reception/orientation housing unit should be located near the admissions and medical areas. Movement between this unit and the general population should be limited. A self-contained unit for the housing, program, and testing/evaluation requirements of newly admitted residents is preferred.

General housing

ACA Standards note that "the [housing] units are the foundation of facility living and must promote the safety and well-being of both residents and staff."

Housing units include living areas and dayrooms. The dayroom can be located immediately adjacent to the sleeping areas, or it may be designed as a separate area, typically located near the supervisor. Depending on the amount of space provided, the dayroom may be divided into quiet and active areas. It is designed to encourage interaction between youth and staff and to be easily observed by supervision staff.

Support areas may include multipurpose and group rooms, interview rooms and counselor's offices, and distributed classrooms.

Housing is also needed for special holding for those who require protection and separation or close supervision for reasons related to offense, criminal record, or behavior.

Programs

The treatment programs of training schools include the provision of academic, vocational, industry, and specialized programs (e.g., life skills, individual study programs, etc.).

Academic programs

In most states, residents of juvenile training facilities are expected to attend school for approximately 6 hours each day.

Classrooms are typically designed for small student populations (10–15 or fewer), and toilet facilities are located nearby to limit movement. Classrooms should be designed to meet environmental requirements of standard classrooms and should be designed with natural light, controlled access and egress, and technological support for videoconferencing and distance learning.

Vocational programs

Vocational programs require the combination of practical lab and training areas with academic or classroom areas. Vocational areas should be designed for small student populations (10–15 or fewer), with toilet facilities located adjacent to or near labs to limit movement.

Vocational areas should also be designed to meet environmental requirements of the Occupational Safety and Health Administration (OSHA) and other standards for ventilation and safe

▲ *Split-level dayroom in housing unit, San Luis Obispo County Juvenile Services Center, San Luis Obispo, California. Patrick Sullivan Associates. Photo: Nick Wheeler.*

use of chemicals and toxic materials. Rooms should be designed to provide natural light, controlled access and egress, and direct observation from hallways to enhance supervision, and with technological support for videoconferencing and distance learning. Secure storage is required for tools.

Additional programs

- *Juvenile industry programs.* Different spaces are required for assembly programs, computer repair or other repair programs, and document processing programs.

- *Library and law library access.* Space should be provided for tables for reading and studying, as well as a supervisor or librarian's work area. Book stacks should be low and arranged to allow visual supervision by staff.

- *Religious programs and services.* Design should permit clear sight lines for staff supervision of all group assembly/worship areas. If a chapel is provided, it should be located in an area with easy access for residents and volunteers. All worship areas have in common the need for safety and security, storage, comfort, and supervision.

Recreation

A variety of recreation and physical exercise programs should be accommodated in training schools and other juvenile correctional facilities. Individual and team activities, challenge and/or obstacle courses, weight training, and general recreational games are customary.

Most facilities provide one or more full-size indoor gymnasium(s) designed for several types of full-court games or partial-court uses. Outdoor recreation and team sports fields are typically provided. There may also be space for rope courses and other special activities. Storage space for equipment is essential.

In some facilities, small recreation yards are located adjacent to housing units for use by unit residents. In others, larger

yards for soccer, baseball, football, and running tracks are provided. These areas require gated fencing, and security systems are often used to supplement direct staff observation at the perimeters. These larger areas may be shared by multiple units or by an entire training school or correctional institution.

Medical services

Medical areas in training schools vary, depending on the security level and size of the facility. Small institutions may provide only a simple nurse station/examination area, whereas large ones may provide hospital-type facilities with inpatient rooms and outpatient examination and treatment areas.

Increasingly, medical facilities are designed for evaluation and diagnosis by use of video and data links to outside agencies, which can provide improved access to services without patients leaving the facility.

Food services

The size of the kitchen is determined by the capacity of the housing units and the

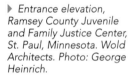

▶ Entrance elevation, Ramsey County Juvenile and Family Justice Center, St. Paul, Minnesota. Wold Architects. Photo: George Heinrich.

number of meal periods required to serve the population of the school. Food service support spaces, including storage spaces, delivery, cleanup, and staff support areas, vary widely in size and requirements, based on the service delivery options in each facility. Most training schools make use of central dining areas with cafeteria-style serving lines.

Laundry services

Laundry and storage spaces, and equipment and supply requirements, vary according to the number of changes provided each week. Modern dispensing systems are used in central laundries to increase safety and security in the use of supplies and chemicals.

Commissary/canteen services

In some locations, commissary and canteen services are used as part of an overall treatment and normalization program.

UNIQUE DESIGN CONCERNS

The three main categories identified here—courts, detention facilities, and training schools—have different architectural design requirements, and all differ from their counterparts that are designed for adults.

Juvenile and Family Courts

Site selection and design

Chapter 4, "Courthouse Facilities," notes criteria for site selection and design that are also relevant to juvenile and family courts facilities. Among these criteria, proximity to a good public transportation system that can convey people to the facility directly, as well as good roadways and adequate parking for people who travel by private car, are especially important. Site design should also anticipate the movement of people back and forth

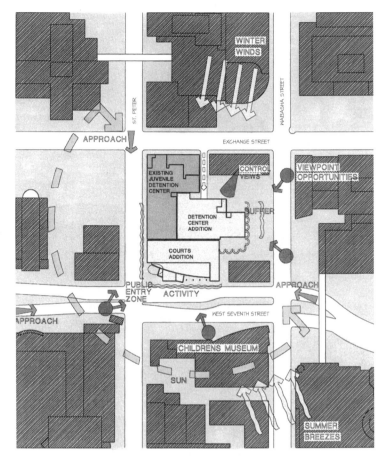

▲ Site plan showing relationship to existing juvenile detention area and street grid. Ramsey County Juvenile and Family Justice Center, St. Paul, Minnesota. Wold Architects.

across the site's perimeter during evenings and weekends for court and court-related activities.

Organization of the building

The jurisdictional organization of these courts varies from one system or location to the next. Some systems have entirely separate and specialized juvenile courts, or family courts, or juvenile and family courts combined. Other systems operate with juvenile and family divisions created within a general jurisdiction court. The resulting physical infrastructure for these courts varies in a mix-and-match fashion in some systems.

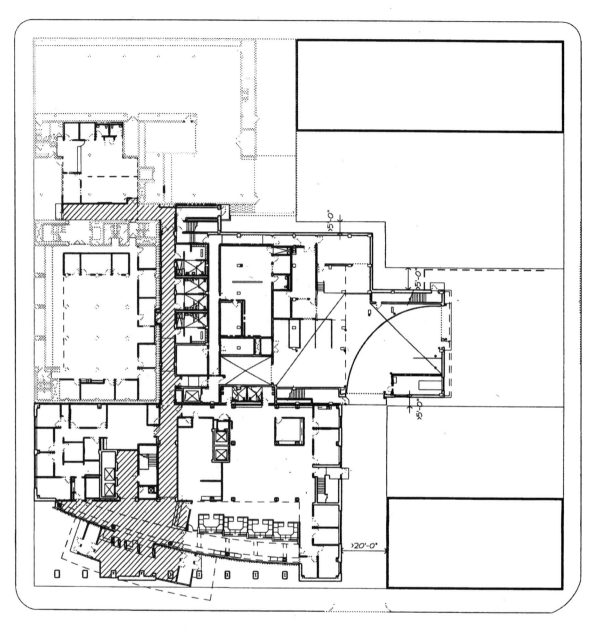

FIRST FLOOR

▲ Plans, entrance level and fourth floor showing
relationship of courtrooms and detention housing
pods. Ramsey County Juvenile and Family Justice
Center, St. Paul, Minnesota. Wold Architects.

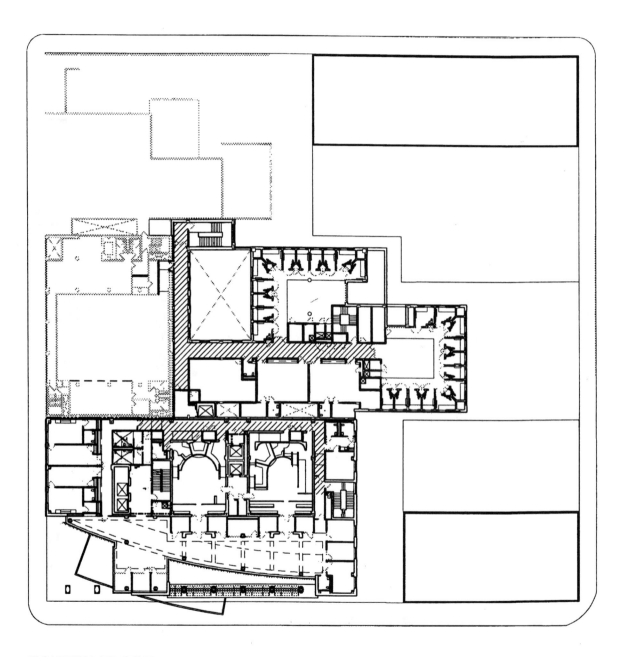

FOURTH FLOOR

0   10   20   40   80

The planning and design of new facilities should reflect the principles outlined in Chapter 4, "Courthouse Facilities," with respect to the organization of court sets and court floors, the location of high-volume public spaces at or near grade level, and controlled, three-way circulation paths for public, private, and secure movement.

In addition, there are several extra design considerations to be kept in mind along with the principles given in Chapter 4: (1) the special characteristics of the user groups involved, (2) the added security risks that exist, and (3) the need for flexibility to accommodate changing operations in the future.

Diverse user groups

Virtually all juvenile and family courts serve a wide variety of users, including children, family members, staff, judges, law enforcement personnel, and service people.

The users arrive both individually and in groups of two persons or more. Normal peak times are between 8:00 and 10:30 A.M. and again just after 1:00 P.M., but there can be considerable activity in the evenings and on weekends. Activity during nontraditional hours is a distinguishing feature of such buildings.

Access to the site and the building from all public transportation and parking areas should therefore be well lit, open, and safe at any time of the day or night. The facility's entrance, parking, and public areas should be designed to provide clear orientation and easy use by everyone.

Security requirements

Security provisions for juvenile and family courts often exceed the provisions for security for general jurisdiction or other limited jurisdiction courts. The threat of spontaneous outbreaks of violence can be greater in disputes between family members.

Security during "precourtroom times" is of special importance. These are specific and identifiable risk periods. Observation, control, and separation are essential at these times. Control of visitor areas may require the assignment of reception staff to specific waiting areas for public visitors and participants in trials.

The security screening checkpoint at the public entrance should be able to handle a large number of people, including children, so that no excessive congestion occurs. Three-path public/private/secure circulation systems should be provided, and surveillance or a security presence should extend throughout the building and its entry point(s) to the outdoor parking areas. It should be possible to maintain visibility and control of all areas, including exterior paths of approach.

Flexibility for future change

Juvenile and family court facilities should be designed for changes in operation and jurisdiction over time. Provisions should be made for alterations and expansion on the site and in the building.

Future changes in the jurisdiction of cases may include the eventual need for juries (and jury boxes and deliberation rooms) in courtrooms and buildings that do not use juries today. More cases and people are involved each year in juvenile and family proceedings. Facility designs should therefore anticipate more openness, larger accommodations for the public and staff, and an increase in the size of courtrooms and hearing rooms for future activities.

Exterior design

Juvenile and family court facilities should

convey a welcoming civic presence. The scale of the building should be appropriate to the physical context and reflect the community's role in the proceedings. The scale and image should respect the wide variety of users and be approachable, rather than intimidating.

The design of the facility may also reflect the specific jurisdiction of the court. If juvenile detention cases are heard, the architecture should promote a sense of dignity and the importance of the judiciary and the legal system. If divorce and child support matters are heard, the design should be family-oriented and give special attention to providing separate areas for the parties involved and their extended family members.

Interior design

Public space

Like the public spaces in the general jurisdiction courts discussed in Chapter 4, the entrance lobby, corridor, and waiting areas in juvenile and family facilities can be vulnerable to cost-cutting measures because they are often not considered tenant space. Lobby, corridor, and waiting areas should be designed with generous amounts of daylight and openness. The high volume of traffic in these areas also requires that durable materials and finishes be used.

Lobby and public corridor areas often offer opportunities for the display of art by and for children.

Signage for wayfinding should be easy to see and understand in English and other relevant major languages. Touchscreen display systems can be used to supplement other information systems indicating where certain hearings are scheduled on a given day, for example, but they should not be relied on as the

▲ Entrance lobby circulation inside security screening. Ramsey County Juvenile and Family Justice Center, St. Paul, Minnesota. Wold Architects. Photo: George Heinrich.

primary source of direction for people entering the building. A public information counter should be easily visible to visitors as they pass through the screening checkpoint.

Victim/witness separation and waiting areas. The provision of separate and controlled waiting areas is essential for victims and witnesses who are in the building before, during, and after hearings and trials. The separate waiting areas must be able to accommodate multiple cases and parties. Furniture sizes and seat-

▶ *Waiting area outside courtrooms. Ramsey County Juvenile and Family Justice Center, St. Paul, Minnesota. Wold Architects. Photo: George Heinrich.*

ing arrangements should anticipate the presence of children.

The location of the waiting areas should consider the amenity of daylight and view, as well as sound control and safety. Waiting areas for families and children that are oriented inward toward an atrium space, or on mezzanine levels with railings and overlooks, risk being excessively noisy and unsafe.

Victim/witness waiting areas should be easily observable by security staff, and the presence of uniformed staff in the building can serve as an additional deterrent to violence. Small conference areas in which attorneys can confer in private with their clients should be located near the waiting areas.

Adjudication space

The image of the courtroom is critical in juvenile and family facilities. It should be "dignified but not intimidating."[2] Over

[2]Hunter Hurst, *Shaping a New Order in the Court: A Sourcebook for Juvenile and Family Court Design* (Pittsburgh, Pa.: National Center for Juvenile Justice, 1992) pp. 3–5.

the past 20 years, a number of juvenile courts with "living room" courtrooms have been designed—low, casual, and conference-room like. Some judges today believe this design approach has not worked, particularly in serious juvenile and contested family court proceedings. They believe instead that the process of making weighty decisions is helped by a dignified facility and courtroom.

In proceedings involving dependency cases (as compared with delinquency cases), it is especially important that courtrooms and hearing rooms be designed to feel safe and secure and to minimize the sense of intimidation.

Either corner-bench or center-bench courtrooms may be appropriate for juvenile and family proceedings, depending on the jurisdiction and the preferences of the judges and the court.

Courtroom layout. The layout of the courtroom should enable all parties to see and hear each other easily. There should be clear lines of sight between the judge's bench, witness stand, and all positions at the counsel tables. However, designs should not force eye contact between victims, witnesses, and the accused.

The clerk should be positioned next to the judge, within easy reach and conversation distance. The court reporter position should permit a clear line of sight to the witness stand, counsel tables, and judge, and the courtroom should accommodate easy movement of equipment if the court reporter must change positions. Separate entrances should be provided for the public, the judge, the staff, and the in-custody individual (adult or juvenile).

Accessibility. Juvenile and family courts accommodate people of all sizes, ages, and physical capabilities. The design of the courtrooms must therefore respond to the widest possible range of physical characteristics. These differences in users affect the size and scale of the courtroom and its individual areas, as well as the materials selected. Because children of young ages may participate, the design and ergonomics of the witness stand must be able to handle different physical sizes and the corresponding sight lines.

The courtroom design should meet, and in some ways exceed, requirements for handicapped accessibility as outlined in Section 11 of the Americans with Disabilities Act Accessibility Guidlines (ADAAG). Most positions in the courtroom (including the witness stand, public areas, and counsel tables) should be designed for use by both adults and children. The positions should accommodate persons with physical, mental, and social disabilities of all kinds.

Technology. Provisions should be made for appropriate audio and video equipment (sound reinforcement, audio/video-conferencing, remote deposition, and evidence presentation). These systems are important in family and juvenile courts,

▲ *Courtroom with center bench and tables for the parties in a case. Ramsey County Juvenile and Family Justice Center, St. Paul, Minnesota. Wold Architects. Photo: George Heinrich.*

particularly because allowances may be made for child testimony from remote locations. Sound systems and room acoustics must be designed to support quiet speech by small children.

Juvenile Detention Facilities and Training Schools

Although they are secure, juvenile detention facilities are less institutional in appearance than those for adults. The designs encourage youth to gather, with appropriate visibility and supervision by counselors or staff. Even in facilities

▶ *Aerial view, West Valley Juvenile Hall, Rancho Cucamonga, California. Patrick Sullivan Associates.*

▼ *Site plan, West Valley Juvenile Hall, Rancho Cucamonga, California. Patrick Sullivan Associates.*

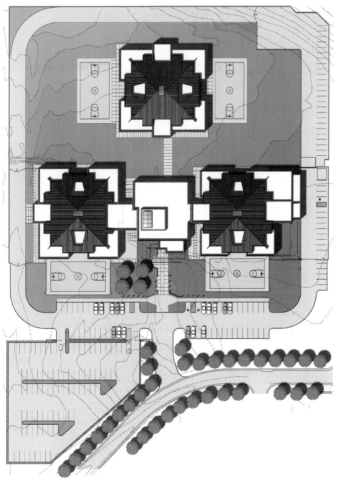

designed for higher-security holding, the security measures tend to be less obtrusive.

Site selection and design

Chapter 3, "Adult Detention Facilities," notes criteria for site selection and design that are relevant to juvenile detention facilities and training schools. The sites selected for juvenile detention, especially, should not be remote from treatment programs that involve community-based resources and nonresidential settings. Facilities should be located close to or in the heart of the community. For training schools relatively less linked to family and community-based resources, more remote places can be considered.

Organization of the building

Detention facilities with 20 or fewer beds are usually designed on one level. Access to all areas is easy, but the site footprint is large. A number of juvenile detention facilities have also been designed with multiple levels. Residential units can be split, stacked, or arranged in tiers. In these units, passive dayrooms may be located on each level, with active areas shared on a central level. The building

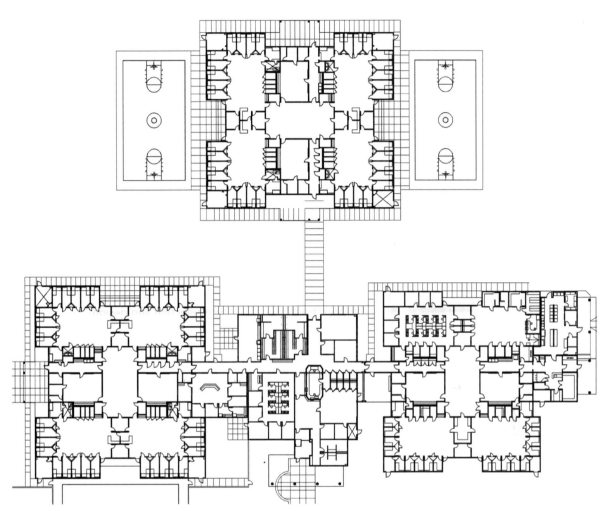

footprint can be smaller in these configurations. In some cases, service or support functions can be located on other levels.

Training schools in most states are designed within campus complexes or as single buildings. Single-story facilities are preferred.

Housing

Early juvenile facilities were similar to jails and prisons, with long double-loaded corridors organized around dayroom control centers. Today, juvenile housing units are generally designed in three primary configurations—podular, linear, and combination.

Podular. Podular layouts typically have the dayroom space adjacent to the front of the resident rooms. The podular design concept groups three or four small housing units (rooms and dayrooms, with active recreation areas) around a central

▲ Plan of podular housing clusters with interior classroom and program spaces, "two-fer" direct supervision stations, and adjacent outdoor recreation. West Valley Juvenile Hall, Rancho Cucamonga, California. Patrick Sullivan Associates.

177

▶ Section drawings through typical housing pod cluster. West Valley Juvenile Hall, Rancho Cucamonga, California. Patrick Sullivan Associates. Photo: Nick Wheeler.

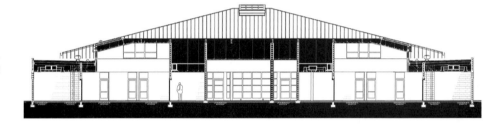

▶ Interior of multipurpose room at center of pod, featuring natural light overhead and at perimeter wall beyond. West Valley Juvenile Hall, Rancho Cucamonga, California. Patrick Sullivan Associates.

active area and a primary control or staff station. This configuration allows staff to both supervise and interact with individuals and groups. It allows direct visual supervision from a staff station of all youth room doors during night shift operations. The primary concern in podular design is the ability to effectively separate youth who are acting out from the rest of the group. A linear configuration makes observation more difficult.

Linear. Linear design concepts feature residential units configured as individual or paired areas along a circulation corridor. Residential units may be on one level, on split levels, or stacked. Dayrooms can be on the same levels as the sleeping rooms or on other levels. The central circulation area is typically on the entry level.

Combination. Facilities can be designed with a mixture of types of units, depending on the size of the resident population and its supervision, program, and other classification requirements.

Exterior design

Juvenile justice facilities tend to have a more residential nature and scale than facilities for adults. Although large facilities have been designed and constructed, many recent ones resemble small schools or campus projects with aggregate groupings or clusters of buildings. Many look like special-function schools and offer community-based services.

Facilities of this kind seldom feature extensive use of concrete on the exterior. Although security barriers are preserved, the general architecture strives to be nonintimidating. Construction materials may be masonry, stone, and concrete, but the massing and blocking are smaller

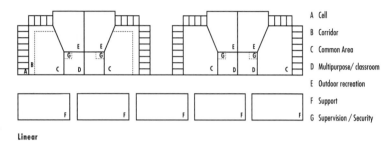

	A	Cell
	B	Corridor
	C	Common Area
	D	Multipurpose/ classroom
	E	Outdoor recreation
	F	Support
	G	Supervision / Security

Linear

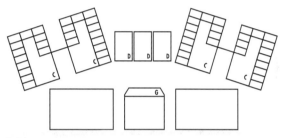

Podular

▲ *Typical unit design concepts for juvenile housing. Units generally may be linear, podular or a combination.*

and low rise, often with pitched roofs and windows and skylights to bring in natural light.

City and county juvenile facilities often combine multiple functions, including both residential and community-based programs. They have both an outward and an inward focus. A facility's public side may present an image of discipline and order and, particularly if court functions are included, of the dignity and stability of the court. The staff and juvenile holding areas, in contrast, may promote a sense of openness and transparency. Designing facilities with a feeling of openness is important in smaller, nonurban facilities that are used for short-term detention, especially of juveniles under the age of 14.

The design of high-security facilities for serious offenders, particularly juveniles

JUVENILE AND FAMILY JUSTICE FACILITIES

▶ *Aerial view, Regional youth detention center prototype, State of Georgia, Department of Juvenile Justice. Patrick Sullivan Associates.*

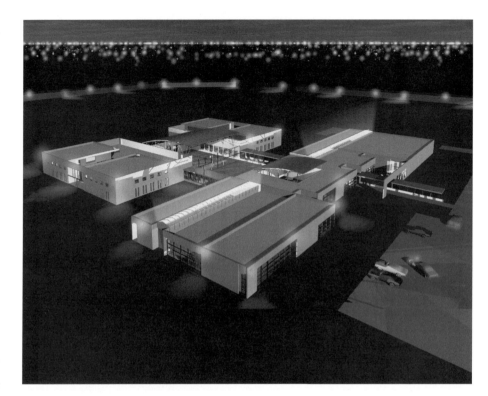

▼ *Exterior elevation studies showing low-rise character of the facility. Regional youth detention center proto-type, State of Georgia, Department of Juvenile Justice. Patrick Sullivan Associates.*

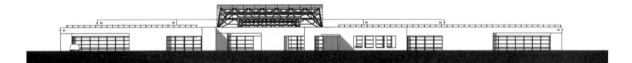

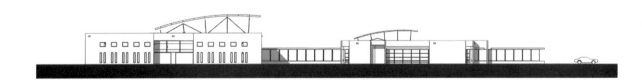

between the ages of 14 and 16, involves different issues and criteria. There is an active debate regarding appropriate design solutions.

Interior design

Juvenile facilities should be designed and furnished to minimize opportunities for suicide. This is critical in spaces where youth are not under constant supervision by staff, such as sleeping rooms and bathrooms. Furniture; lighting; heating, ventilating, and air-conditioning (HVAC) louvers and grilles; bathroom fixtures; plumbing grilles and grates; and all other items or elements present in juvenile facilities should be carefully selected and installed.

Specific requirements for suicide-resistant design include the following[3]:

- No interior bars or windows
- Securely mounted fixtures without slits or protruding objects
- Removable or detachable hinge pins in doors
- Securely mounted air grilles, not larger than ⅛ in., with frames flush to the wall
- Screen covers on diffusers and vents that permit adequate ventilation but prevent youth from fitting fingers or cloth through them
- Recessed showerheads
- Beds that do not have openings or projections

- Drinking fountains without protruding mouth guards or drain slots
- Breakaway hooks
- Nonbreakable mirrors mounted flush to the wall
- No electrical outlets in rooms
- No access to plumbing chases

Experts note that the design should "avoid any surface, edge, fixture, or fitting that can provide an attachment for hanging."[4] There are a number of other key issues that must be addressed:

- Towel holders should be ball-in-socket or indented clasp, not pull-down hooks or bars.
- Beds, desk surfaces, and shelves should have no sharp edges and be configured to prevent attachment. Beds should be totally enclosed underneath.
- Light fixtures should be recessed and tamper resistant.
- Door handles, faucets, fire sprinkler heads, and door hardware inside the rooms should all be recessed, designed to prevent attachment or to break away under a light load.

3. Kenneth Ricci, Laura Maiello, and Shelly Zaviek, "Juvenile Housing," in Leonard R. Witke, ed., *Planning and Design Guide for Secure Adult and Juvenile Facilities* (Lanham, Md.: American Correctional Association, 1998).

4. Patrick Sullivan, "Violent Kids: Environmental Responses/Architectural Challenges," *Journal of the Environmental Design Research Association* 30 (1999), p. 8. See also David Lester and Bruce Danto, *Suicide Behind Bars: Prediction and Prevention* (Lanham, Md.: American Correctional Association, 1993) and the work of Randall Atlas. The ACA has produced several instructional videos, including "Suicide in Juvenile Justice Facilities: The Preventable Tragedy Video" (1990). Joseph R. Rowan, Diane Geiman, and Denise Flannery have developed *Suicide Prevention in Custody: Self-Instructional Course* (Lanham, Md.: American Correctional Association, 1991).

▶ Outdoor recreation area. Regional youth detention center prototype, State of Georgia, Department of Juvenile Justice. Patrick Sullivan Associates.

Normative design

Standards and ideas supported by the American Bar Association recommend that the interior design of juvenile facilities foster a sense of community and personal space. This is achieved in part through normative design techniques that:

- Accent differences between the parts of the building through varying spatial characteristics, room shape, lighting, floor level, ceiling height, etc.

- Allow for changing the furniture layout. Furniture should not be of a uniform color and type, but should vary from room to room.

- Use a variety of textiles, colors, and patterns for walls, floors, furniture, drapes, shades, and finishes.

The normative environment inside a facility is often the most stable one that the young resident has ever experienced.

Individual sleeping rooms should have an open space of 35 sq ft unencumbered by room furnishings and should be at least 7 ft wide in the shortest dimension. Natural light should be provided directly through a window on the exterior wall or from a source within 20 ft of the room. Sleeping rooms typically should be furnished with a bed and a desk with appropriate seating, although some rooms for sleeping only are designed without desks and chairs.

Natural light in all the living areas (sleeping rooms, dayrooms, activity areas) is an important feature. Normative design features can include carpeting, wood furniture, curtains, and increased access to television and recreational equipment. All features should be designed to be durable, heavy, and comfortable, with solid construction and parts that are not easily removed. Where security levels and program objectives have allowed, some facilities completed in the past decade have featured the use of movable beds, colored accent walls, storage modules, bean bag chairs, and various types of carpet.

▶ Klamath Falls County Courthouse, Klamath Falls, Oregon. Kaplan McLaughlin Diaz and James D. Matteson Architects Photo: Michael O'Callahan.

▼ Courtroom. Klamath Falls County Courthouse, Klamath Falls, Oregon. Kaplan McLaughlin Diaz and James D. Matteson Architects Photo: Michael O'Callahan.

▲Douglas County Jail, Lawrence,
Kansas. Treanor Architects, P.A.
Photo: Steve Swalwell Architectural
Fotographics.

◀ Public entrance lobby. Douglas County Jail, Lawrence, Kansas. Treanor Architects, P.A. Photo: Steve Swalwell Architectural Fotographics.

▼ Housing unit dayroom with direct supervision station. Douglas County Jail, Lawrence, Kansas. Treanor Architects, P.A. Photo: Steve Swalwell Architectural Fotographics.

▲ New York State, Division for Youth, Louis Gossett Jr. Residential Center, Lansing, New York. Patrick Sullivan Associates Architects Photo: Nick Wheeler/Wheeler Photography.

◀ Housing unit dayroom. New York State, Division for Youth, Louis Gossett Jr. Residential Center, Lansing, New York. Patrick Sullivan Associates Architects Photo: Nick Wheeler/Wheeler Photography.

▲ *Typical sleeping room. New York State, Division for Youth, Louis Gossett Jr. Residential Center, Lansing, New York. Patrick Sullivan Associates Architects Photo: Nick Wheeler/Wheeler Photography.*

EXIT

◀ Daycare room. Ontario Provincial Police Headquarters. Salter Farrow Pilon Architects Inc./Dunlop Farrow Inc. Architects Photo: Design Archives/Bob Burley.

▶ Public entrance lobby. Ontario Provincial Police Headquarters. Salter Farrow Pilon Architects Inc./Dunlop Farrow Inc. Architects Photo: Design Archives/Bob Burley.

▼ Law Enforcement Museum. Ontario Provincial Police Headquarters. Salter Farrow Pilon Architects Inc./Dunlop Farrow Inc. Architects Photo: Design Archives/Bob Burley.

▲ Ontario Provincial Police Headquarters. Salter Farrow Pilon Architects Inc./Dunlop Farrow Inc. Architects Photo: Design Archives/Bob Burley.

◀ Law library. Edward W. Brooke Courthouse, Boston, Massachusetts. Kallman McKinnell Wood Architects. Photo: Steve Rosenthal.

▶ Judge's chamber. Edward W. Brooke Courthouse, Boston, Massachusetts. Kallman McKinnell Wood Architects. Photo: Steve Rosenthal.

▲ Courtroom. Edward W. Brooke Courthouse,
Boston, Massachusetts. Kallman McKinnell Wood
Architects. Photo: Steve Rosenthal.

▶ Balcony overlook at entrance
rotunda. Edward W. Brooke
Courthouse, Boston,
Massachusetts. Kallman
McKinnell Wood Architects.
Photo: Peter Vanderwarker.

▲ Edward W. Brooke Courthouse, Boston, Massachusetts. Kallman McKinnell Wood Architects. Photo: Steve Rosenthal.

◀ Atrium. Edward W. Brooke Courthouse, Boston, Massachusetts. Kallman McKinnell Wood Architects. Photo: Peter Vanderwarker.

▲ New 22-story facility with strong civic
landmark attributes. Carl B. Stokes U.S. Federal
Courthouse, Cleveland, OH. Kallman McKinnell
Wood Architects. Photo: Robert Benson.

▲ Grand Valley
Institution for
Women, Kitchener,
Ontario. Kuwabara
Payne McKenna
Blumberg Architects.
Photo: Steven Evans.

▶ Interior. Grand
Valley Institution for
Women, Kitchener,
Ontario. Kuwabara
Payne McKenna
Blumberg Architects.
Photo: Steven Evans.

▲ *Classroom. Grand Valley Institution for Women,*
Kitchener, Ontario. Kuwabara Payne McKenna
Blumberg Architects. Photo: Steven Evans.

▲ *Typical housing unit porch. Grand Valley
Institution for Women, Kitchener, Ontario.
Kuwabara Payne McKenna Blumberg
Architects. Photo: Steven Evans.*

CHAPTER 7

MULTI-OCCUPANT FACILITIES

Multi-occupant facilities are those in which different justice operations, and often other tenants, are housed together, either beneath the same roof or on such a closely co-located basis that they may be considered part of the same project. The terms *multiple use* and *mixed use* are sometimes used to designate these facilities. We prefer the term *multi-occupant.*

There is a long tradition of multi-occupant justice facilities in the United States at the federal, state, and county levels. Numerous federal buildings contain both courts and other government offices, for example, often including a U.S. post office. In many counties, the local seat of government is a courthouse with space for the sheriff, the jail, the mayor or other elected official's office, and perhaps even the fire department.

Many of these multi-occupant facilities have grown up in an additive way over the years. Such a facility may have begun as a nineteenth-century structure designed for a single purpose, but has been added to and internally reshuffled several times in subsequent decades. Some may be clusters of buildings or spaces that have been patched together on a make-do basis as budgets and other resources allowed.

Older versions of multi-occupant facilities tend to be small or medium-sized in scale. They were designed to do simpler things and to serve correspondingly smaller communities. Today, some multi-occupant facilities can be quite large, and their various elements are often designed and constructed all at once or as part of a master plan that schedules growth in phases.

ABSENCE OF DESIGN GUIDANCE

There is no planning and design guidance literature that focuses directly on multi-occupant facilities. Virtually all design guidance resources address the justice system on a piecemeal basis in terms of its discrete elements—law enforcement, adult detention, courts, corrections, juvenile and family facilities. As in the preceding chapters, each set of resources in the literature speaks to one main facility type or another, and operational concerns are often emphasized over brick-and-mortar issues.

Supplementary guidelines that address specialized issues (e.g., security, courtroom technology, etc.) are available, but these, too, vary greatly by focus and currency of use. The design decision maker has little to go on beyond personal experience and project-specific circumstances when faced with the challenge of a multi-occupant facility.

▲ *Laclede County Government Center, Lebanon, Missouri. ASAI Architecture. Photo: Architectural Fotography.*

TECHNICAL AND IDENTITY CHALLENGES

The absence of design guidance literature is unfortunate, because multi-occupant facilities can pose serious challenges that are both technical and identity-related. The simple question, "What happens when different kinds of justice operations go together under the same roof?" touches on everything from different materials and construction methods to competing points of view about what a justice facility should be in the first place.

Technical Challenges

Different pieces of a multi-occupant facility may require different approaches to the various building systems. Each type of occupancy within the building will have its own program requirements, and different codes and standards may apply.

One portion of a facility may require the most advanced telecommunications infrastructure to support technology-intensive operations on a 24/7 basis, whereas other parts may consist chiefly of reinforced concrete. One part of a project may need blast-resistant exterior wall systems, security glazing, and custom interior finishes; another may only need space designed to office building standards. Integrated building systems controls may be called for in one case and independent controls in another. When different occupants pay separately for their shares of the total operations and maintenance costs, each may require its own controls.

Technical challenges can be compounded when different occupancies must fit within existing buildings that are modified to accommodate them, or when they are inserted on a site that includes exist-

ing buildings. Complications may increase if one or more elements in the multi-occupant combination are likely to expand at a faster or less predictable rate in the future than the others. The issue of growth and designing for flexibility may be a greater priority with one element than with another.

Putting an accurate price tag on a multi-occupant project can require more detailed cost estimating than usual. More than one project has gotten into trouble when the variations in cost for its separate parts have been miscalculated or misunderstood by funding sources.

Identity Challenges

The designer must ask:

- What kinds of adjacencies are appropriate?
- Are all possible combinations of occupants equally desirable?
- Should the courts and police, for example, be next to each other?
- When different occupants are beneath the same roof, and perhaps sharing the same floor, who controls the ambience?
- Who or what determines the character of the facility as it is perceived by the public?
- Does it make a difference if the facility has multiple identities, or no distinct identity at all?

The question of appropriate adjacencies is a vital one for the judiciary, the third branch of government. Its authority as an independent and impartial entity can be reinforced or undermined by the way it is physically housed. When the courts are joined in multi-occupant combinations with other kinds of justice, justice-related, or nonjustice operations, the resulting project may or may not succeed in instilling public confidence in the workings of the system.

The appropriateness of different combinations of occupants should be weighed when decisions are made about what kind of facility to approve for construction, and about how it should be planned and designed in detail. Other issues involve functionality, cost, and convenience, and the specific circumstances of a project, from the site to the local politics. Ideally, all such considerations will be resolved during the program and design phases into a harmonious whole that is consistent with acceptable conceptions of justice.

TYPICAL PATTERNS OF MULTI-OCCUPANT FACILITIES

Multi-occupant facilities typically involve one or more of the following kinds of combinations:

- Justice-only occupants
- Justice and justice-related occupants
- Justice and nonjustice occupants from the public sector
- Justice and nonjustice occupants from the private sector

Justice-Only Occupants

Justice-only multi-occupant facilities combine two or more of the major justice operations beneath the same roof or close together as part of the same project. The combination of corrections and detention facilities is not unusual. There are some projects that house adult inmates, male and female, as well as juvenile detainees and inmates of all security classifications, and even from a mix of federal, state, and local jurisdictions.

The most common combination of justice-only occupancies involves the courts, law enforcement, and detention. The ability of law enforcement to hold persons in custody requires space for cells or a jail. The ability to transport prisoners to and from a criminal trial courtroom safely and cost-effectively has become an argument for locating a jail and a court together.

The relative sizes of each element in this combination—courts, law enforcement, detention—can have a dramatic effect on the overall character of the facility in every respect, from its technical requirements to its image. As the sizes of each element vary, the spectrum of possibilities ranges from facilities that are primarily courts-based, with supportive law enforcement and detention in a subordinate role, to the opposite case in which the facility consists overwhelmingly of a jail in which there is a small courts component. In some cases, the courts component is swallowed up by the other occupants to the point where it is no longer architecturally legible from the exterior.

Where the elements are more or less equal in size, the architectural identity of the project can be especially challenging. Familiar architectural solutions tend to emphasize the appearance of separateness for the elements within an otherwise unified whole. This is easier to accomplish when the court operations and the jail and law enforcement operations are co-located but not contiguous. A classic diagram for the relationship between the courts and the jail is the Venetian "Bridge of Sighs," in which a linking bridge connects the two main elements for the purpose of conveying prisoners back and forth.

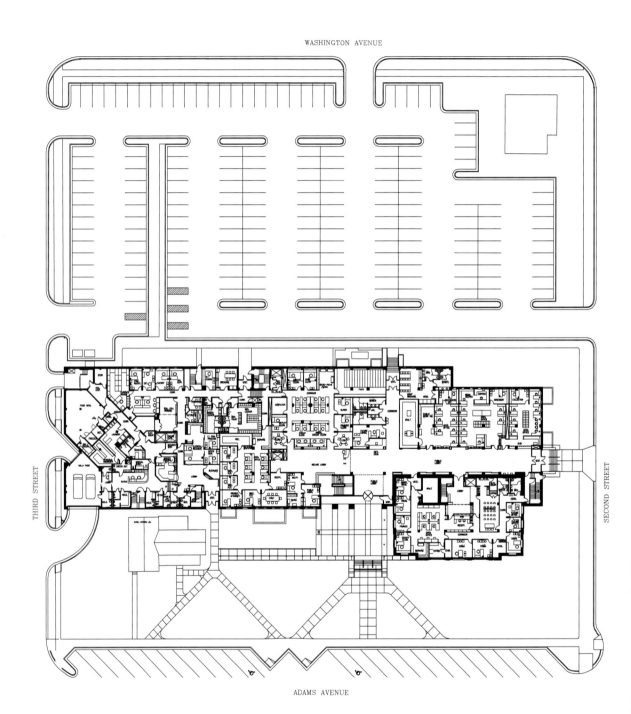

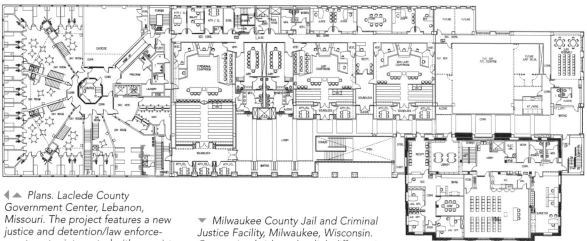

◀▲ *Plans. Laclede County Government Center, Lebanon, Missouri. The project features a new justice and detention/law enforcement center integrated with an existing county courthouse dating from the 1920s. ASAI Architecture.*

▼ *Milwaukee County Jail and Criminal Justice Facility, Milwaukee, Wisconsin. Connecting bridges that link different justice buildings together are often used, especially for the movement of persons in custody from holding areas to courts. Venture Architects. Photo: Howard Kaplan, Architectural Photography, Inc.*

Justice and Justice-Related Occupants

The justice-related occupants that often become major program elements show up noticeably in the courts and the juvenile and family arenas. These occupants include prosecuting attorneys, public defenders, and probation officers. The number of such allied professionals, as well as the confidential nature of what they do, can necessitate treating them as separate occupants who require space, often in large amounts, that is clearly set off from the other parts of the facility.

Juvenile and family justice facilities tend to involve diverse program elements. The different occupancies in a single project may include courts, housing for different genders and security levels, educational facilities, freestanding treatment centers for substance abuse and psychological counseling, a medical clinic, and the like. The facility as a whole may be developed as a low-rise project in a campus setting in which different occupants are in different buildings. The operations in some of these buildings, and in some cases the buildings themselves, may be managed and owned by private contractors.

The major design tasks in projects with various justice-related occupants involve finding appropriate combinations of free and restricted access for the mix of users, including individual citizens and families, who come to the facility, often during evening and weekend hours.

Justice and Nonjustice Occupants from the Public Sector

Justice operations are often housed alongside other public sector occupants that are not related. The presence of other government entities is common. At the federal level, court buildings may contain offices for such tenants as the U.S. General Services Administration or the Department of Veterans Affairs. When the courts component remains primary,

▶ Federal Building and Courthouse, Oakland, California. The scale and location of this facility, housing more than two dozen federal and state agencies, make it a prominent landmark on the skyline. Kaplan McLaughlin Diaz Architects. Photo: Imperial Color Labs, Inc. (Richard Barnes and Ron Starr).

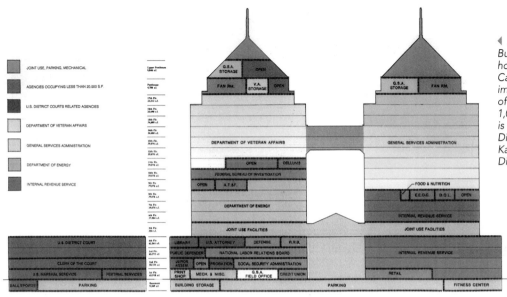

Legend:
- JOINT USE, PARKING, MECHANICAL
- AGENCIES OCCUPYING LESS THAN 20,000 S.F.
- U.S. DISTRICT COURTS RELATED AGENCIES
- DEPARTMENT OF VETERAN AFFAIRS
- GENERAL SERVICES ADMINISTRATION
- DEPARTMENT OF ENERGY
- INTERNAL REVENUE SERVICE

COURT ANNEX   SOUTH TOWER   NORTH TOWER

◀ Section, Federal Building and Courthouse, Oakland, California. Approximately 15 percent of the facility's 1,050,000 total GSF is devoted to U.S. District Courts. Kaplan McLaughlin Diaz Architects.

the architectural character of the project overall can present a judicial appearance.

Government centers, however, rather than justice buildings, can be the result when the justice component is overshadowed by the volume of square footage devoted to other public sector occupants. When government centers are developed as single large buildings or as several buildings together, their scale and prominence as landmarks may cause urban design priorities to be paramount. The architecture is driven by influences apart from justice.

At the state and local levels, the mix of justice and other public sector occupants is often more diverse. Some law enforcement operations may be beneath the same roof as the fire department, and they may include an emergency medical service unit (EMS) and an emergency operations center (EOC).

More typically, combinations of courts, law enforcement, and detention in vary-

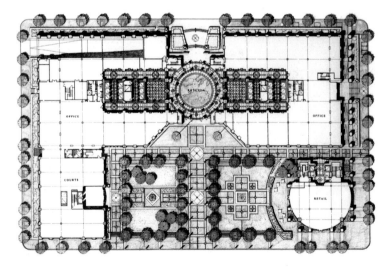

▲ Site plan, Federal Building and Courthouse, Oakland, California. Kaplan McLaughlin Diaz Architects.

ing proportions may be housed with offices for state, county, and/or city government (e.g., county board and manager, and city council and mayor), as well as such entitites as the Department of Parks and Recreation, Finance, Planning and Zoning, and so on.

189

▶ Ocean City Public Safety Building and Court, Ocean City, Maryland. Court and law enforcement operations, and juvenile services, are combined with emergency medical services and an emergency operations center (EOC) in this facility. It is designed to handle increased activity during summer vacation months, and to coordinate responses to natural disasters such as hurricanes. The EOC is located on the upper level to withstand washout flooding at the lower level. Ayers / Saint / Gross Architects. Photo: Alan Karchmer.

▲ Holding cells, Ocean City Public Safety Building and Court, Ocean City, Maryland. Ayers / Saint / Gross Architects. Photo: Alan Karchmer.

◀ Courtroom, Ocean City Public Safety Building and Court, Ocean City, Maryland. Ayers / Saint / Gross Architects. Photo: Alan Karchmer.

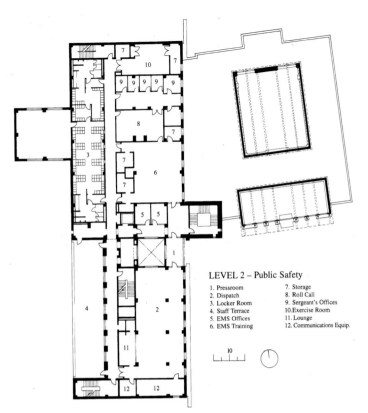

◀ *Plans showing relationship of public safety areas to district court areas, Ocean City Public Safety Building and Court, Ocean City, Maryland. Ayers / Saint / Gross Architects*

LEVEL 2 – Public Safety

1. Pressroom
2. Dispatch
3. Locker Room
4. Staff Terrace
5. EMS Offices
6. EMS Training
7. Storage
8. Roll Call
9. Sergeant's Offices
10. Exercise Room
11. Lounge
12. Communications Equip.

10

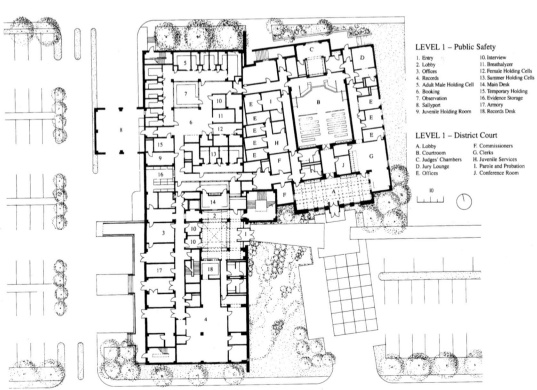

LEVEL 1 – Public Safety

1. Entry
2. Lobby
3. Offices
4. Records
5. Adult Male Holding Cell
6. Booking
7. Observation
8. Sallyport
9. Juvenile Holding Room
10. Interview
11. Breathalyzer
12. Female Holding Cells
13. Summer Holding Cells
14. Main Desk
15. Temporary Holding
16. Evidence Storage
17. Armory
18. Records Desk

LEVEL 1 – District Court

A. Lobby
B. Courtroom
C. Judges' Chambers
D. Jury Lounge
E. Offices
F. Commissioners
G. Clerks
H. Juvenile Services
I. Parole and Probation
J. Conference Room

10

The resulting challenges for planning and design range from achieving a coherent architectural image, rather than a jumbled and chaotic one, to developing a suitably zoned infrastructure of building services that can support different agencies or departments, some of which may work on a 7/24/365 basis. Large portions of the facility may be in service only during normal daytime working hours, whereas other portions may never shut down.

Justice and Nonjustice Occupants from the Private Sector

A number of justice facilities have recently been designed with significant amounts of square footage set aside for leasing to tenants from the private sector. Both office space for rent and retail space have been programmed into the projects from the beginning. Such space may or may not be designed to be recaptured by the justice or other public sector occupants in the future. Developing lease space can be a skillful way of ensuring room for the growth of justice operations. Alternately, the private tenants may be viewed as a permanent revenue-generating resource.

There are extra costs and security issues when private sector tenants are allowed to circulate through the facility and to occu-

▼ *Middletown Police Headquarters, Middletown, Connecticut. Plan showing ground floor of law enforcement facility designed for extensive retail space. Jeter Cook Jepson Architects, Inc.*

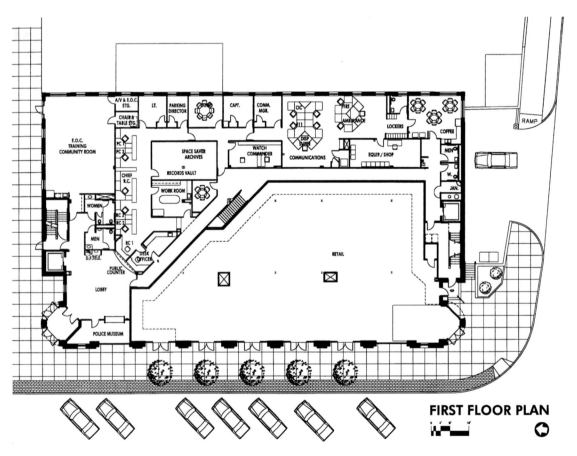

FIRST FLOOR PLAN

py it after normal business hours. When the lease space is at the sidewalk level and limited primarily to the zone along the perimeter, it can be easier to control. The more demanding design issues in such cases may involve image. The task may be to preserve an appearance of dignity while providing a commercial storefront.

If private sector lease space is located on upper levels in a high-rise tower, a separate and costly vertical circulation core may be necessary, primarily for security. If underground or nearby parking spaces are also provided to private tenants, security risks can be heightened by the potential for an explosive device to be hidden in an unmonitored car.

There has been increasing interest in public-private partnerships for project financing in some cases. Public entities have occasionally found it advantageous to work with the private sector in rent and lease-purchase arrangements. Private sector developers, in turn, may determine that it is in their interest to encourage more combinations of governmental and private activities within a multi-occupant project, thereby adding to the number of these hybrid facility types in coming years.

MULTI-OCCUPANT JUSTICE FACILITIES IN THE FUTURE

Multi-occupant facilities will continue to challenge design decision makers in both familiar and new ways. Meeting such challenges will entail upgrades of and additions to existing facilities, as well as the construction of new ones.

When growth occurs on existing sites that are large enough to accommodate it, chances are that new buildings will be co-located with the old ones. Where new sites are developed, the jurisdiction may

▲ Middletown Police Headquarters, Middletown, Connecticut. Elevation along retail storefront. Jeter Cook Jepson Architects, Inc. Photo: Woodruff / Brown Photography.

operate with a master plan that calls for several occupants to be housed in a single large complex or on a campus that is constructed in phases. No single pattern of multi-occupant combinations can be identified as a dominant trend, but it is reasonable to assume that all of them will be more complicated.

Cost and Convenience

Cost and convenience will be among the issues considered in any multi-occupant project. Conventional wisdom in former times often argued that costs could be reduced and efficiency enhanced if different operations were put together in a single package, rather than being treated separately. This may or may not be true today, depending on the specific justice operations and other facilities being housed together. Multi-occupant facilities are not necessarily the most efficient or least costly to construct and operate.

Convenience, too, can be a difficult and divisive issue. Convenience for whom, and to what end? What lawyers and other justice-related professionals regard as convenient for themselves may or may not correspond to what citizens would prefer. The latter may be more concerned about good public transportation to and from a justice facility, or with keeping an unwanted project out of their community.

The idea of "one-stop shopping" has arisen in recent years in connection with courts and juvenile and family facilities that attempt to provide as many services as possible in one place. There are different points of view within the justice community about the definition and desirability of the one-stop shopping approach. When the idea is broadened to include other public services provided in the same location, the result is often the government center.

Information Technology

New kinds of multi-occupancy facilities may appear in the next several years as information technologies continue to influence ideas about physical space, time, and geographic distance. Advances in the ability to handle information electronically will continue to spark new ways of thinking about what programs and facilities need to be joined.

One possibility is that some justice facilities will be streamlined and more widely dispersed in distributed networks supported by centralized data, records, or work processing facilities off-site. The use of centralized support facilities may make it possible to reduce the size of some buildings.

Streamlining or reductions in scale may, in turn, make it easier for the designer to develop an appropriate architectural image and relationship to context, giving rise to an entirely new set of opportunities to restore the distinctive identity of justice-only facilities.

As distributed networks of smaller-scale justice operations become more viable, countervailing trends toward more consolidation may also appear. Justice and other government buildings may be increasingly conceived as integral to a mix of activities involving health, education, transportation, and culture that are brought together to help sustain a critical mass of community services.

A certainty facing design decision makers is that many, if not most, of the facilities for tomorrow already exist today in some form. The amount of existing building stock is such that many of the justice projects developed in the future will necessarily grow out of or alongside what is in place now. At the least, technical issues associated with adaptive reuse will be major concerns.

Another certainty is that the debate over appropriateness inherent in any multi-occupant facility for the judiciary and the justice system as a whole will intensify. It will be an open-ended discussion with no single set of answers.

PART II

SYSTEMS AND ISSUES

LIGHTING AND ACOUSTICS

Planning and design for lighting and acoustics in a justice facility must be addressed from the initial design of a project, because the building mass, volume, configuration, and orientation have a major impact on lighting requirements. Similarly, the basic attributes of all spaces—height, volume, and configuration—dramatically alter acoustic needs and conditions.

Moreover, basic design requirements and those for lighting and acoustics are intertwined. For example:

- Lighting controls must respond to operational requirements for security and control in detention and correctional environments.

- Lighting controls must respond to the changing requirements and special conditions of court proceedings.

- Wall construction must achieve acoustic goals while responding to other functional requirements, including security and special construction requirements.

- Acoustic design of interior spaces must support the intended activities planned for the spaces. The acoustical systems are typically designed to work as an integrated system with special audio-video and data-telecommunication systems.

The following sections summarize key requirements and initial planning concepts for a number of conditions found in justice facilities.

◀ *Rotunda, The Municipal Justice Center, Aurora, Colorado. Skidmore, Owings and Merrill, Washington, D.C. Photo: Michael Griebel.*

LIGHTING SYSTEMS

Basic Planning Requirements

The design of a lighting system has a dramatic impact on the initial and life cycle costs of virtually any justice facility. Energy costs, durability and maintenance, and initial fixture prices are all contributing factors.

Because of the extended operational periods typical of justice facilities, the critical nature of their work, the need for high performance by many people in standard, peak period, and emergency situations, design for lighting and daylighting must incorporate the best principles of design for comfort, reduced glare, and quality of light.

Proper lighting design

- Helps to define functional areas

- Enhances spatial configurations

- Accentuates materials and surface characteristics

- Alleviates blandness

- Establishes a visual hierarchy within an area, featuring particular activities and/or elements.

Typical lighting systems in justice facilities use integrated systems incorporating fluorescent, incandescent, and high-intensity discharge (HID) sources with energy-efficient ballasts. Incandescent sources are used where color rendition is critical, instant illumination is required, or the use of other sources is impractical.

Good lighting design is especially critical in courtrooms and hearing rooms, control centers, communication centers, and conference rooms, including rooms designed specifically for video systems. In these spaces, areas must not be over- or under-lit, and the color rendition of lights and reflectances of surfaces (and the impact of color in the environment) are crucial.

Light levels

Recommended lighting levels (illumination levels, or measurements of the amount of light falling on surfaces) have been published by the Illumination Engineering Society (IES) for a variety of spaces and functions found in modern justice facilities.

Lighting design involves more than simple calculations, however, because the human eye responds to color and luminance contrasts, rather than illumination. Basic amounts of light are needed to see, but the human eye responds to the average intensity, not the total intensity of light in the field of view. Therefore, our sense of sight depends on contrasts, and the ability to see depends on both the amount of light and the relationships between brightly lighted and darker surfaces.

Lighting requirements are not the same for all people and functions. Spaces designed for use by those over 45 years of age should consider the changing needs of middle-aged and elderly persons. As the eye ages,

- Greater amounts of light are required to perform tasks.
- The lens of the eye tends to yellow.
- The adaptation process slows, making it more difficult for the eye to recover when going from bright to dark spaces, from dark to bright, or to adjust to bursts of bright lights.
- Glare sensitivity increases.

In general, lighting levels fall into low, medium, and high ranges. The table on page 199 presents key areas and spaces in various justice facilities, indicating the typical ranges that should be used as design targets for lighting levels. In many situations the lighting should be provided according to a designed scheme incorporating direct and indirect light, ambient and task lighting, and daylighting to provide appropriate color rendition and intensities (providing sufficient contrast without creating veiling reflections, glare, and so forth).

Specific areas of key rooms should be spotlighted—for instance, presentation areas should be more highly illuminated for better legibility of presentation materials. Design concepts should provide appropriate and natural color rendition in all areas in which recognition of a person or close scrutiny of gesture and nuance is important (e.g., lineup rooms, courtrooms, hearing rooms, presentation areas, and visitation areas).

Building exterior lighting

Lighting requirements for building exteriors include general lighting for parking, pedestrian access, and the site in general. Area lighting should be sufficiently high for good visibility, typically at or above levels used in commercial shopping centers, inasmuch as access between buildings and parking areas and/or public transportation areas should provide a sense of safety for a facility's staff and the public.

Special attention should be given to the ground areas on all sides of the facility within 25 ft of the building (or enclosed fences or other perimeters). These areas should be kept clear of concealing plantings and other site elements and illuminated to provide visibility for surveillance and protection against unauthorized

RECOMMENDED LIGHTING LEVELS, BY TYPE OF SPACE

Task/Activity	Illumination Target (fc)	Classification	Comments
Movement/circulation areas	10–20	Low	
Control rooms	20–30	Low–medium	Multiple video monitors
Storage areas	10–20	Low	
Inmate housing	5–30	Very low–medium	Night/daytime
Conference/office areas	30–50	Medium	
Courtroom—spectator seating	30	Medium	
Courtroom—litigation area	50–90	Medium–high (see text)	
Precision work areas	75–100	High	Detail work

entry. This is particularly important in facilities where the primary security perimeter is the exterior wall. Light fixtures in these areas should be placed to provide proper illumination without causing problems with stray light (entering cells or housing areas, for example).

Perimeter security lighting is provided at the final security barrier of detention and correctional facilities, which usually consists of the perimeter fence or wall. Lighting levels in these areas should be 2–6 fc and designed specifically to allow staff (and/or closed-circuit video equipment, CCVE) to detect and recognize a person at or near the perimeter.

In all exterior installations, fixtures should be placed to reduce glare and minimize potential for the light source to be within the field of vision of the staff (or equipment) who monitor and supervise the area. Spill light, or light which illuminates unintended areas, can be a significant problem, and glare must be

▼ Exterior entry, Kane County Juvenile Justice Center, Geneva, Illinois. Wight & Company in association with HDR. Photo: George Lambros.

▶ Exterior lighting at housing unit, Osceola County Detention Facility, Kissimmee, Florida. HLM Design. Photo: Scott McDonald, Hedrich-Blessing.

considered, because typical exterior lighting luminaires can create intense light.

Interior lighting

Justice facilities include many unique areas and functions (courtrooms, control rooms/centers, communication centers, guard towers, and the like) with specific lighting and control requirements.

Additional challenges arise because of security requirements. Special security-type fixtures and equipment used in inmate-accessible areas (particularly medium- and maximum-security areas or areas to which inmates are permitted unsupervised access), must balance requirements for security with basic requirements for lighting. Because lighting fixtures can be used as places for concealment, fixtures are often designed with hard, unbreakable lenses securely mounted in steel frames with security fasteners. To make such lenses unbreakable, manufacturers may use polycarbonate or similar types of materials, which yellow with age and with increased exposure to light.

Care must be taken in the initial design and in maintaining the facility to select appropriate fixtures and lighting fixture distribution schemes that

- Provide good color.

- Deliver an appropriate balance of distributed illumination with sufficient highlights to improve clarity of vision.

- Provide appropriate levels of illumination for the activities conducted within an area—the range of activities in some areas can be very wide.

- Require low energy use.

- Serve in typical situations and in emergencies, meeting requirements for safety and emergency operation, particularly lighting during emergency situations or exit conditions.

- Minimize or reduce maintenance costs and allow easy access to fixtures and bulbs for replacement or repair.
- Allow appropriate standardization of fixtures and bulbs (avoiding obsolescence and reducing the numbers and types of bulbs needed for replacement).

Inmate holding and housing areas (cells and dormitories) should be provided with maximum-security, vandal-resistant wall- or ceiling-mounted light fixtures with energy-saving, long-life fluorescent lamps. These lamps should have circuitry for night light, controlled by housing control staff or by programmed switching with manual overrides.

Lighting in medical areas should support medical requirements as well as security levels. In examination rooms and medical patient holding or housing areas, fixtures should be designed for both security and illumination.

Local switching should be used except where remote control is required for security or operations. Where multiple tasks are anticipated in an area, multiple-level switching should be provided.

In court facilities, a range of lighting levels is needed in many areas, as users of the spaces will vary from very young to elderly people, the legibility of copy and print will vary widely, and the range of materials used and presented will vary.

For example, in a courtroom a single trial process may involve testimony from both young and old, and the age span between an attorney, a witness, a juror, and the judge—all of whom need to see, understand, and react to evidence—may be 60 or more years. Evidence used in a trial can range from indistinct pencil drawings to video presentations and reenactments, and in-person and video conference testimony may also be used. Particularly in courtrooms with natural light—with or without views provided by windows or skylights—lighting control, quality, intensity, and reflectances are crucial. Because participants in trial settings are located on all sides of the litigation area, lighting must be designed to meet requirements in all directions—and directional wall and ceiling lighting design must be carefully studied from all critical angles.

In addition, the architect should use lighting to support the design intention of the building. In courtrooms, the symbolic importance of the judge's bench and other key areas of the room must be enhanced by lighting, particularly in some contemporary courtroom configurations, which must achieve an appropriate image without the help of the traditional architectural devices (procession, orientation, biaxial symmetry, and height) present in historical courtrooms.

Light Reflectance Values

In many environments, useful light reflects from walls, ceilings, floors, and other interior surfaces onto work surfaces. This is particularly true with indirect systems, where a large portion of light is directed toward ceilings or walls. High-reflectance finishes, such as white and off-white surfaces, maximize the use of available light. As finishes grow darker, they absorb proportionately more of the light that hits their surfaces.

The amount of reflection from surfaces can and should vary somewhat, according to the specific functions and types of spaces. The table on page 203 summarizes typical ranges of surface reflectances

▲ *Courtroom, Kane County Juvenile Justice Center, Geneva, Illinois. Wight & Company in association with HDR. Photo: George Lambros.*

◄ *Video conference room. Indirect and direct lighting supports use of monitors, laptop computers, and V&VOIP (Voice and Video Over Internet Protocol) system. Technology and photography: DOAR Communications, Inc.*

that should be considered for the efficient use of light in justice facilities.

With the widespread use of CRTs and audio-video equipment in justice facilities, specific criteria for the design of teleconference centers should be incorporated into courtrooms, hearing rooms, communication and control centers, and rooms designed specifically for videoconferencing and training (jury assembly rooms, briefing/roll call rooms, and the like). In these areas, designers should consider not only light reflectance value, but color selection for interior surfaces, because color and color contrasts will affect legibility of text and video camera performance.

Specially designed fixtures may be incorporated into courtrooms and public spaces, particularly in historic renovation

or restoration projects, in federal, state appellate, or supreme courts, or in large city or county projects where the cost of developing unique or specialized fixtures can be justified.

Controls

With the increased use of audio-video systems, justice facility architects must plan for multilevel switching and dimming systems. In addition, the use of energy management controls, including daylighting, photocells, time clocks, and occupancy sensors (infrared or movement sensors), is an important feature of twenty-first-century justice facilities. All of these systems have appropriate uses and should be incorporated into the lighting plan for a facility during the early design stage. In many situations, it is important to pro-

RECOMMENDED REFLECTANCE LEVELS, BY SURFACE TYPE*		
SURFACE	**REFLECTANCE (%)**	**TYPICAL MATERIAL**
Floors	10–20	Medium- to light-colored carpet
		Medium- to light-colored wood
		Medium shades of tile
Work surfacess	20–50**	Light woods
		Medium- to light-colored laminates
Window treatments	30–50	Medium- to light-colored fabrics
		Medium- to light-colored blinds
Walls	30–50	Medium- to light-colored paint
		Medium- to light-colored vinyl wall coverings
		Light-colored fabrics
Ceilings	70–90	White/off-white acoustic tile
		White/off-white gypsum
		Other light-colored surfaces
Office Partitions	25–45	Medium- to light-colored fabrics
		Medium- to light-colored laminates
Other furniture/ equipment	20–50	Medium- to light-colored surfaces

*Assuming matte finishes.
**As work surface reflectances move toward 50 percent, designers should carefully study the angle of light on a work surface to minimize glare.

vide these systems with individual room controls and overrides to allow flexibility and adaptability in the use of spaces and to permit staff to make decisions as needed regarding appropriate lighting levels.

In detention and correctional facilities, the location and design of controls is crucial to security. Switches for light control should be placed within inmate-accessible areas only where deliberately selected (such as light control within an inmate cell in a direct-supervision medium- or minimum-security housing unit). Generally, lighting control is maintained for all fixtures by the control room or console position. Where controls are located within inmate-accessible areas, security-type switches (with key control or other type of control) must be provided.

Dimming controls provide flexibility in illumination levels, but have other effects as well. Dimming an incandescent light source increases the life of the lamp, but as the lamp is dimmed, the light migrates toward the orange-red end of the spectrum.

Dimming fluorescent lamps requires the use of special dimming ballasts, and only rapid-start fluorescent lamps can be dimmed. An option for reducing light levels in settings with fluorescent luminaires is to provide separate switching for lamps within the fixtures. If dimmers are used, fluorescent lamps cannot be dimmed all the way, because at very low levels the lamps create a flicker or spiral pattern. Color shifts also can occur in

dimmed lamps, particularly if the luminaire is used in a cooler location or in an air-handling fixture.

Daylighting

Providing natural light has been an important factor in the design and configuration of justice facilities over the past few decades. The key to providing natural light is to balance the requirements for views, natural light, and security in an appropriate solution for the facility and for specific functions.

Today, experts advise that habitable areas of buildings should be within 30 ft of natural light and views. Particularly in housing areas, standards for detention and correctional facilities outline requirements for natural light in inmate areas.

Yet direct sunlight entering interior spaces must also be carefully controlled. Direct sunlight produces very high luminance levels and can create extreme luminance differences, resulting in poor visibility, discomfort, and fatigue. Indirect skylight, however, is natural light without these disadvantages. As a result, indirect skylight can be useful in recreation areas, corridors, casual activity areas, and, with appropriate screening, in task areas.

Skylights, windows, and clerestories can be used to provide natural light. Regardless of the opening, light control should be considered in the design. Various methods can be used to control light, including the use of diffuse glazing materials, tinting, screens and shields, and general orientation. For example, high openings allow light to penetrate more deeply into the interior spaces, and high-entry light can be spread and softened by the use of exterior shading devices, interior horizontal

▼ *Dayroom. Natural light is provided to dayroom space through combined use of skylight and windows on multiple levels.*

Four variations for controlling natural light through windows. Minimize east-west windows to reduce glare from low sun angles. Exterior solutions can be more expensive, but are an important alternative to secure (inmate-accessible) areas where natural light is provided

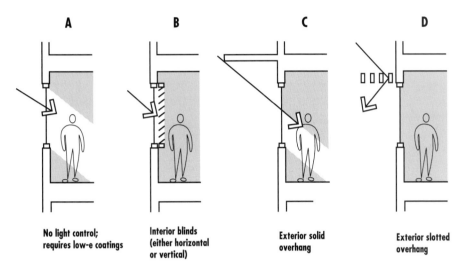

A

B

C

D

No light control; requires low-e coatings

Interior blinds (either horizontal or vertical)

Exterior solid overhang

Exterior slotted overhang

◀ *Lighting control/ shading device options.*

light shelves, and deep window wells. Skylights can introduce daylight into upper floors directly, and into lower floors through atria and light wells.

In all cases, orientation of openings to the north produces softer and more uniform light, but high-quality illumination can be provided with other orientations with effective and appropriate daylight controls.

ACOUSTICS

People need to hear the spoken word, especially critical discussions and instructions, in many areas of justice facilities. Audibility requirements for such facilities are very high, as well as complex. In a courtroom, for example, jurors must hear audio evidence that may be indistinct, and parties at attorney tables must conduct private conversations without being overheard by jurors. The challenge is compounded because many functions are often compressed into relatively compact areas.

Designing for acoustics cannot be left until late in the process; acoustic design must be incorporated into the planning from the earliest stages of design. Buildings and spaces must be designed with proper spatial relationships, volumes, and shapes.

Basic Principles

People can hear a wide range of sounds —sounds that vary widely in frequency (pitch) and intensity (sound levels). Yet not all people hear equally well, and the ability to hear may change as people age. The human ear can detect individual sounds against a complex background of loud noises, but speech perception is nearly impossible above 80 dBA.[1]

There are various types of sound sources. Sound waves created by a "point" source, such as a voice, act like spheres of sound that radiate outward from the source, losing strength rapidly as the distance from the source increases. Sound intensity drops at the inverse square of distance from a point source; in other words, the sound level is one-fourth as intense as the distance doubles.

Many sound sources are point sources. Others are considered "linear." Examples of these sources include railroad trains and interstate highways. The sound intensity of a linear sound source does not diminish as quickly as that of a point source, and the sounds associated with highways and railroad trains can present a significant challenge where sound-sensitive areas (courtrooms and the like) are located on exterior walls with windows or skylights.

1. J. C. Webster, "Noise and Communication," in *Noise and Society,* D. M. Jones and A. J. Chapman, eds. (New York: John Wily & Sons, Inc., 1984). The decibel scale is a logarithmic scale measure of sound intensity relative to the threshold of human hearing. It is often used to show changes in sound intensity levels. Loudness is a subjective measure of what the human ear perceives. Since the ear does not respond equally to all frequencies, the "a-weighted" scale (dBA) was created to obtain a single number that could represent the sound level of a noise containing a wide range of frequencies. The dBA scale is based on the actual dB values for a 1000 Hz note, and using the dBA scale, a 200 Hz tone with the same dBA value as a 1000 Hz tone will be perceived as having the same loudness, although the actual intensity will be very different.

Especially important in building design are "area" sources, produced by linear sound sources (e.g., rows of cheering spectators or multiple pieces/types of mechanical equipment in a single area with large radiating surfaces). There is little reduction of sound energy produced by the distance of the area source to the adjacent spaces. In these areas, wall, ceiling, and floor isolation and separation are necessary to limit sound transmission to adjoining spaces.

Absolute silence is not a goal of good acoustic design. Instead, the goal is to provide an environment in which background sounds are regular, not too loud, and not disruptive, and to design a space in which people can hear what and when they should. Yet a space should also provide appropriate sound absorption and separation to allow privacy when and where needed.

Common Sounds in Decibels

Painfully loud or deafening sounds (jet engines during takeoff, hard rock bands, nearby thunder, and the like) may be 110–140 dBA or more in intensity. The intensity of very loud sounds (crowd noises, loud printing or mechanical equipment, automobile horns, and the like) can be 90–100 dBA. Loud noises (from cafeterias with reflective surfaces, crackling of food wrappers from 2 ft, sound levels inside commercial aircraft cabins) are 80–90 dB in intensity.

Normal speech usually falls between 50 and 70 dB in occupied rooms (with background noises of 25–35 dBA). Most office activities are in a range between 45 and 55 dBA, but background noises of 40–50 dBA are loud enough to annoy people, even if continuous.

Soft music levels in residences and quiet settings may range between 30 and 40 dBA. Background sounds in a residence late at night may measure 25–30 dBA. Quieter sounds, such as whispers and the rustle of leaves in a breeze, are typically measured between 10 and 20 dBA.

Critical Issues in Acoustic Design

The critical issues to be addressed in acoustic design for justice facilities include the following:

- Distance and separation from the sound sources. Functions that can be disturbed by intrusive noises should be located away from the sources of the sounds.

- Design of the individual spaces —shapes, heights, profiles, volumes.

- Background sound and noise levels. By definition, unwanted sounds constitute noise. Any abrupt, intermittent, or fluctuating sound can be annoying, and it is especially hard to disregard sound that contains spoken words or music. On the other hand, regular and low sounds (produced by air outlets, etc.) can create a regular background, which can be coordinated with sound isolation to mask unwanted sounds.

- The pitch of the sound, which has an effect on its perceived loudness and the disruption it causes. High-frequency sounds are generally more annoying than other sounds, because human hearing is less sensitive to low-frequency sounds.

- Selection of materials and the absorptive characteristics of the materials (see "Sound Absorption" on page 208).

- Sound transmission through mechanical systems. Sound travels in ducts independently of airflow direction. The isolation of noise transmitted by ducts must be planned, using sound-attenuating mufflers and linings. Turns must be smooth so that disturbed flows can dissipate. Systems must be designed to eliminate inappropriate cross talk (sounds transmitted from one room to adjacent rooms through common air ducts). Similarly, water piping systems must be designed with pipe and pump isolation mounts, pads, and hangers.

- The construction of walls, floors, and ceilings (see "Sound Isolation" on page 208).

In general, a number of areas in justice facilities should be designed so that external noise (whether airborne or structure-borne) is not intrusive to listeners. In smaller rooms, such as offices and conference rooms, this can be accomplished by (1) locating noisy areas (elevators, mechanical equipment rooms, and the like) away from the critical areas (courtrooms, etc.) and (2) providing appropriate wall, floor, and ceiling construction around the critical areas to reduce sound transmission between the areas by 50 dB or more.

In special areas and rooms required for justice facilities (courtrooms, jury assembly and other large training/assembly spaces, etc.), acoustical design issues become even more important, as it is essential that the judge, attorneys, and witnesses be heard clearly by all occupants of a room at all times. As a result, the overall sound level in the room should be low; that is, the ambient noise level should be low.

Privacy of speech must be achieved between a number of areas in a justice facility (because of the confidential nature of many of the conversations, the constitutional protection of privacy in attorney-client conversations, and other protections). Speech privacy in both enclosed and open office areas is based on the signal-to-noise ratio between the steady background sound (noise) and the desired speech level. Background noise is commonly created by a combination of the heating, ventilating, and air-conditioning (HVAC) system (airflow sound), general office activities, and electronic sound systems.

In enclosed offices, sound levels within a room can be considered constant because of the typically small size of such spaces, but sound-absorptive surfaces within the room can help reduce sound intensity levels. Wall, ceiling, and floor construction is crucial to sound transmission, and room-to-room attenuation (noise reduction measured in dB) should reduce sounds 35 dB or more in offices to provide privacy (more in chambers and offices with substantial requirements for confidentiality).

In open offices, sound-absorbing ceilings and floors are crucial for controlling sound. Speech-level privacy is provided at a rate relative to distance from the source and the effectiveness of the ceiling and floor treatment. In other words, sounds can be heard between desks in open offices, and speech privacy depends on two factors: the presence of a consistent and stable background noise level; and the use of sound-absorptive surfaces and materials on walls, cubicles, ceilings, and floors. Background noise must be uniform so as not to be noticeable.

Sound Isolation

Sound transmission between ceilings, walls, and floor systems is a crucial design issue for justice facilities. In general, heavier homogeneous construction materials provide better sound isolation. The sound transmission coefficient (STC) of a homogeneous material increases by more than 5 dB for each doubling of weight. The initial doubling of a material provides the most practical improvement. A solid concrete wall, for example, has an STC of 44 if it is 4 in. wide, and 48 if it is 8 in. wide.

The sound isolation efficiency of materials depends on stiffness; an ideal sound-isolating construction would be heavy and limp. Because this is not practical for most justice facility applications, typical high-performance walls use double-wall constructions with wide separations between layers. Sound leaks must be prevented, inasmuch as sound travels through openings with little loss; small openings act like speakers between rooms. The more sound-tight the wall, the more serious the sound leak (e.g., a 1 sq in. hole in a 100 sq ft partition can transmit as much sound as the rest of the partition). As a result, partition cracks and joints must be sealed, electrical outlets cannot be back to back, and all wall penetrations for pipes, ducts, and the like must be sealed. Caulking the perimeter of a gypsum board base layer on both sides of a partition can increase the STC performance of the wall by 20 dB. Doors should be designed with threshold gaskets or drop seals where STC wall performance is critical, and double-pane vision panels should be provided where necessary.

Sound Absorption

Sound absorption is an important consideration in room design. Sound levels within a room can be reduced by the effective use of sound-absorbing materials such as acoustic ceiling panels, curtains, and carpets. Without treatment, sound energy created by speech, office equipment, and other sources reverberates within the space. With treatment, less sound is heard because reflected sounds are reduced, but direct sounds remain unchanged and can still be heard.

Different materials vary considerably in terms of sound absorption and performance. Their thickness has a significant effect on the efficiency of porous sound-absorptive materials, if such materials have interconnected pores. Combinations of porous materials and volume resonators or vibrating panels can provide nearly uniform, or "flat," sound absorption at a wide range of frequencies.

The efficiency of sound-absorbing materials is also affected by their location, particularly if materials are spread into "checkerboard" patterns rather than uniformly distributed, because of the "area effect" caused by the additional absorption provided by exposed panel edges.

Reverberation control is particularly important in justice facilities, where the intelligibility of speech is very important. Typically, the larger the room volume (as in a courtroom or dayroom space), the longer the reverberation time. Doubling the total amount of absorption in a room will reduce reverberation time by half and will help to create the sense that the sound comes directly from the actual (direct) source.

Special Requirements

Courtrooms

Courtrooms should be located away from highways, flight paths, and noisy equipment rooms. Do not locate HVAC equipment, mechanical equipment, rest rooms, and other noisy spaces adjacent to courtrooms or sharing a common wall (to avoid structure-borne transmission of sound). Wherever possible, use sound-lock vestibules and corridors, storage rooms, or other "buffer" areas to isolate the courtroom from noise. To be effective, surfaces should be heavily treated with sound-absorbing materials to control noise buildup.

TYPE	STC RATING	DESCRIPTION
A	50	Minimum 200mm normal weight CMU, unfilled.
B	50	Shaftwall construction - 25mm gypsum liner panels with metal studs, two layers 15mm gypsum board on opposite side, with insulation full height in the stud cavities.
C	55	Two layers 15mm gypsum board one side, three layers opposite side of metal studs extending into structure. Insulation full height in stud cavities.

CMU to Structure

Examples of acoustic partitions. Diagram illustrates three common acoustically rated wall types found in justice facilities.

209

All doors to courtrooms should be solid, heavy, and gasketed around their entire perimeters when closed. Background noise should be low (25–30 dBA) and should not obscure or mask conversation or evidence presentation. Reverberation times should be low (less than 0.6 seconds) to accommodate special requirements of sound reinforcement systems (integrated voice/video and/or four-channel recording systems).

Typically, sound-reflecting material is used behind the judge's bench and the witness stand (to reflect sound into the litigation area), and absorptive surfaces are used on all other walls (behind the jury, in spectator seating areas, etc.). The use of absorptive ceiling and carpeting should be integrated with the selection of furnishings for the spectator seating area.

Judge's chambers
The judge's chambers should be furnished with highly sound-absorptive carpeting, drapes, and furniture, which will reduce the ambient noise level.

Grand jury room
It is critical that no one overhear grand jury discussions, presentations, or deliberations. The room should be located away from highways, flight paths, and noisy equipment rooms. Do not locate HVAC equipment, mechanical equipment, rest rooms, and other noisy spaces adjacent to the grand jury room or sharing a common wall (to prevent structure-borne transmission of sound). Wherever possible, use sound-lock vestibules and corridors, storage rooms, or other buffer areas to isolate the room from other noises. Adjacent areas should be heavily treated with sound-absorbing materials to control noise buildup.

All doors to grand jury spaces should be solid, heavy, and gasketed around their entire perimeters when closed. Background noise should be low (25–30 dBA), and should not obscure or mask conversation or evidence presentation. Reverberation times should be low (less than 0.6 second) to accommodate the special requirements of sound-reinforcement systems (integrated voice/video and/or four-channel recording systems).

In formal grand jury spaces, sound-reflecting material may be used behind the witness stand and jury foreperson position (to reflect sound toward jurors), and absorptive surfaces are used on all other walls. The design ambient sound level within the room should be 30–35 dBA. Doors should not open into areas where people congregate.

Jury deliberation areas
As discussed in relation to grand jury rooms, it is critical that no one overhear jury deliberations. Provisions for sound control include the use of a sound-lock vestibule, construction with high sound transmission loss and an ambient sound level of 35 dBA within the room. Doors should not open into areas where people congregate.

Support offices (probation, public defender, prosecutor)
The sound transmission loss of private offices for senior staff and appointed and elected officials should be similar to that of judicial chambers. The rooms should be furnished with highly sound-absorptive carpeting, drapes, and furniture, which will reduce the ambient noise level. Other offices and spaces should be designed for acoustic performance similar to that of corporate office areas, based on functional requirements and requirements for privacy and confidentiality. Office areas should also use carpet and highly absorptive ceiling materials, with

absorptive materials on cubicle or work-station surfaces where staff conduct in-person or phone conversations and disruptions should be minimized.

Prisoner holding and security areas

The prisoner holding and security areas of a court (sheriff's department, U.S. marshal areas) are typically constructed with highly reflective and reverberant surfaces and, as a result, must be designed to provide sound absorption for comfort.

Detention/correctional environments

Design for acoustic control of detention and correctional facilities is crucial to maintaining a sense of management and control, particularly in prisoner holding areas. Control of reverberation and reflected sound is particularly important in housing areas, because housing unit designs are governed by specific needs for (1) hard materials for durability and security and (2) direct sight lines from control stations, which often require rectilinear spaces and hard glass partitions.

Acceptable sound levels in housing units and dayroom areas will vary based on the time of day and the activities allowed. Sound levels should be designed to be below 45 dBA in any area in which inmates sleep. During daytime periods, and particularly where dayrooms are used for passive activities, sound levels of 70 dBA may be allowed. Reverberation times in dayrooms should be limited to 0.6–0.8 seconds to improve speech intelligibility and communication.

Controlling unwanted sounds is an important aspect in overall sound control in these areas. The volume of television sets must be limited, and background sound introduced by mechanical systems and other sources should be limited to 35 dBA or less.

To achieve reduced sound levels, day-room areas are frequently provided with acoustical ceilings and wall panels and commercial carpet with high noise-reduction coefficients. Irregularly shaped areas can help in achieving appropriate sound levels and controlling reflection.

In some cases, the need to provide sound separation between different groups in a detention or correction facility requires that inmates be housed in different areas of the facility. Because of the requirements for direct observation and the typical details of security door construction (with ½–1 in. door undercuts), it is difficult to achieve adequate sound separation.

With appropriate design of walls and mechanical systems, it can be possible to locate dissimilar inmate populations in adjacent units if sound-lock vestibules are provided. Moreover, different supervision methods (direct supervision, intermittent supervision) will dictate separation requirements, even when housing units are located in a common cluster of such units.

For additional information, see *Acoustics in Corrections, A Guide to Addressing Problems in Correctional Facilities.*

Juvenile facilities

Noise reduction is important in juvenile detention and training school facilities, particularly in housing areas and in day-rooms or passive recreation areas. Noise should be controlled through the use of acoustical materials on ceilings and walls and the use of carpeting in dayrooms. Additional measures should be considered, including the use of sound-reducing pads on door frames and sound-deadening cores on metal doors, if used.

Mechanical rooms and equipment

Mechanical rooms should be designed

NOISE CRITERIA, STEADY BACKGROUND NOISE*

Type of Space	NC Curve
Courtrooms, hearing rooms, grand jury room, jury assembly	20-25—very quiet
Large conference/training rooms, chambers	25-30—quiet/very quiet
Private offices/conference spaces	30-35—quiet
General office areas	35-40—moderately quiet
Public areas, cafeterias, reception areas	35-40—moderately quiet
Detention/correctional facility dayroom areas	30-35—quiet

*The numerical designation of the NC curve is the arithmetic average of the respective sound pressure levels at 1,000, 2,000, and 4,000 Hz (critical frequencies for speech perception).

RECOMMENDED SOUND TRANSMISSION CLASSES, PARTITIONS

SPACE	PARTITION OR PANEL BETWEEN	APPROXIMATE ISOLATION REQUIREMENT*	
		Quiet	Normal
Courtroom, hearing room, mediation room	All areas	STC 55	STC 50
Chamber suite, and judge's private chambers; elected official office	All areas	STC 55	STC 50
Jury deliberation suite, outer wall	All areas	STC 55	STC 50
Jury deliberation room	Sound-lock vestibule	STC 50	STC 45
Large conference room	All areas	STC 50	STC 45
Private offices, appointed officials, senior or deputy director staff	Demising partitions and other nonrelated department spaces or public areas	STC 50	STC 45
	Other private offices or open office areas within the agency or department	STC 45	STC 40
Mechanical equipment rooms	All areas	STC 55	STC 50
Toilet rooms, particularly rooms with multiple fixtures, staff or public	All areas	STC 55 or higher; structural isolation should be reviewed	STC 50

*Background level in room considered.

with appropriate isolation from adjoining spaces (adjacent, above, and below). Beyond wall isolation, however, these rooms should be designed for control of structure-borne sound, inasmuch as vibration can travel in columns, beams, and floor slabs. Mounts should be used to isolate vibrating equipment (air-handling units, fans, boilers, transformers, cooling towers, pumps, chillers, compressors, and the like). Vibrating equipment should be positioned away from the center of long floor spans to positions near columns or load-bearing walls (for stiffening).

CHAPTER 9
MECHANICAL, ELECTRICAL, AND STRUCTURAL SYSTEMS

This chapter presents key concepts regarding initial planning and design of the mechanical, electrical, and structural systems in modern justice facilities.

Engineering systems represent 30 percent or more of the first cost of a correctional or detention facility. The central plant must function to ensure that critical operations are maintained throughout all areas of the facility, particularly in justice facilities that must function 24 hours a day, 365 days a year.

Proper planning for a central plant must consider appropriate location of the facility, security, reliability and maintainability, and access to emergency and uninterruptible power to serve critical mechanical and electrical equipment, including boilers, chillers, electrical switch gear, pumps, and other equipment. In addition, many mechanical and electrical areas—particularly central utility areas—should be designed to accommodate a logical expansion of major components.

Key issues to keep in mind regarding engineering system design in justice facilities include the following:

- Utility requirements for justice facilities differ from those of other types of facilities. The number of showers and toilets is great, and the use patterns often are restricted. Installed bars or other screens can affect flow rates.

- Special attention must be given to construction methods and installation techniques to control or eliminate places for the potential concealment of weapons or contraband.

- A high level of coordination between disciplines is needed during the construction and occupancy phases of a project to ensure that special requirements are met (proper installation of systems, bars, grilles, ductwork, and fixtures, often with special security fasteners).

- Because of the integration of systems and security requirements, field coordination and timely installation of components is crucial to meet schedules and to avoid delays and claims.

STANDARDS

Mechanical and electrical systems should be designed to comply with the requirements of all applicable national and regional codes, standards, and guidelines, including those outlined by the following:

- National Electrical Code (NEC)
- National Fire Protection Association (NFPA 70)
- Various handbooks published by the American Society of Heating, Refrigerating, and Air-Conditioning Engineers (ASHRAE)
- Occupational Safety and Health Administration (OSHA)
- Americans with Disability Act Accessibility Guidelines (ADAAG)
- State and local codes, laws, and ordinances
- Facility/operators standards

The best general sources of information on heating, ventilating, and air-conditioning systems today are the 1999

ASHRAE Handbook—Applications, the 2000 *ASHRAE Systems and Equipment Handbook,* and the 2001 *ASHRAE Handbook—Fundamentals.* The ASHRAE handbooks are guidelines that are referenced in many codes. Together, they provide an introduction to major issues and summarize typical systems and approaches to system design. Among other criteria, ASHRAE standards specify mechanical ventilation of interior justice facility areas.

Specific guidance regarding mechanical and electrical system requirements for detention and correctional facilities can be found in the American Correctional Association (ACA) standards, which identify requirements for water, power, waste disposal, and ventilation. Over the past decade, new standards have been adopted which specify requirements for ventilation for acceptable indoor air quality. During this period, many detention and correctional facilities have been designed with air-conditioning systems for staff, public and visitor areas and, increasingly, for inmate areas, particularly in climates where heat and/or humidity levels can create problems in the management of inmates.

MECHANICAL SYSTEMS

Mechanical systems should be designed to provide essential heating, cooling, and ventilation to all areas of justice facilities, including many areas that must maintain desired environmental conditions 24 hours a day, 365 days a year. The systems must be designed to maintain appropriate comfort levels for staff, visitors, and inmates.

Design Criteria

The minimum summer indoor design temperature is typically about 75°F, according to most local, state, and federal regulations. Similarly, the maximum winter indoor design temperature is typically no more than 72°F. In equipment- or treatment-sensitive areas, the summer design indoor temperature range may be 70°–76°, and the relative humidity (RH) 40–60 percent; winter design indoor temperatures for sensitive areas may be 70°–76°, with 30–60 percent RH. These ranges can vary to some extent, and court facilities tend to have the most restrictive range in temperature and humidity targets, partly because of the increased need to control temperature and humidity in order to maintain the architectural millwork and finishes in courtrooms, chambers, and public areas.

Heating, ventilating, and air-conditioning (HVAC) systems designed to maintain humidity levels must be fully justified because of their high operational and maintenance costs. Humidity control is typically reserved for critical computer and electronic equipment systems. Because maintaining a maximum RH level of 60 percent is relatively easy with standard HVAC equipment, architectural finishes sensitive to humidity levels below 30 percent RH should be minimized.

Indoor air quality should be carefully considered in the design of mechanical systems. Several recently occupied court facilities have experienced problems with air quality. Although the causes of these problems are varied, many problems can be addressed in both new construction and renovation projects by designing to meet the criteria outlined in ASHRAE Standard 62-2001, "Ventilation for Acceptable Indoor Air Quality." In particular, mechanical system air intakes and building or vehicular exhausts should be separated, materials and systems should be selected that reduce the presence of volatile organic compounds (VOCs), and improved air-filtration systems should be provided.

In addition to code requirements, design criteria used in justice facility design should comply with industry standards regarding noise levels, noise transmission, smoke containment and/or evacuation, and controls.

Mechanical System Selection

Mechanical system design is subject to wide variances between different regions of the country. Successful design must balance requirements for comfort in typical and emergency situations with life-safety requirements. Above all, systems should be easy to understand and maintain, and system selection must consider the availability of qualified operational and service personnel.

In general, systems must be designed to be appropriate to their intended use, particularly in regard to a justice facility's 24/7/365 and peak load requirements. Criteria to consider in selecting an appropriate system include the following[1]:

- Temperature, humidity, and air pressure requirements
- Capacity requirements
- Redundancy
- Spatial requirements
- First cost
- Operating cost
- Maintenance cost
- Reliability

[1]American Society of Heating, Refrigerating, and Air-Conditioning Engineers, *2000 ASHRAE Handbook—Systems and Equipment* (Atlanta: Heating, Refrigerating, and Air-Conditioning Engineers, 2000), 1.1.

- Flexibility
- Life-cycle analysis

Typically, HVAC systems are selected on the basis of life-cycle cost analyses, frequently balancing equipment selection requirements with energy usage requirements. This is particularly true in justice facility designs, in which facilities are designed for long life and are frequently located in more remote (nonurban) areas, and where the consequences of system failures can be considerable.

Heating and cooling loads narrow the choice of systems for any project. These loads must be calculated according to the type of space and its use, location of the project, solar exposure, and anticipated changes in activities, weather, and times of use. The following factors must be considered in the final selection of a system:

- The extent of zoning, the degree of control required in each zone, and the space required for individual zones.
- Requirements for cooling and humidity control, particularly if large quantities of outside air are needed for ventilation or to replace air exhausted from the building,
- The need for effective distribution of heat or cooling. Some systems may offer high efficiency and comfort for cooling, but do not perform well for heating.
- The size and appearance of the equipment and terminal units (e.g., diffusers, fan coil units, radiant panels).
- Space available for equipment, location of this space, and/or space available for horizontal or vertical pipes and ducts.
- Acceptable noise levels in the occupied areas.

In addition, weather-related concerns that may affect final system selection include considerations of seismic activity and issues related to temperature ranges or humidity in the locality.

Typical Systems in Justice Facilities

Central utility plants

Power plants and utility plants for major justice facilities (large prison campuses and the like) are typically designed to support the needs of the institution alone. In some cases, power plants or portions of the utility services can be shared with other users and for other uses. For example, power can be provided from a nearby central power plant. In remote locations, facilities may have their own wastewater plants or may depend on a municipal wastewater system. The potable water supply may be provided by the institution or by a nearby water department.

Although construction of a central utility plant (CUP) is cost-effective for a large campus or where land values and configurations may create special requirements, provision of an electric power-generating plant (cogeneration or other) is typically beyond the scope of standard building mechanical systems. Construction of such plants should be considered only if power from a standard supplier cannot be brought to the site cost-effectively.

Centralized equipment and distribution systems

In large campuses and medium-to-large consolidated facilities, central plant equipment (boilers, chillers, heat exchangers, cooling towers, and pumps) is used to create and distribute chilled water and hot water as the cooling and heating media.

As a rule, greater operational efficiency can be acheived with a large utility plant than with small, distributed utility functions. In some facilities, large equipment may be located in a single area. In others, cooling towers may be located on building rooftops or remote from the central utility plant, with boilers, chillers, and pumps co-located in a central plant. Whether the large equipment is located in one or two areas, heating (hot) water and chilled water are typically pumped to individual air-handling units.

Air-handling units (AHUs) in justice facilities may be centralized or distributed. These units may be located within the building or on rooftops (either standard or custom-package units), depending on the design of the facility and the requirements for the specific unit. System design and zoning are typically based on occupancy types; floor area covered; standard, extended, or 24-hour operations; building program functions and scheduling flexibility; distribution plans and building configurations; and other variances in load requirements.

Mechanical systems designed to provide appropriate zone temperature control in justice facilities may incorporate variable air volume (VAV) systems, bypass multizone systems, dual-duct constant volume systems, and constant volume variable temperature systems. In prisons and detention facilities, many systems are capable of taking advantage of "free cooling" through the use of dry-bulb or enthalpy sensors that allow economizing cycles during times of moderate outdoor conditions.

It is important for some areas of justice facilities—notably those associated with housing, holding, and treatment of restrained persons—to be designed with extraordinary provisions for backup and reliability of ventilation and temperature control. For example, in inmate housing and infirmary areas, the zones served by specific AHUs should be limited, and additional sets of supply and return fans may be required to provide minimum environmental conditions and reduce the effects of equipment failure when the facility is operating in an emergency mode.

In general, in areas in which inmates are present, mechanical systems should be located in secure areas and should be vandal resistant, offer no hiding places for contraband, and provide no escape routes. Thermostats and control sensors should not be exposed in inmate-accessible areas. Outside air intakes should be protected and located in areas that prohibit contamination of the air system, either accidental or intentional. All grilles (supply, return, and exhaust) in inmate areas should meet or exceed the standards of the American National Standards Institute (ANSI) or the American Society for Testing and Materials (ASTM) for detention/correctional applications.

Proper installation of mechanical systems is critical for both security and maintainability. Particularly in security areas of justice facilities, access points and paths must be designed to provide adequate access without compromising security. Ductwork should be concealed or constructed of heavy-gauge materials if exposed. Barrier bars must be provided in ductwork and behind grilles in security areas.

Office areas

Office-type justice facilities (police stations, courthouses, administrative buildings for detention/correctional facilities that are located outside security perimeters, and the like) frequently employ some version of a VAV system for distribution of conditioned air throughout the building(s).

Special areas of these buildings, such as control/communication rooms and centers, emergency operation centers, and data processing or telecommunication areas, may be provided with self-contained air handling and cooling units to meet the strict requirements for maintaining temperature and humidity.

Housing and inmate cell areas

Housing areas and inmate cell areas in detention and correctional facilities may incorporate the use of VAV systems or, depending on the design of the building and the system, may feature the use of constant-volume HVAC systems to maintain proper ventilation rates and to eliminate system terminal devices (which are inherent in VAV systems). These devices require periodic maintenance within close proximity of the spaces they serve and, depending on the design of the building, regional variations in climate conditions, and other features, may be difficult to service.

Specific requirements

Inmate housing and processing areas are typically served by separate HVAC zones, which are frequently served by separate AHUs. Although minimum requirements for exhaust air must be met, the exhausting of air in inmate areas—especially in housing and intake/processing areas—may be increased to reduce accumulation of odors. The following are typical systems and requirements, by area:

- Inmate cell and holding rooms—100 percent outside air, constant volume,

Exterior Plumbing Chase

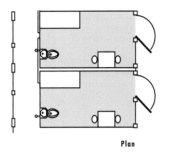

Interior Plumbing Chase

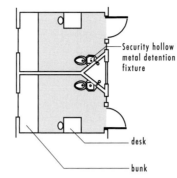

Security hollow metal detention fixture

Plan

desk

bunk

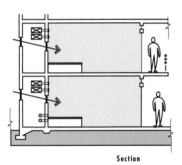

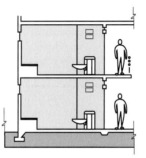

Section

▲ *Alternate service chase locations in inmate areas. These diagrams illustrate interior and exterior plumbing and mechanical service chase locations in inmate housing areas.*

variable temperature, and multispeed fans. Heating and cooling systems must consider the bunk location and the effect of the supply location on a sleeping inmate, particularly in extremely hot or cold climates and seasons.

- Dayrooms and program areas at the housing units—35 percent minimum outside air, single zone, VAV system.

- Control rooms—100 percent outside air, constant volume, return air recirculated through toilets and exhausted to outdoors.

- Kitchen and dining areas—served by dedicated air-handling units and exhaust fans.

In security control, housing, intake/transfer/release, and medical areas of detention and correctional facilities, smoke filtration systems should be provided, consisting of supply fans, HEPA filters, activated charcoal filters, distribution ductwork, and appropriate automatic dampers and control devices.

Special-purpose facilities

Mechanical systems designed to serve special-purpose justice facilities (medical examiner facilities, detention/correctional health care, ballistics and other laboratories, 24-hour operational or control centers) have specific and stringent requirements that may either add to or supercede the technical requirements of other justice facilities. Medical infirmaries in detention and correctional facilities should be designed to accommodate high levels of exhaust and infection/disease control within a security environment, which often mandates the use of grilles, louvers, and equipment that limit/restrict the flow and movement of air. Security provisions must not be overlooked, particularly in medium- and maximum-security environments, inasmuch as every area of the facility must be carefully designed to deter, detect, and prohibit escape and concealment of contraband and to limit opportunities for inmates to harm themselves or others.

Consequently, constant-volume systems, including bypass multizone and subzone reheat with selective area controls or individual room controls, may be provided. In some areas, constant-volume systems with terminal reheat and terminal humidification are a good choice.

Mechanical System Controls

Most justice facilities, whether single- or multiple-building campuses, incorporate electronic programmable logic controllers based on 4 to 20 milliamp monitoring signals and capable of stand-alone operation to provide an efficient energy management and equipment control system.

ELECTRICAL SYSTEMS

The purpose of the electrical services in a justice facility is to provide normal and emergency power to all critical systems, meeting all normal and emergency service requirements, and security systems, lighting, and all equipment, including convenience receptacles throughout the facility.

Typical Systems in Justice Facilities

Typically, electrical services are provided to the building, or to each building in a justice complex, at medium-voltage potential from the local municipality through an underground on-site utilities distribution system (to reduce potential threats to overhead service). Electricity is distributed through switch gear and transformers to the main electrical room of the project.

Systems are typically designed with distribution from a central location outside the security perimeter. In justice projects with multiple building locations, distribution of power at each location is usually provided via underground ductbanks from service points to buildings, and services are provided from pad-mounted transformers to the building's switchboard. Interior electrical distribution equipment is typically installed in secure closets and located for efficient distribution of electrical services through the building(s).

Most moderate-to-large justice facilities are supplied with 480/277 V, three-phase, four-wire service. In older facilities, 208/120 service may be used if higher voltage is not available. Where provided, the 480 V service is used for the larger loads in the building (chillers, air-conditioning equipment, elevators, pumps, and air-handling units). Motor control centers are located in the mechanical rooms and are served from the main switchboard.

Lighting systems are frequently designed to use 277 V single-phase service, served from the main electrical switchboard to panel boards located in electrical closets distributed throughout the building(s).

Power for convenience receptacles, special equipment, and selected lighting is generally provided with dry-type transformers and lighting and appliance panelboards supplying 120/208 V, three-phase, four-wire service. Transformers are housed in distributed electrical closets to provide 120 Vpower for the distributed outlets and circuits (for offices and workstations, general use/convenience outlets, and dedicated circuits).

Selected areas and requirements with high density loads, including food preparation areas, laundries, and central maintenance and laundry areas, should be served by dedicated panel boards.

The building section diagram on page 220 presents an example of how electrical, mechanical, and specialty system closets and spaces should be vertically and horizontally aligned in a multistory justice facility such as a courthouse. See the section "Areas and Spaces" later in this chapter for additional information on specific space and technical requirements of all critical areas in justice facilities.

▶ *Diagrammatic section through building. Illustrates the typical vertical alignment of key mechanical, electrical and data-telecommunication system spaces in a multi-story justice facility.*

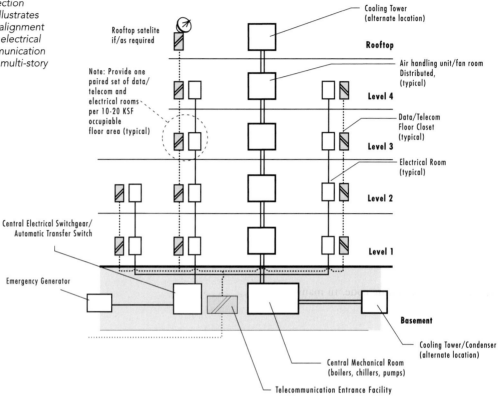

Rooftop satelite if/as required

Note: Provide one paired set of data/telecom and electrical rooms per 10-20 KSF occupiable floor area (typical)

Central Electrical Switchgear/ Automatic Transfer Switch

Emergency Generator

Cooling Tower (alternate location)

Rooftop

Air handling unit/fan room Distributed, (typical)

Level 4

Data/Telecom Floor Closet (typical)

Level 3

Electrical Room (typical)

Level 2

Level 1

Basement

Cooling Tower/Condenser (alternate location)

Central Mechanical Room (boilers, chillers, pumps)

Telecommunication Entrance Facility

In most cases, buildings are provided with a service-entrance-rated main switchboard or main distribution panel board for each normal or emergency service provided. Metering of normal services is handled at service entrances.

Standby Electrical Power (Emergency)

The building loads that are essential to the safety of life, egress from the building, communication, security of the facility, and other loads deemed necessary to maintain minimum functionality of the building are fed from the emergency power distribution system. The distribution system is fed from one or more auto-matic transfer switches, which are fed from both the normal utility power source and the standby emergency generator. When any transfer switch senses a loss of utility power, it automatically signals the emergency generator to start and switches to the emergency generator when this power source is available.

The time delay between sensing loss of utility power and switching to emergency power is somewhere between 6 and 10 seconds for a life-safety system. Continuous power must be available for critical computer-related and security-related functions in most detention and correctional facilities. For the most critical loads, a central uninterruptible power supply (UPS) is typically provided. The UPS is connected to the standby power system, with batteries provided to ride through the short-term loss of power. The UPS system should be designed to support the control centers, communication systems, security systems, and other critical loads for a sufficient time until generator power is on-line or a controlled shutdown is complete.

Emergency generators may be diesel or natural-gas fueled (or both), and fuel supplies are typically housed on site for 12- to 24-hour operation at the rated loads.

The generator should be sized to support the security control and console systems, site lighting, life-safety systems, smoke evacuation, and other functions as required by the building code. In many cases, generators are sized to support functions that would be required for reduced operations in detention and correctional facilities, including food service equipment, medical service areas, ventilation fans and limited cooling systems, and lighting in some program areas. Frequently, provisions are made for a secondary or backup generator, especially in large facilities or where power reliability is a problem.

Emergency power requirements for facilities not designed for 24/7/365 operation can be reduced to life-safety requirements alone. In these cases, typical loads include exit signs and light fixtures designed to serve the paths of exit travel. In smaller facilities, it may be more cost-effective to provide emergency power to required exit lighting by means of local battery packs.

Whether designed to be connected initially or after a delay, the emergency systems in a justice facility should be designed to support the following:

- Life-safety and security lighting (generator system)
- Exterior security lighting (generator system)
- Fire alarm and detection systems (UPS and generator systems)
- Fire pumps (generator)
- Security systems, including door, closed-circuit video equipment (CCVE), access control, and intercom systems (UPS and generator systems)
- Communication systems (UPS and generator systems)
- Data/telecommunication areas, including entrance facility, main distribution frame, and intermediate distribution frame rooms (UPS and generator)
- Control rooms and consoles (UPS and generator)
- Selected elevators (generator)
- Selected heating and cooling control systems and equipment, including air-handling equipment for designated areas (generator, as dictated by project needs)
- Elevator lighting, signaling, and control (generator, as dictated by project needs)
- Selected loads associated with medical areas (patient isolation rooms, nurse call, medical gas systems)
- Sump pumps (generator)
- Smoke control systems, including all air-moving equipment serving smoke evacuation, containment, and filtration systems (generator, but verify per applicable code)
- Supply and exhaust fans for holding, housing, isolation, and security control rooms (generator, but verify per applicable code)

- Selected food service equipment in facilities housing inmates or detainees (generator)
- Kitchen refrigerated and freezer storage (generator)

PLUMBING SYSTEMS

Plumbing systems provided in justice facilities include domestic water, sanitary waste, vent, plumbing fixtures and equipment, and storm drainage (including site and internal storm drainage systems). Stringent water quality standards must be met, and requirements for filtration and water softening should be reviewed for each project, based on water content and supply. If required, water softener equipment should be located in central mechanical/pump rooms.

Water Supply

Water supplies may be provided to justice facilities through municipal water systems or through wells or a reservoir system (in remote areas). If a facility has its own water supply, a water treatment plant must be provided, staffed by qualified operators.

Water systems for justice facilities include domestic water supplies, fire protection/sprinkler systems, and irrigation systems and may include non-potable water systems. The system should be designed to reliably provide appropriate quantities of water, meeting stringent quality standards, to all areas of the facility and site. Storage tanks should be provided in most correctional and detention projects to ensure water supplies in case of emergencies, typically for three days at minimum. Where water is stored for emergencies, a system should be designed to keep the stored water potable.

Water supplies are usually piped to a central location in or near the utility plant. In detention and correctional facilities, receiving and distribution piping should be designed to allow visual and metered monitoring and control.

Wastewater Treatment

The treatment of wastewater must comply with all governing codes, rules, and regulations. Wherever possible, wastewater treatment is achieved through connection to a municipal system. Where this is not feasible, an independent, on-site sewage treatment plant may be required. A treatment plant should be sized to handle at least 80 percent of the total water consumption of the facility, and qualified operators are required to staff the plant.

Typical Plumbing Systems in Justice Facilities

In most justice facilities, domestic hot water is generated and stored by steam-to-water heaters located within central mechanical/pump rooms. Hot water is provided for staff use throughout a facility at 120°–140°, and hot water provided for inmates' fixtures may be restricted to 105° at the point of use. Where lower temperatures are provided at inmates' points of use, systems must be designed to maintain water quality and limit opportunities for development of legionella or other contamination. In larger facilities, recirculating pumps may be installed to provide instantaneous hot or tempered water at all outlets during periods of low demand.

Fixtures

In justice facilities, institutional or high-grade commercial porcelain or vitreous china plumbing fixtures are provided in staff, public, and general-purpose toilets and rest rooms and break areas. Institutional fixtures are provided in maintenance and housekeeping support areas (in public, private, and restricted-access areas of virtually all justice facilities).

In inmate-accessible areas of many medium- and maximum-security facilities, stainless steel security-type fixtures are provided for inmate toilets, showers, and cells. Security-type water closets are typically equipped with low-maintenance metering valves. Showers are usually controlled by metered valves or by electric solenoid valves with timers to limit shower length.

Recently, inmate-accessible areas in minimum- and some (predominantly direct-supervision) medium- and maximum-security facilities have been designed using institutional porcelain or vitreous china plumbing fixtures. The choice of fixtures should be decided on the basis of security and observation requirements and according to directions to the design team from the inmate management and supervision staff.

Plumbing systems must be designed to support security and maintenance needs. Plumbing systems serving fixtures in inmate housing/holding areas are typically designed to be accessible from outside cell areas and from within a dedicated and secured mechanical chase area. Sanitary drains in many facilities require constant maintenance because of inmates' attempts to clog toilets or drains or to pass contraband. As a result, easily accessible clean-outs should be provided for toilets, floor drains, and hose bibs. Plumbing chases often contain supply or exhaust air ducts, and careful coordination is required to ensure adequate access to all equipment.

FIRE PROTECTION SYSTEMS

Fire protection systems must be designed in compliance with state and local building codes and NFPA requirements (including NFPA 101). In most justice facilities (with the exception of federal projects under specific requirements), fire protection system requirements must be verified during the design and construction phases with the appropriate state and local fire marshals. It is important that fire pumps and all air-moving equipment serving smoke evacuation, containment, and filtration systems be provided with standby (emergency) power.

Fire protection systems included in most justice facilities consist of detection devices, smoke and fire dampers, and the required standpipe and automatic sprinkler systems. Smoke evacuation and containment systems must comply with state and local codes. Air-handling units in most justice facilities must include automatic smoke purge cycles with manual overrides. Sprinkler system operation (wet versus dry system) and sprinkler head selection (standard, concealed, pre-action, security) should be appropriate to the facility type and the particular area of the facility. Special design considerations are important for security control and computer equipment areas.

Fire pumps with access to municipal water supplies and/or internal water storage tanks are usually provided in the central mechanical/pump rooms to serve sprinklers and standpipes. Although there are codes governing the locations of standpipes and sprinklers, special provisions for institutional-type, vandal-resistant security sprinkler heads should be made in inmate-occupied areas of justice facilities.

▸ *Rooftop cooling towers behind architectural screen. New courthouse project. Syska Hennessy Group: Mechanical, Electrical & Plumbing Engineers. Photo: z. jedrus.*

▸ *Central boiler plant. New courthouse project. Note the steel cross-bracing. The structure for this building (cross-bracing, deep beams, etc.) made coordination extremely critical for the equipment layouts and duct runs. Syska Hennessy Group: Mechanical, Electrical & Plumbing Engineers. Photo: z. jedrus.*

AREAS AND SPACES

Typical Areas

The total mechanical and electrical space required for most justice facilities ranges between 6 and 10 percent of the gross building area. This allocation of area includes provisions for centralized and distributed equipment rooms. Spaces required for vertical shafts typically add another 1–2 percent of floor area, depending on system design requirements and specific systems selected for the project.

A central location in the building will minimize duct, pipe, and conduit runs and sizes and can centralize maintenance and operations. Depending on the type of system selected, however, not all electrical and mechanical equipment should be centrally located. For example, in some systems, air-handling units are more appropriately distributed into rooms closer to the areas served.

Most large equipment rooms should be 12–18 ft high (clear ceiling height).

Typical mechanical and electrical areas include central utility plant areas, central electrical transformer and switchgear rooms, emergency generator rooms or areas, uninterruptible power supply equipment rooms, central mechanical rooms, distributed fan rooms, and distributed electrical closets.

Central utility plant

The utility plant for a building frequently houses the main equipment, but additional rooms may be required for air-handling equipment, electrical panels and transformers, and distributed data/telecommunication or fire/security equipment spaces. Equipment and system requirements and, consequently, space requirements vary greatly across the United States (and worldwide), and overall space requirements must be developed on a project-by-project basis.

Utility plants are typically located outside the security perimeter of a prison or jail, often near a loading dock, garage, or warehouse. In smaller facilities and those serving lower-security prisoners, the central plant may be located inside the perimeter, near maintenance areas. This arrangement can help to reduce staffing, as in many prisons and jail facilities one full-time plant engineer must be on duty at all times to maintain operations of critical utility systems and an engineer located outside the security perimeter may not be fully utilized.

The location of a utility plant should be selected so as to reduce the required length of runs for utility service. In urban facilities or justice projects that comprise a single building, utility areas should be centrally located on a lower level of the building with convenient access for large equipment and replacement components and service.

Although such central locations are convenient for site design and for service vehicle access, care must be taken to design utility areas in such a way that a nonrelated accident or mishap will not create a security or service problem for the plant or equipment. In facilities located on tight urban sites, mechanical (air) distribution equipment and intakes should not be located in or near central utility plant or mechanical room areas. Central electrical rooms and vaults should be located in buildings in such a way that a vehicle mishap or accident (intentional or not) will not affect service operations, the generators, or generator fuel supplies.

Cooling towers

Space should be planned on the site—or in urban projects, on rooftop—for cooling towers. If located on the ground, air- or water-cooled towers or condensers should be located at least 100 ft from the building and parking lots so as to reduce noise and keep discharge air and moisture away from the building. For either rooftop or ground-level units, provisions should be made for some degree of enclosure (on sides). Specific allowances should be made in the budget for the structural costs associated with cooling tower locations, and for provision of adequate area and appropriate enclosure for the equipment.

Central mechanical room

Typically, boilers, chillers, pumps, and domestic water heating equipment should be located in an enclosed room, usually on the lower levels of the building, to reduce the costs associated with service access to the building from the site perimeters and to reduce the impact of vibration and noise associated with the equipment. The room(s) should be planned to provide sufficient clearance to allow easy access for service and replacement of major parts as needed.

Areas should be provided for central boilers, boiler feed units, chemical treatment equipment, pressure-reducing equipment, control air compressors, and miscellaneous equipment. The refrigeration equipment areas should house chillers, chilled water and condenser water pumps, heat exchangers, air-conditioning equipment, control air compressors, and other miscellaneous equipment. ASHRAE guidelines specify that chillers are to be located in rooms separated from other equipment. Other areas should be

designed to house equipment related to the fire suppression and the domestic hot water system, including hot water heaters, pumps, fire pumps, storage tanks, and other equipment.

In many situations and projects, specific rooms will be required for the air-handling units (AHUs) that serve occupiable areas of the building, including areas on

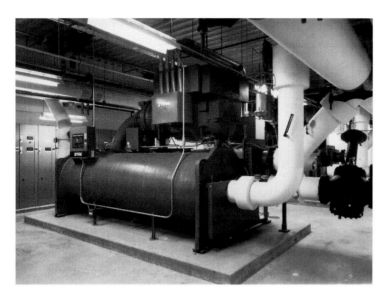

▲ *Central chiller plant. New courthouse project. Syska Hennessy Group: Mechanical, Electrical & Plumbing Engineers. Photo: z. jedrus.*

state and local codes provide criteria regarding fire and smoke detection, management, and dampers. Wherever fan rooms are located, they should have good access to outdoor air and exhaust air and for replacement of equipment. The number of fan rooms included depends on the system selected, total floor area of the building and areas that should be served by the system, and the design criteria for an efficient system. For initial planning of justice facilities, designers can assume that typical AHU rooms should be 500 or more NSF in size to serve a 15,000–20,000 sq ft floor plate in office or court occupancies.

the lower level(s). System designs often provide separate rooms for each office, court, or detention area or floor level. These rooms typically require 400 sq ft or more per area. Note: A centralized single AHU with one or two fans to serve the building is usually not recommended for court facilities because of the need to provide efficient after-hours and partial operations and to reduce the potential for a single failure point for the building.

Distributed fan rooms

Air-handling units may be located in designated rooms or other areas (above ceilings or in other spaces). Wherever possible, AHUs should be located in rooms that can be readily accessed for service (filter replacement, routine and major service, including replacement of major shafts and coils).

Fan rooms may be located in virtually any area of the building. It is crucial that life-safety requirements be met in locating fan rooms; national guidelines and

Central electrical switch gear room

The central electrical service entrance/ transformer/switch gear room may range from 200 NSF for a small electrical service room in a small facility to 1,000 NSF or more in a large correctional complex. This area is typically located on the service-entry level of the building and should be located as close to the incoming electrical service as practical. This area should not be subject to flooding.

Emergency generator room/area

In the event of a power disruption, an emergency power generator should start automatically and should support life-safety and egress lighting, the fire alarm system, duress alarms, the public address system, and other essential operating equipment in the facility. Status monitoring of the emergency generator should be provided in the building central control.

The designers should allow 600–1,000 NSF or more for a generator room or area, depending on generator size, fan/ventilation requirements, and storage/reserve tank requirements. This area is typically located on the service/entry-level of the building, but may be located on a separate pad or on a different level because of requirements for noise abatement and separation. It should generally not be located more than several hundred feet from the electrical switch gear.

Uninterruptible power supply system (UPS) room

The UPS area may be required to house central switch and battery equipment, particularly if a central building-wide UPS is provided. Although package units may be located in various areas, centralized building-wide systems are not uncommon in justice facilities. Where provided, these systems serve a wide range of areas of the building, including prisoner detention areas (institutional restrained areas), security control centers (building security control and prisoner security control), data/telecommunication entrance facilities; central computer room(s), floor communication closet, and often audio-video system equipment rooms.

Electrical closets

Providing a definable area for the design of systems and service zones is especially important in electronically enhanced buildings because better performance of computers and electrical systems can be achieved when building telecom and power systems serve parallel "zones" or areas of a building. This approach allows individual electrical and telecommunications closets to serve reasonably sized floor areas with similar horizontal distribution, vertical stacks, and cross-building ties without the problem of additional interference on data lines that is created

▲ Emergency generator plant. New courthouse project. Syska Hennessy Group: Mechanical, Electrical & Plumbing Engineers. Photo: z. jedrus.

when equipment is connected to different power sources or transformers.

Where building floors are larger than 10,000 sq ft in size, multiple pairs of closets should be provided on each floor. This ensures redundancy in vertical cores and allows for cross ties on each floor for secondary pathways. Although different buildings and designs may locate systems above or below floors, the key to continued flexibility and adaptability in the future is to provide easy access to these interstitial areas.

Electrical and data/telecommunication closets should be grouped together in pairs and designed to serve approximately 10,000 sq ft from one pair. Typical floor plates in court buildings should be conceived in terms of "blocks" of space that are defined by reasonable walking, wiring and service distances (often 100' × 100'), or approximately 10,000 sq ft.

OTHER ISSUES AND CONSIDERATIONS

Energy Efficiency

With the development of operationally effective housing unit design (podular concepts, designed for direct or indirect supervision), the square footage per inmate in justice facilities increased dramatically between the mid-1950s and the mid-1970s. With the 1973 oil embargo came increased interest in cutting energy costs and consumption in all government facilities. Special attention was focused on mechanical and electrical systems, including heating, ventilation, air-conditioning, lighting, domestic hot water, and the overall large equipment used to support the building (pumps, motors, etc.).

Specific changes in the design of mechanical systems in justice facilities since the mid-1970s include the following:

- Widespread adoption and use of building automation and management systems (BAMS or BMS) with direct digital controls and monitoring of temperatures, airflows, and systems throughout all operational periods, with enhanced ability to adjust to compensate for changes in requirements as needs arise and during likely periods of increased use

- Improved zoning of areas served and matching of AHUs and distribution system designs with the size of the zone, solar orientation (internal versus facade zones) and functional requirements — including use of variable-speed pumping, requirements for extended hours or 24/7/365 operation, and use of room-by-room controls

- Reducing power required by the fans, through use of a wide variety of variable-speed fans or fan drives and high-efficiency motors on HVAC equipment

- Proper sizing of boilers and chillers to better match heating and cooling design, with modular design to accommodate low or partial loads as well as peak demands

- Incorporating the use of heat-recovery systems to reclaim value from the exhaust heat for incoming cold air intakes (or the benefit of exhaust cooling for incoming hot air), including flue heat recovery and dampers, and dual-fuel and high-efficiency combustion systems

- Using warm-up cycles during fan start-up periods

- Increased use of energy-efficient separate domestic hot water heaters to allow large boilers to be shut off during warm and hot weather

- Operating with lower hot-water temperatures (typically 120° versus 140°), while considering health and safety issues (Legionnaires' disease and the like)

Energy efficiency in mechanical/electrical systems is supplemented by improvements in building design over the past decades:

- Improved lighting systems and design, including use of high-efficiency ballasts and lamps and improved directed and/or task lighting fixtures

- Use of low-energy fixtures for exit lighting, and high-intensity discharge (HID) lamps (i.e., high-pressure sodium and metal halide) in parking lots and for perimeter lighting (where appropriate)

- Use of programmable lighting control systems with daylighting and other automatic sensors
- Maximizing use of daylight in the building
- Use of Low-E coatings on windows
- Emphasizing replacement of windows (in existing facilities)
- Integrating passive solar design concepts into the architectural and site design

STRUCTURAL SYSTEMS

The selection of a structural system for any building must be based on a careful analysis of many different factors. Some of the most important are bay size and shape, cost, availability of materials, local practice and speed of construction.

The bay size is a major factor. Every structural system has a practical span range. The use of a structural system for spans above its practical range will make the system expensive or even unworkable, as it may be impossible to achieve the required strength or stiffness. The use of a structural system for spans below this range will make the system unnecessarily expensive. The shape of the bay is an important factor as well. A square bay will be more conducive to the use of two-way systems, systems that work in two directions like flat slabs or waffle slabs; for rectangular bays, it is usually more appropriate to use one-way systems or systems that work mainly in one direction like one-way joists.

Cost is obviously an important factor. For any building, there are various structural systems that can meet all the requirements of the applicable codes and all additional requirements of the owner. The goal is to find the system that will meet all requirements at the minimum cost. Local practice and availability of materials are factors that will have a direct effect on the cost of the building.

In addition to the aforementioned factors, every building type has its own set of requirements that must be considered, as they can have a major impact on the selection of a structural system. The following paragraphs describe these requirements, as well as the most common structural systems for two types of justice facilities: courthouses and detention facilities.

Courthouses

Among the specific issues to consider in the design of courthouses are the long spans, the control of floor vibrations, and the blast design and force entry requirements.

Bay size

The length of the spans is a function of the required courtroom width. The typical span across the width of a courtroom is on the order of 40–45 ft. The span in the other direction does not have to be as long and varies according to the layout of all the different spaces in the building, but it can be in the range of 20–30 ft.

The long span requirement makes some concrete systems impractical. Among these are the flat plate and flat slab systems, for which the maximum practical spans are on the order of 35 ft and 40 ft, respectively. In addition, the rectangular shape of the typical bay makes a one-way system more appropriate than a two-way system; therefore, a one-way joist system that has a span range up to 50 ft is usually more suitable than a waffle slab system. Post-tensioned concrete slab systems can also span these distances while safely carrying the prescribed design loads. A steel framing system with floor beams and girders can easily meet these span requirements as well.

Floor vibrations are important, especially in courtrooms. Vibrations are produced mainly by mechanical equipment in the building and by people walking in the corridors, offices, and courtrooms. The structural design must be such that the vibration levels in the building cannot be perceived by people in the offices and courtrooms. Concrete systems usually result in acceptable vibration levels because they are inherently stiff. Steel framing systems, which are more flexible, may result in levels of floor vibration that can be perceived by the users of the building if vibration control is not considered in the design of the structure. However, vibration levels can be easily controlled when they are considered in the design. In this case, the size and/or spacing of the steel beams may be controlled by the vibration requirements.

Blast design and force entry requirements, at this writing, are mandatory only for federal courthouses. A separate section on blast design and force entry is included later in this chapter.

Concrete and steel systems

Concrete and steel systems are feasible structural systems for courthouse buildings. Although many factors must be considered in making a selection, a one-way joist slab may be the most appropriate system if reinforced concrete is used. In this case, the joists are supported by reinforced concrete beams that span between the columns in the direction perpendicular to the joists. Ideally, the depth of the beams will match the depth of the joists; if so, the formwork will be greatly simplified.

If structural steel is used, steel beams spaced between 8 and 12 ft apart are supported by steel girders that frame into the columns. The typical slab construction consists of corrugated composite metal deck with concrete topping. The concrete slab works in composite action with the steel beams and girders and participates in carrying the gravity loads. The composite action between the slab and the steel beams is achieved by welding shear connectors to the top flanges of the beams and girders. The thickness of the concrete slab is usually governed by the fire resistance requirements specified by the applicable building codes. A certain thickness of concrete must be provided to achieve a given fire resistance unless the metal deck is fireproofed. Usually, lightweight concrete is used, because the slab thickness necessary to achieve the required fire resistance is considerably less if lightweight concrete is used instead of normal-weight concrete. The reduced weight of the slabs results in a reduction of the loads that must be carried by the floor framing, columns and foundation. As stated earlier, the size and spacing of the steel beams may be governed by the vibration control requirements.

Detention Facilities

The most common structural systems for detention facilities are precast concrete cells, masonry bearing walls with precast concrete plank floors, and cast-in-place concrete frames with nonbearing reinforced masonry walls.

The precast concrete cells are typically fabricated as two-cell modules with one utility chase. The modules are five-side boxes with four walls and ceiling. The ceiling of one module serves as the floor of the module above. The modules can be stacked to approximately eight stories and are connected to the modules above and below with pins that are grouted into embedded inserts. The lateral connections to adjacent modules are usually made through welded plates. All the furniture, plumbing fixtures, light fixtures, windows, and doors are installed at the shop. The completed cells are then transported to the site and erected.

The main advantages of this system are quality, speed of construction, and reduced cost. The quality of the finished product is improved because most of the construction is done at the shop, where there is obviously better quality control. The construction can be completed very quickly because the precast cells can be fabricated while the site work and foundation are being completed. The potential for cost savings is more obvious for bigger projects for which the number of identical cells to be fabricated is large. In small projects, in which the number of cells is small and there are several different types of cells, a different structural system may be more appropriate. The structure of the day space between groups of cells, with spans that vary approximately 20–50 ft, can be done in many different ways: precast double-tees, precast hollow-core slabs, cast-in-place concrete, and steel joists with metal deck are among the most common.

Masonry bearing-wall systems are also common. Because secured walls are necessary, it makes sense to use those walls for the structural support of the building. The reinforced masonry walls between cells are then used as bearing walls. The floor system usually consists of precast concrete plank floors, hollow or solid, depending on the requirements of the applicable codes. A disadvantage of this type of construction is that it is slow to build.

Cast-in-place concrete frames with non-bearing reinforced masonry walls are also common. In this system, the floor construction over the cells is usually flat plate and the day space between groups of cells, for the longer spans, is one-way joists or, in some cases, waffle slabs.

Steel construction has also been used, although it is far less common than concrete for detention facilities. Prefabricated steel cells are relatively new and not very common at this time.

As in any type of building, the selection of the structural system is greatly influenced by local practice and the availability of materials in the area at the time of construction.

Blast Design and Force Entry Protection of Courthouses

United States courthouse facilities are designed and constructed to adhere to the provisions of the U.S. General Services Administration (GSA) Security Design Criteria. These criteria are intended to reduce the hazard to occupants in the event of an explosive terrorist threat. The goals of the specific provisions are to provide an increased setback from the street curb, reduce the potential for progressive collapse, reduce the hazard of impact from flying debris, isolate occupants from direct blast pressures, maintain critical life-support facilities, and aid in the rescue of victims. Although the primary goal of the GSA Security Design Criteria is to minimize injury to occupants, passive protection will reduce the likelihood of a catastrophic event and limit the extent of damage resulting from an explosive threat. However, physical security alone will not guarantee a desired level of protection; a combination of technical and operational security is required to maintain access control and screening of packages and parcels entering the facility. The appropriate balance of security services will constitute the desired level of protection.

Site conditions

The secured perimeter represents the closest distance a potential threat, in the form of a vehicle bomb, can advance toward the targeted structure. In order for the secured perimeter to be effective, bollards, planters, hardened street architecture, or retaining walls, capable of resisting the impact of the specified vehicle traveling at the maximum practical approach speed, must be installed. The standoff distance, measured from the secured perimeter to the closest point on the structure, coupled with the explosive charge weights corresponding to the specified GSA Security Criteria protection level, establishes the blast design requirements for the building.

In addition to the required protection against stationary exterior vehicle bombs, provisions must be made to protect the vehicle entranceways to the site. These perimeter entry points must be equipped with retractable hydraulic bollards also capable of resisting the impact of a moving vehicle traveling at the maximum practical approach speed. At these locations, a combination of hydraulic and stationary bollards must be utilized to provide a continuous anti-ram barrier and prevent vehicles from gaining access to the site.

Facade

The building's exterior is its first real defense against the effects of a bomb; how the facade responds to this loading will significantly affect the behavior of the structure and its ability to protect the occupants. To establish the blast design

criteria, pressure and impulse maps are developed for each of the four sides of the building reflecting the detonation of an explosive charge at the secured perimeter of the site. These maps define the blast environment to which the structure's facade and structural system must be designed. However, the GSA Security Criteria impose a limit on the maximum blast design load for exterior facades.

The use of protective glazing and a hardened facade, properly designed and detailed to provide the protection specified by the GSA Security Criteria, will effectively reduce the hazard to all occupants of the facility. To meet the GSA Security Criteria, the single-pane glazing or the inner lite of an insulated glazing unit must be made of laminated glass. If the glazing is adhered to the mullions with structural silicone sealant, the facade will be able to sustain greater deformations while retaining the glazing within the mullions. The window mullions must be sufficiently sized and detailed to support the blast loading on the glass and transfer that load to the supporting structure. Similarly, the nonglazing portions of the facade and anchorage must be properly sized and detailed to transfer the blast load to the structure. Employing these protective design features will reduce the risk to occupants of impact from flying debris. Injury from exposure to direct blast pressures will also be dramatically reduced.

In sizing window systems, stronger mullions are typically required to conform to the glass-fail-first philosophy of protective design. In this method of design, the glazing is allowed to fail in a safe manner, but the mullions, frames, and anchorage must be designed to survive the collected forces. According to the statistics of glazing resistance, this corresponds to a nominal 750-break-per-thousand capacity of the glass.

Although a curtain wall may appear to be a very fragile facade, great strides have been made in developing an enhanced curtain wall system that offers the required protection to occupants. Such curtain wall systems have been shown, through explosive testing, to be remarkably resilient. When properly designed and constructed with attention to detail, the curtain wall system provides a relatively low-frequency response to the short-duration blast load. This low-frequency response permits the curtain wall to dissipate a significant portion of the blast energy through deformation.

However, the performance of this system requires the mullion sections and the connections to be detailed to allow deformations to develop. Curtain wall systems for the Las Vegas Federal Courthouse were explosively tested at the large blast thermal simulator (LBTS) at the White Sands Missile Range (WSMR) and were found to exceed their design requirements. Not only was the flexibility of the system beneficial to the survival of the frame members, it also improved the apparent capacity of the glazing to withstand the blast load.

The curtain wall frames must be designed to withstand the effects of the collected blast pressures. The design loads may be determined through a dynamic analysis of the system. In addition to the dynamic benefits of low-frequency systems in withstanding high-frequency shock loads, the allowance for inelastic deformations will further reduce the apparent equivalent static loads on the curtain wall. The equivalent static loading is limited by the capacity of the glazing, which is a function of the size and thickness of the lites. For the design of the framing members, the glass-fail-first phi-

losophy of protective design is employed. The 750-break-per-thousand capacity of the glazing must be used in determining its limiting capacity. Furthermore, to hold the glazing within the window wall frame, the glazing must be completely set in place with structural silicone sealant.

Structural protection

Lateral system

The lateral bracing systems in conventional structures are designed to resist only wind (and seismic loads where applicable). However, in the case of blast-resistant structures, the blast-induced base shear forces can easily exceed the capacity of structural members designed to resist conventional load conditions. The magnitude of the lateral blast-induced base shears depends to a great extent on the amount of inelastic deformation the structure is permitted to sustain. Therefore, an acceptable level of lateral deformation must be specified, and the corresponding blast-induced base shear must be compared with base shears associated with wind and seismic forces. The largest base shear will govern the design of the lateral system. However, for the design to be effective, the floor slabs, acting as horizontal diaphragms, must be able to transfer the blast forces collected by the facade to the lateral structural system, which, in turn, transfers the loading into the foundation.

Progressive collapse

Progressive collapse is defined as the spread of an initial local failure from element to element, resulting in the collapse of a disproportionately large part of a structure. In other words, a progressive collapse occurs, for example, when the loss of a single column results in the destruction of a large portion of a building. To prevent progressive collapse, the key elements of the structure can be designed so that a localized structural failure does not occur.

This approach, referred to as the method of specific local resistance, is formulated for a specific charge weight, and, as a result, the structure is vulnerable to a bomb larger than the specified threat. Conversely, the structure can be designed to redistribute the loads in the event that a key element, such as a column, is destroyed. In this approach the adjacent columns, beams, and girders are designed to support the surviving loads.

This alternate load path method ensures that the floors above and/or adjacent to the damaged column do not crash down into the failure zone. It is important to note that the surviving floors may sustain significant damage. However, the upper floors will not collapse, and rescue personnel will be able to gain access and evacuate the area.

To guard against progressive collapse, a conventional structure is improved by a combination of structural redundancy and increased ductility through the use of seismic detailing.

A properly designed structure will be able to absorb large displacements, redistribute the loads, and, although damaged, remain standing. After being subjected to a bombing, all structures will require some repair, and in many cases complete reconstruction. The goal in protective design, however, is to ensure the safety of the occupants, prevent the occurrence of additional injuries and casualties, and allow life-safety personnel to assist victims. The protection is not provided for the sake of saving the structure.

The use of seismic detailing alone does not provide a guarantee against progres-

sive collapse for the specified blast loads. Seismic detailing does, in general, increase the amount of ductility available for connection deformations, therefore enhancing the performance of a connection under deformations exceeding its elastic capacity. However, other structural aspects such as floor slab reinforcement, span lengths, and column heights are also significant in assessing the risk of progressive collapse. For example, a satchel charge detonated inside may damage the floor slabs above and below the explosion, significantly increasing the unbraced length of an adjacent column. Although such columns should be designed for a two-story unbraced length, their damaged state may lead to instability, initiating a failure and possible collapse. In anticipation of this scenario, the columns surrounding the failed column should be sufficiently sized and detailed to withstand the additional loads and deflections without failure.

Structural elements

Critical structural elements that may be subjected to blast loads, including beams, columns, and slabs, must be analyzed to determine their capacity to withstand the blast loads. This analysis is both dynamic and inelastic and takes full advantage of the material's capacity to deform prior to failure. The design of the structural elements and the determination of the equivalent static forces for detailing the connections requires the determination of the worst-threat scenario at the location of each element and the iterative sizing and corresponding evaluation of the blast effects. This process must be applied to the structural elements at the building's perimeter and within the uncontrolled areas into which a terrorist threat may be introduced.

CHAPTER 10

SPECIALTY SYSTEMS

This chapter presents an introduction to integrated and communicating systems and emphasizes the importance of design for a shared infrastructure to support them. The chapter addresses some basic planning requirements, system design concepts, and special issues associated with data/telecommunication and audio-video systems.

Justice facilities today are technology-intensive environments. As justice-related agencies and operations increase their use of computers, the amount of equipment and the locations in which that equipment is used continue to grow. Virtually all justice facilities must accommodate PCs and terminals or controls at every staff or public counter workstation. In many justice facilities, the number of computers equals or exceeds the number of staff in the building at all but peak periods. And this is just the beginning. Justice facilities nationwide are already being designed for wireless systems.

Today's justice facilities must be sufficiently flexible to handle constant change in actual work and organization, as well as changes in equipment. New justice facility design must be based on processing information rather than processing people or paper. In these facilities, information will move electronically and paper will be used as a display medium instead of a storage medium.

The facilities themselves will change as a result. When information flows to people, instead of people moving to information, physical locations within the facility become less important, allowing functions to be geographically dispersed. This has important implications for both the organization and the overall spatial needs of the courts, police stations, detention/correction centers, and their support offices.

For instance, such facilities can be smaller. Jurisdictions around the country are discovering that electronic storage of documents reduces space requirements for the storage of paper documents, and records rooms are shrinking in size. Likewise, workstations must change. The use of imaged documents creates new demands, as many positions must be designed to accommodate 21 in. monitors to provide views of full-page imaged documents.

The use of videoconferencing is increasing. Many facilities have videoconferencing capability, and the use of hands-free teleconferencing should be accommodated in many areas, ranging from conference rooms and public areas to virtually all staff workstations.

Employee work areas are evolving. Computers and peripherals continue to shrink in size, and equipment is increasingly portable. This is a real benefit to various professionals in the justice community, including prosecutors and attorneys, who carry portable computers. Probation officers, pretrial officers, and social workers today use laptop computers. Many carry handheld personal digital assistants (PDAs) and palmtop computers to various locations to take notes and prepare reports while out of the office.

These trends have an effect on the interior environment. The use of hands-free telephones requires privacy, which increases the importance of the textures and materials used for carpets, screens, and

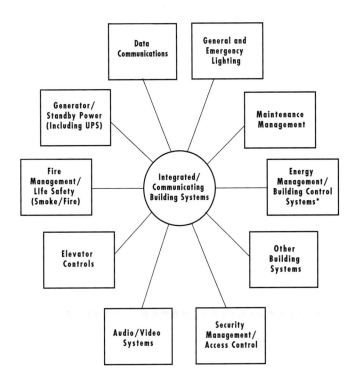

* including temperature monitoring systems, and control systems on packaged equipment

▲ Integrated/ Communicating Building Systems. Ten or more building systems should be integrated or communicating in current justice facilities.

and, increasingly, are combined with the actual day-to-day justice management systems to create a new, blended integrated system (i.e., where systems come to life "as needed," based on information input into justice tracking or case management systems).

INTEGRATED AND COMMUNICATING SYSTEMS

Many building systems and equipment today are designed with integral microprocessor controls. Much like the microprocessors used in today's automobiles that improve performance in all conditions, these microprocessors allow better control and monitoring of systems in buildings. All new justice facilities should be planned and designed with building management or control systems that enhance building operations and maintenance, provide more user control, and provide system responsiveness at the individual workstations.

Systems can be fully integrated, but this is not a requirement. In many jurisdictions, codes and construction practice tend to separate some systems (security and fire systems, for example) through the use of completely independent devices, infrastructure, and controls. This separation is intended to enhance reliability and provide redundancy for the other systems incorporated in justice facilities.

Whether integrated or independent, systems should communicate with each other to enhance building performance and provide more flexibility for today's operations and changing requirements in the future. In general, the following systems should communicate:

• Energy management and building control systems (EMS/BMS), including temperature monitoring systems

wall coverings. Normal privacy between open-office workstations can be provided with the use of highly sound-absorptive ceilings, moderately high screens, and sufficient ambient sound (either via general sounds in the office or by the use of an electronic sound-masking system). At times when confidentiality is essential, full privacy is very difficult to achieve and requires the use of tall screens, highly absorptive ceilings and floors, and the use of electronic sound masking.

Building technologies themselves continue to evolve. In addition to sophisticated security and fire/smoke detection systems, justice facilities today feature integrated and communicating building systems for improved building performance. These systems serve the building

(TMS) and control systems on packaged equipment, including chillers, boilers, computer room heating, ventilating, and air-conditioning (HVAC) systems, kitchen/laundry equipment, and laboratory equipment

- Generator or standby power systems, including provisions for uninterruptible power supply (UPS)

- Emergency lighting and general lighting control systems

- Data and telecommunication systems (including traditional PBX or voice/video over Internet protocol (IP) systems)

- Fire management (life-safety) systems, including smoke and fire detection and control devices

- Security management and access control systems

- Maintenance management systems

- Miscellaneous building systems

- Elevator control systems

SYSTEM CONTROL LOCATIONS

The control of various systems is provided in multiple locations in justice facilities today. In detention and correctional facilities, the system central control panels and displays are consolidated and co-located with the staff security control centers. This provides a single point of response for decision making as various situations and emergencies arise. Large police facilities and courthouses typically provide security control centers for detention area control, with separate day-to-day building control centers for mechanical and electrical systems. Smaller facilities may have a separate office or control room, or systems controls may be located in the mechanical room.

Increasingly, controls for systems are being provided within the office and work areas—put in the hands of the users of the space. Communicating or consolidated systems allow the use of individual PCs or touch-screen devices for individual control of room lighting, temperature, and data/audio/video systems.

Local controls are provided in various locations of justice facilities to control the lighting, temperature, sound volume, and audio-video equipment from a single keyboard or touch screen. In courtrooms, for example, these systems allow users to control multiple systems with one touch. Frequently, control of courtroom lighting and temperature is provided at the judge's bench and/or the Court Clerk's position, with motorized shades on windows and integrated control of presentation technology.

This puts room controls into the hands of the people working in the room. It also allows the room to support different

▲ *Temperature control panel, new courthouse project. Local control panel for the automatic temperature control system (DDC). Each panel can be addressed by a laptop unit and from a central control panel located in the engineer's office. Syska Hennessy Group: Mechanical, Electrical & Plumbing Engineers. Photo: z. jedrus.*

functions at different times of the day. With these systems, it becomes easier to use special rooms (e.g., training rooms, conference areas, assembly rooms, court-rooms, briefing rooms) for a variety of activities that rapidly change and adapt day to day or hour to hour, ranging from trial proceedings to general use by clerk and support staff when the judge is not on the bench, and even for use as a train-ing room (complete with distance-learn-ing capabilities) during after-hours or scheduled periods.

FOCUS ON THE INFRASTRUCTURE

To provide these capabilities, justice facility design is focused on the underly-ing infrastructure—the areas located out of sight (behind the walls, above the ceil-ings, under the floors). It is in these

areas that the integrated system of cabling, pathways, and spaces that sup-port the building's data/telecommunica-tion and specialty systems wiring must be provided.

A justice facility should be designed with simple and straightforward vertical and horizontal alignments and connec-tion pathways and spaces. This applies not only to the movement of people (ele-vators, escalators, corridors, stairs, lob-bies, etc.), but also to the engineering systems (mechanical ducts and runs and the electrical and electronic systems). Designing good vertical and horizontal pathways and spaces is critical in plan-ning a courthouse and is the key to flexi-bility and adaptability in the future.

Systems and spaces must connect in clear and simple ways to allow a building to change and adapt over time. In modern

▼ *Vertical Zoning of Systems. This section of a typical office or court floor area illustrates a preferred, vertically zoned approach to hori-zontal distribution of HVAC, plumbing, electri-cal, data/telecommunica-tion, audio-video, and other building systems.*

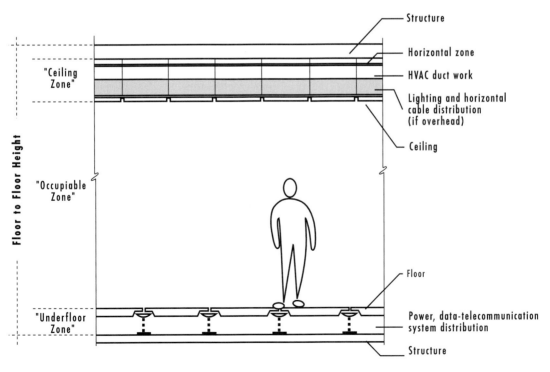

justice facilities, the full run of all wiring systems—the pathways and spaces for data/telecommunication, security, fire detection/alarm and suppression control, and so forth—should be designed for easy access and changes by authorized staff.

The systems should be designed to expand in place with minimal disruption. The initial design for the main fixed elements of the building infrastructure (including HVAC and plumbing systems and electrical and electronic systems) should accommodate the immediate and short-term needs of the occupants and at the same time anticipate and handle major changes that may occur over a longer period (10–40 or more years).

Whether a justice facility is designed as a single floor or as a multifloor building, typical floor plates should be conceived of in terms of "blocks" of space that are defined by reasonable walking, wiring, and service distances (often 100' × 100'), or approximately 10,000 sq ft (a "zone"). Electrical and data/telecommunication closets should be grouped together in pairs designed to serve approximately 10,000 sq ft. This is particularly important in electronically enhanced buildings, because computers and electrical systems perform better when they serve the same zone. Network performance drops when equipment is connected into outlets served by different transformers. This approach allows individual electrical and telecommunications closets to serve reasonably sized floor areas with similar horizontal distribution, vertical stacks, and cross-building ties without the problem of additional interference on data lines that is created when equipment is connected to different power sources or transformers.

Where building floors are larger than 10,000 sq ft in size, multiple pairs of closets should be provided on each floor. This provides redundancy in the vertical cores and allows for cross ties on each floor for secondary pathways. Although some buildings and designs may locate systems above or below floors, the key to continued flexibility and adaptability in the future is to provide easy access to these interstitial areas.

In justice facilities, security zoning often creates special restrictions to the pathways and spaces. See Chapter 11, "Security Systems," for additional information on specific requirements.

DATA/TELECOMMUNICATION SYSTEMS

Basic Planning Requirements
Building planning and design should comply with the following:

- American National Standards Institute (ANSI)/Electronics Industry Association (EIA)/Telecommunications Industry Association (TIA)—568: "Commercial Building Telecommunications Wiring Standard"

- ANSI/EIA/TIA—569: "Commercial Building Standard for Telecommunications Pathways and Spaces"

- ANSI/EIA/TIA—609, "Building Standards on Bonding and Grounding"

The general system of areas and spaces required for data and telecommunication systems include the entrance facility, floor distribution closets, computer rooms and/or file server rooms, rooftop access points, and the horizontal and vertical pathways. Direct vertical alignment and appropriate locations and distribution of floor electrical and telecommunication closets are critical for appropriate building zoning and service distribution.

The entire system of pathways and spaces should be considered in the planning and design phases of a project, and the design should accommodate the immediate and short-term needs while providing an infrastructure that can accommodate longer time frames (20 or more years).

Horizontal pathways

Horizontal pathways are provided for installation of telecommunications cable from the telecommunications closet to the individual outlets in individual or team work areas. A number of different systems can be used for horizontal pathways, including the following:

Underfloor duct

Underfloor duct systems are pathways for containing cables and wires for services such as telecommunications and electrical power. These systems typically consist of rectangular distribution and feeder ducts embedded in the concrete floor. Ducts may be used in single, double, or triple runs and may be intermixed in combinations of large and small ducts to provide increased or decreased capacity. Access points should be placed in duct runs to permit changes in direction and provide access for pulling wires.

Embedded underfloor ducts may be single- or two-level systems. Flush-duct systems include those systems in which the upper surface of the ducts and access unit covers are level with the top concrete surface. Multichannel raceway systems have internal barriers to provide a separate section for each type of service

within a single raceway. These are designed to be used in reinforced concrete construction systems where a minimum of 3 in. is required to bury a system.

Typically, distribution duct runs are located 5–6 ft apart at the midpoint of the building module. After the parallel distribution runs have been established, the cross runs and access units are determined by the density of the service requirements and the area to be supplied from each telecommunications closet. Refer to ANSI/EIA/TIA — 569, "Commercial Building Standard for Telecommunication Pathways and Spaces," for additional information.

Cellular floor

A cellular floor is an underfloor system in which structural members act as the formwork to support the concrete floor slabs, with the cells becoming the distribution raceways. The feeder ducts are set at right angles to the direction of the cells and are contained within the concrete pour. Steel and concrete cellular floor systems are generally available. Some steel systems are specifically designed with increased capacity requirements for telecommunication system distribution. See ANSI/EIA/TIA — 569, "Commercial Building Standard for Telecommunication Pathways and Spaces," for additional information on cellular floor distribution cells, feeder ducts, access points, layout requirements, inserts, service fittings, and installation requirements.

Access floor

Access flooring is composed of modular floor panels supported by pedestals with or without lateral bracing or stringers. It is used in general office areas, computer rooms, and equipment rooms and is available in combustible, noncombustible, and composite panels. It can be designed for seismic and other special conditions.

Access flooring is typically available as:

1. A stringered system with lateral bracing between pedestal supports

2. A freestanding system with panels supported solely by the pedestal supports with no mechanical fastening (usually restricted to access floor of 12 in. or less)

3. Cornerlock systems, in which panels are supported only by pedestals, but with the panels mechanically fastened to the pedestal heads at each corner to add stability

The use of access flooring requires depressing floor slab heights to equal the height of the finished access floors. Where slabs are not depressed, ramps to the access floor areas must be provided, compliant with building code and accessibility requirements.

See ANSI/EIA/TIA—569, "Commercial Building Standard for Telecommunication Pathways and Spaces," for additional information on fire requirements, installation guidelines, wire management, and outlet locations.

Access floor systems are widely used in Europe. They are frequently used in a variety of special areas in justice facilities (in control centers, communication/911 centers, and computer or file server rooms in virtually all justice projects). In addition, their use is not uncommon in courtrooms (although the system may be limited to the litigation area of the courtroom). A number of recent justice projects have been designed and constructed with access floor systems provided in

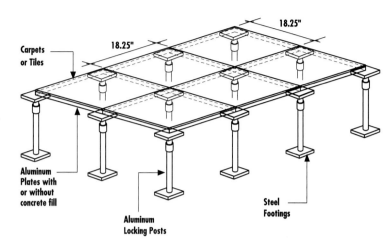

Clerk's offices, jury assembly areas, and other office-type occupancies.

Other systems, including cellular deck systems (Robertson or Walker duct or the like) have been included in courtrooms and other spaces in justice facilities nationwide; they provide a solid floor surface for various conditions while allowing flexibility in a variety of locations for power, audio-video systems, and telecommunications/data outlets throughout a room.

Specific solutions are required for a number of specialized rooms included in justice facilities (briefing/roll call, 911 or communication centers, large assembly/training/conference rooms, courtrooms and hearing rooms, jury assembly and multipurpose rooms, grand jury areas, etc.). For example, the floor system at the bench in a courtroom and at the built-in millwork may be a raised floor (concrete-filled panel) system. Options for wiring should be evaluated case-by-case, and decisions should be based on cost, installation control, and ability to accommodate changes in cabling and access points over the life of the building.

▲ *Basic Components of a Cornerlock Access Floor System*

Backbone wiring

Backbone wiring provides interconnections between telecommunication closets, equipment rooms, and entrance facilities in the wiring system structure. This wiring consists of the transmission media, intermediate and main cross-connects, and mechanical terminations. Backbone wiring may include transmission media between buildings. In most new justice facilities, the primary backbone of the building consists of optical fiber cable. In planning the routing and support structure for the backbone cabling, care must be taken to avoid areas where there may be sources of high levels of electromagnetic interference, such as motors and transformers.

Horizontal wiring

Horizontal wiring is the data/telecommunications wiring system that extends from the work area outlet(s) to the closets. This wiring includes the telecommunications outlet in the work area, the mechanical termination for the horizontal cables, and cross-connections located in the telecommunications closet.

The pathways and spaces that accommodate horizontal wiring should be designed to permit access. Designing these pathways and spaces also is important in controlling the effects caused by equipment that generates high levels of electromagnetic interference (EMI), such as motors and transformers used to support the building's mechanical systems and copiers and large printers used in typical office work areas.

Horizontal wiring between the telecommunications closets and specific outlets should be designed as a "star topology." This means that an individual outlet should be wired directly back to a telecommunication closet patch panel. The ANSI/EIA/TIA standards also specify that horizontal wiring should contain no more than one transition point between different forms of the same cable point. This means that, wherever possible, a direct and continuous (unbroken) telecommunication wire should be provided between every outlet and the patch panel. It is this simple organization of termination points that provides the flexibility to allow "plug-and-play" uses at different locations in the building.

Horizontal wiring in a building—from telecommunications closet to telecommunications outlet—should not extend more than 90 m (approximately 300 ft), regardless of the media type. This provision in the standard is designed to allow maximum performance of unshielded twisted pair cabling. Longer runs may be provided for backbone wiring, depending on the media selected.

Today, unshielded twisted pair cables (UTP) meeting specific ANSI/EIA/TIA performance standards (CAT5E, CAT6 or CAT7) are typically used in justice facilities. In some locations and for some purposes, optical fiber (glass or plastic) may be used. In all projects, the final determination of the cable plant for the horizontal wiring should be reviewed and finalized during the schematic and design development phases of the project. Whatever cable is used, all horizontal runs should be reviewed to verify that cables are not bent improperly or on too tight a radius.

Grounding considerations

Grounding systems are normally an integral part of the specific signal or telecommunications wiring system that they protect. In addition to helping protect personnel and equipment from hazardous voltages, the grounding system may reduce the effect of EMI to and from the telecommunications wiring system. Improper grounding can produce induced voltages, and these voltages can disrupt other telecommunications circuits.

The grounding instructions and requirements of electrical codes and equipment manufacturers should be followed. It is important to note that grounding requirements of specific data and telecommunication networks can exceed the grounding requirements of national or local regulations or practices. Typically, each telecommunications closet, equipment room, and entrance facility has an appropriate grounding access, and that grounding is available for cross-connects, patch panel racks, telephone and data equipment, and equipment required for maintenance and testing.

To meet these standards, the building should comply with the requirements of ANSI/EIA/TIA—609, "Standards on Bonding and Grounding."

Areas and Spaces

Programming staff

Space should be provided in justice facilities for programmers associated with criminal justice information systems (CJIS) and other systems and projects. In large jurisdictions, offices for system programmers may house 15 or more staff with the required support areas (printers, copiers, meeting/work areas, and reference/resource materials). Often, these groups can be located almost anywhere in the building, but should be provided a

quiet location with controlled access to natural light and views (with windows, but controlled light).

Network and computer support staff

In large facilities, space may be required for data and telecommunication staff. These staff typically prefer to be located near the data/telecommunication entrance facility/main distribution frame room. However, the office and cubicle workstations do not have to be located in the computer room (on an access floor). Support areas for these staff should include a workroom for new installations, such as to accommodate new personal computers or servers. In large facilities, workroom areas should be provided with benches, and nearby equipment storage, as well as staging and breakdown areas.

Data/telecommunication entrance facility (EF)

The entrance facility houses equipment supplied by local service providers (data, telecommunication, and cable television—cabling, switch and associated cross-connect equipment, etc.). The entrance facility should be located with the power entrance room to improve the overall performance of the telecommunications system. It should be planned to terminate wiring for the public switched network and to house building-level electronics and cross-connected inter- and intrabuilding cabling systems, using wiring distribution frames/backboards, protective blocks, and other equipment required by the telephone and cable utilities.

Main distribution frame (MDF) room

An area should be provided in each facility for an MDF housing rack for network equipment and servers. Depending on the electrical design, space may be provided for package uninterruptable power supply (UPS) systems in such areas. There are special requirements for air-conditioning in these areas, and workstations should be provided in the equipment rooms for network management. In large installations, associated rooms may be provided for vendor space (conference and office work area, reference storage, and equipment/supply storage).

Public branch exchange room (PBX)/operator office

Depending on the service requirements in any area, space will be needed for a public branch exchange (PBX) system or Voice-over Internet Protocol (VOIP) system. If a separate PBX room is required, nearby space should be provided for an equipment storage room, layout, and set up. Increasingly, justice facilities are being designed with VOIP solutions. In these facilities, the PBX areas should be incorporated into the MDF, and designed equipment areas should be used for housing VOIP servers and associated equipment (for CISCO Call Manager or 3COM systems, or the equivalent).

All three areas—the EF, the MDF, and the PBX room (if provided)—should be planned to support logical expansion in place and to accommodate future equipment and entrance conduits for future expansion. The equipment should be installed in such a way as to provide sufficient access to the backs of equipment panels where cabling is installed. Access to the file server and telecommunication devices must also be ensured for installation, upgrades, and maintenance of equipment.

These areas should be located on a floor level and in an area of the building that is secure and has restricted access, but is readily accessible to the local telephone company, and positioned in an area not subject to flooding. It should not be located near emergency generators, prisoner sally ports, loading docks or other service areas, or other areas that provide opportunity for unsupervised access or potential for damage.

These rooms should be positively pressured to prevent dust infiltration. An ambient air temperature of 72°F and 45 percent relative humidity should be maintained. A backup system to control room temperature and relative humidity is required. The backup system should be connected to the emergency power system.

These rooms should be safe, secure, and dust-free and protected by full-height fire walls with at least a 2-hour rating, with no windows and no false ceilings. Ceilings should be waterproofed. All areas should have an accessible acoustical ceiling and relatively high lighting levels to support maintenance and access.

All areas designed for data/telecommunication systems (including EF, MDF, PBX, floor telecommunication closets, and file server/computer rooms) should be equipped with proper fire extinguisher devices and smoke detectors. A raised floor system for easy access to wiring and cables may be provided. Smooth tiles with raised access flooring should be provided.

Telecommunications closets and rooms

Telecommunications closets are rooms set aside for the exclusive purpose of housing equipment associated with a data/telecommunication wiring system. Typically, telecommunication closets house the mechanical terminations for a portion of the horizontal wiring system and the backbone wiring system. Sufficient space, power, and grounding are required for the passive (cross-connect) and/or active devices (switches and routers) used to interconnect the two systems. Data/tele-communication closets may contain the intermediate or main cross-connects for different portions of the backbone wiring system. In this case, the telecom room should provide space, power, and grounding for the passive and/or active devices used to connect two or more portions of the backbone wiring system.

Closets should be positioned so that it is possible to gain access without disrupting normal office work, and sized to allow an engineer to work within them. Front and back access to the cabinets should be provided, with space for additional wall-mounted data patching frames. Smoke detectors should be provided with an override to avoid unnecessary alarms caused by technicians working in the room. Doors should not open inward and should not swing out-

ward into escape routes. Closets should have waterproof ceilings and no windows. HVAC ducting and pipe work should be kept out of the telecommunications risers.

Closets should be stacked vertically (using common walls) and be interconnected between floors. Floor sleeve penetrations should be sealed at the floor to prevent water leakage to the floor below and to meet the building code and fire code. All sleeves should be treaded and bushed to prevent cable sheath abrasion. Floor penetrations should be sealed. Access floor may be used to accommodate the cables entering from the riser, connecting to the frames, and accessing the secondary distribution system.

Vertical riser areas should be allocated within the room to allow space for vertical risers of the building backbone and vertical cable drops for cable television (CATV) lines or additional cable drops used on an as-needed basis for special or outside media feeds from the courtrooms.

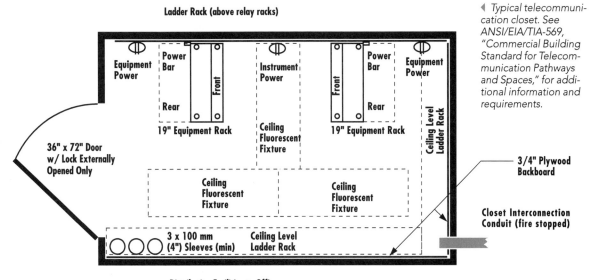

◀ Typical telecommunication closet. See ANSI/EIA/TIA-569, "Commercial Building Standard for Telecommunication Pathways and Spaces," for additional information and requirements.

Ladder Rack (above relay racks)

Equipment Power

Power Bar

Front

Rear

19" Equipment Rack

Instrument Power

Ceiling Fluorescent Fixture

Front

Power Bar

Rear

19" Equipment Rack

Equipment Power

Ceiling Level Ladder Rack

36" x 72" Door w/ Lock Externally Opened Only

Ceiling Fluorescent Fixture

Ceiling Fluorescent Fixture

3/4" Plywood Backboard

Closet Interconnection Conduit (fire stopped)

3 x 100 mm (4") Sleeves (min)

Ceiling Level Ladder Rack

Distribution Facilities to Offices

Although standards dictate that the rooms are designed strictly for use by data/telecommunication systems, in some locations security and fire-alarm equipment panels may be located in these rooms.

Departmental information technology group areas

Justice agencies frequently have designated information technology staff to support training, network access, and other needs. In general, when various agencies are located in a single justice facility, the building should be planned to accommodate distributed file servers (located in each department). Even with this capability, there are advantages to co-locating file server rooms/areas in the building (e.g., shared 24-hour air-conditioning and UPS systems, better access from the entrance facilities, uniform access to the vertical backbone of the building, etc). Other support areas for each group (individual office workstations, workbench and equipment setup areas, training rooms, and required storage areas, etc.) are generally located with their respective agencies.

Typical groups often include staff who handle system administration, setup of PCs, and all applications on the hard drives of the PCs. These groups require offices and/or workstations, with associated storage and setup benches. The setup area should support regular numbers of staff who work on equipment/PC setups. If a training room or shared setup room is available, setups can be scheduled around training sessions. In many justice agencies, setups take several hours per machine. This area should be accessible from a loading area, have space for breaking down and unloading boxes, and have adjacent inventory and parts storage. Benches should support multiple machines with the required electrical and data/telecommunication outlets.

Departmental computer/file server equipment rooms

File server areas should be provided in most justice agencies for central computers and file servers. If several servers are used (WEB server, e-mail server, other application servers), a server management workstation will be needed in the area. Additional space should be provided for the storage of parts, manuals, software, license information, and the like. Servers in the future may be either rack-mounted or freestanding. UPS systems are required. Wiring, power supply, HVAC, and acoustical designs for the file server room should meet individual equipment and systems specifications. General lighting should be provided. Humidity and temperature should be controlled according to the equipment manufacturers' requirements.

AUDIO-VIDEO SYSTEMS

Basic Planning Requirements

Planning for audio-video systems in justice facilities can vary greatly, based on the nature of the agency, its location and relationship to other facilities, and its internal needs within the building. Security intercom and paging systems are discussed in Chapter 11, "Security Systems."

There has been a rapid blurring of the traditional audio-video systems provided in facilities, in general, with the development of Web-based and Internet protocol (IP)–based systems. Increasingly, facilities are being designed to support true plug-and-play systems, whereby any data/telecommunication outlet in the building can be used for video and audio conferencing. With the newest generation of building communication systems, the electronic switches automatically recognize the type of device connected to the jack and provide point-to-point or multipoint conference capability throughout a building without the need for specifically designed rooms and spaces.

It is useful to think about audio-video systems in justice facilities in terms of (1) broad, building-wide systems and (2) individual systems designed to support the functions and operations in specific rooms.

Building-Wide Audio-Video Systems

Key building-wide systems include paging systems, cable/standard television systems, and audio-video conferencing systems, including video systems for arraignments and visitation.

Paging systems

Building-wide paging systems may be provided in addition to the required fire-notification and paging/alarm system. In many situations, these paging systems have been replaced by phone systems, and virtually all staff are given the capability to page to all phone sets, or to select phone desk or handsets for independent paging and communication.

Cable/standard television systems

Cable and standard TV systems are important adjuncts in justice facilities. The distribution of locally available television stations, and a limited number of stations available on cable or from satellite system providers, is common in detention and correctional facilities as a means of reducing stress levels. Both edu-cational and recreational programming may be provided.

In addition, many national and state-wide justice agencies (federal agencies with offices in many locations, or state-wide law-enforcement, court, or correctional agencies) and a number of large justice departments (county sheriff's departments, large law-enforcement/court departments, correctional center training staff, and others) develop programming materials for staff training and education, for communication of a facility's policies and procedures, and for general distribution of various types of programs.

Specific requirements for studio or production support areas should be developed on a project-by-project basis. Typical space requirements can include sound rooms, studio spaces, program support workstations (graphics, video production workstations), equipment areas, storage and supply areas, set preparation and construction areas, reference areas, and the like.

Audio-video conferencing

Audio-video (A/V) conferencing systems are used to provide live two-way or multi-point audio and video transmission between a wide variety of rooms and spaces in justice facilities and other designated local or remote locations. The primary components of an audio-video conferencing system include television cameras; monitors; microphones; speakers; input devices such as SmartBoard or other systems with interactive capabilities; communications and broadcast network, including software and equipment; and fax machines. The communications network can consist of optical fiber, coaxial, or standard data/telecommunication copper cables connecting locations within a building or in nearby buildings, or can be accommodated by digital communication using digital systems and lines for transmission inside or outside a building.

Planning for videoconferencing systems in any justice facility should consider the needs of specific technologies and types of systems. Video systems may be permanently installed, or may incorporate portable or movable equipment to be used as needed. It is important for all new justice facilities to be designed to accommodate the use of videoconferencing at PCs.

General guidelines for installation of A/V equipment focus on the need for sufficient conduits and electrical power and the appropriate location of outlets to provide flexibility. Monitor locations are critical, and careful consideration must also be given to the number and size of monitors and/or screens to give videoconference participants a clear view of the monitors. However the equipment is installed, video signals should be delivered from conference or training rooms to routers, switches, panels, and/or racks to enable the signals to be delivered to other locations as needed either within or outside the building.

Cameras should be discreetly located to minimize distraction and must produce quality images. To reduce distractions, cameras may be provided without lights that indicate which camera is in use. Recommendations for the use of fixed versus pivoting cameras differ among vendors, and a decision between these options should be an important aspect of selecting systems and equipment. Platforms or recessed areas in walls may be required, along with the necessary conduits and electrical power. Controls will be required to manage the materials being exhibited,

and specific controls should be provided to control incoming and outgoing signals and images and other devices that may be used (such as VCRs, PCs, opaque projectors, and the like).

Specific uses of videoconferencing can include general videoconferencing (point-to-point or multipoint meetings) and/or distance education applications, which will include provisions for group and individual systems. Distance learning systems (used in staff training rooms, roll call and briefing rooms, inmate and staff classrooms, courtrooms and hearing rooms, and other large assembly areas) can include audio sound reinforcement and recording, video cameras and recording, the use of VCRs, and other educational display support (SmartBoards, PC-based presentations, document cameras and digital display, interactive software/hardware systems, and the like).

Increasingly, distance learning broadcasts and packages are being provided for small-group or individual use, and content material and formats are being adapted to provide a wide range of standard and interactive teaching systems and content for justice agencies and staff.

Video arraignment systems

Video arraignment or first (initial)-appearance systems have been used for several decades in various jurisdictions in the United States. Today's systems are reliable and offer alternatives to the movement of inmates from security facilities to courts for arraignments or initial appearances (and, conversely, movement of judicial staff to detention or correctional facilities).

Requirements and restrictions on the use of video arraignment systems vary from state to state. As a result, the systems themselves vary. In some jurisdictions, judges or judicial staff may hear matters from courtrooms and/or chambers, with in-custody defendants appearing individually in small booths located in detention facilities (either in central areas or in housing areas). In these situations, the judicial officer must give specific and personal briefings and instructions for each hearing.

In other situations, defendants may be brought to a central location and sit as a group to listen to overall instructions and an orientation given by the judicial officer. Then, each defendant is provided a personal appearance before the judge. This may involve moving the in-custody person to a separate room for the personal appearance, or it may involve the use of a camera with automatic or manual zoom features to focus on the individual and promote a discreet discussion between the judge and each defendant.

Regardless of the type of system, in all cases provisions must be made to allow defense counsel to be present—either at the detention or correctional facility with the defendant or by video from the courtroom. The system must also be designed to protect constitutional guarantees and rights through the use of devices that allow defense counsel to immediately stop the video broadcast and recording and give direct, private, and confidential advice to the defendant without being overheard by the prosecution or the court. These remote interactions can be complicated by the need for original signature documents and the need to have materials signed in court. Increasingly, however, through the use of electronic-signature systems, fax equipment, and the like, remote appearances are being used in court systems nationwide.

Video visitation

Video visitation systems have recently been employed in a number of justice facilities to limit public visitors' access into the security perimeter of detention and correctional facilities. These systems are designed to provide public video and audio contact between authorized visitors and inmates. This, in turn, reduces movement of the general public to the main lobby/visitation area of a facility, and reduces movement of in-custody defendants from secure housing areas to centralized visitation areas. Once in place, video visitation systems can be designed to readily accommodate video visitation from other locations (e.g., from public defender or other attorney offices, or for interviews by authorized law enforcement or court agency staff such as probation or pretrial interview agencies). This capability is intended to supplement, but not replace, in-person meetings and, correspondingly, reduce the requirements for staffing and risk associated with movement of prisoners and the public.

Room-specific audio-video systems

Room-specific audio and video systems are designed to support specific functions and activities. Such systems are incorporated into the planning of a number of key rooms and spaces in justice facilities, including:

- Courtrooms
- Jury assembly spaces
- Grand jury rooms
- Roll call/briefing rooms
- Designated conference and special videoconference/training rooms, and community centers
- Other lecture halls, communication centers, jury deliberation suites, and major spaces

▶ Axonometric illustration of typical audio and video technologies provided in general jurisdiction state and federal courts. Courtesy of Polysonics Corporation.

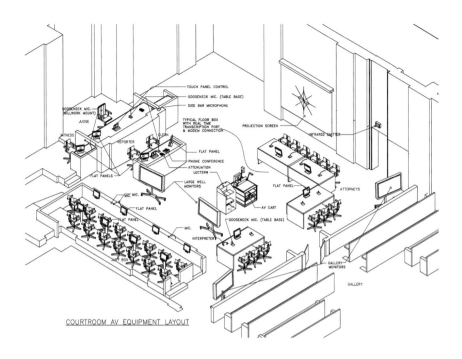

COURTROOM AV EQUIPMENT LAYOUT

TECHNOLOGY REQUIREMENTS, BY COURTROOM TYPE

TECHNOLOGY

	Audio SR / recording	Video conferencing	Evidence presentation	Displays	Security	Lighting	HVAC controls	Motor controls	Other
Federal Courts									
Appellate	√	√	√	√	√	√	√	√	√
District	√	√	√	√	√	√	√	√	√
Magistrate	√	√	√	√	√	√	√	√	√
County / City									
Criminal	√	√	√	√	√	√	√	√	√
Civil	√	√	√	√	√	√	√	√	√
Family / juvenile	√	√	√	√	√	√	√	√	√
Traffic	√	√	√	√	√	√	√	√	√
Other	√	√	√	√	√	√	√	√	√

Courtrooms

Recently, much attention has been focused on courtroom-specific A/V systems. The courtroom is the focal point of courthouse activity and provides an impartial setting for conducting most legal proceedings. Courtrooms may be designed to accommodate general types of litigation or to meet specific requirements for specialized types of trial activity (see Chapter 4 for additional discussion of related issues in courtroom design).

Technologically advanced courtrooms are somewhat different from courtrooms that are not designed to accommodate A/V technology. With additional equipment and specific sight line requirements for the presentation and display of evidence, computer-aided transcription, and/or other presentation systems, courtrooms must meet both the traditional requirements for

◀ District courtroom, Mark O. Hatfield U.S. Courthouse, Portland, Oregon. BOORA Architects, Inc., and Kohn Pedersen Fox & Associates. Courtroom technology and photography: DOAR Communications, Inc.

▼ Demonstration courtroom. An attorney in action at an evidence presentation system lectern at a demonstration courtroom. Courtroom technology and photography: DOAR Communications, Inc.

courtroom configuration and the requirements for clear lines of sight for all participants and must avoid excessive distances and wide sight angles, which affect the ability to hear, observe, maintain concentration, and avoid fatigue.

In addition to the potential differences in the sight lines, size, and configuration of the litigation area, the construction of the walls of the courtroom can vary between traditional courtrooms and those designed to accommodate technology. For example, additional depth may be provided in the walls surrounding a courtroom to accommodate the depth of equipment and screens.

Courtrooms designed for good sight lines for presentations of evidence will require adequate interior ceiling clearances. The height of the courtroom must be considered in the design for acoustics and in establishing mounting locations for micro-

phones, cameras, Assisted Listening System (ALS) emitters, projection screens, fixed or portable monitors, and other equipment. Increased courtroom heights affect distribution patterns and the glare characteristics of lighting fixtures, as well as impact sound

distribution systems, speakers' performances, and the required volume levels.

Wire management in courtrooms can be accommodated via underfloor wiring or by distribution through a combination of wall systems, floor systems, and wiring under built-up elements (judge's bench, witness stand, and the like).

Evidence presentation systems. Modern courtrooms are designed to accommodate a variety of support systems for trials. These include a number of pieces of equipment designed to support evidence presentation, including document cameras, PCs used for presentations (animations, projected presentations, etc.), exhibit retrieval systems, and the like.

Document cameras are vertically mounted cameras that allow trial participants and observers to view documents, photos, X rays, fingerprints, DNA

▲ *Evidence presentation lectern. This product photo of a DEPS (Digital Evidence Presentation System) lectern illustrates key technologies to be accommodated, including laptop computers, VCR and DVD equipment, opaque projectors, and more. Photo: DOAR Communications, Inc.*

▶ *Courtroom. Typical technologies include evidence presentation systems, monitors at counsel tables, clerk, court reporter, and bench locations, and video display systems for jury and public. Mark O. Hatfield U.S. Courthouse, Portland, Oregon. BOORA Architects, Inc. and Kohn Pedersen Fox & Associates.. Courtroom technology and photography: DOAR Communications, Inc.*

autorads, transparencies, and actual three-dimensional objects concurrently through monitors. The technology can allow the presenter to zoom in and highlight critical areas of detail, focusing attention on key or desired areas. Document cameras have their own light sources, and some create a distracting "hot-spot" or high-contrast illumination spot in the courtroom. Care should be taken to position the camera to reduce or eliminate distraction by this light source.

PCs are used to support presentation software and exhibit imaging and retrieval. This requires a connection between the document camera and PC or video-switching and the court's visual display system. The use of computer animations and simulations requires a visual display system capable of displaying them either by means of videotape or directly from a computer. Courtrooms equipped for these demonstrations will require connections between input devices (VCRs, video CD, or PC equipment) and video-switching and the court's visual display systems. Other requirements include proper positioning of monitors for functionality and use by participants, reduction of glare on monitors due to fixed light sources, and provisions for ample and appropriately located data/telecommunication and electrical cabling and outlets.

Real-time court reporting and transcription. Real-time court reporting is an enhancement to the stenotype machine reporting method that permits a trained and skilled stenotype reporter to produce an unedited transcript version of the court proceedings for almost instantaneous review by court participants and interested parties. This requires proficiency in computer-aided transcription

(CAT). In these systems, the court reporter's shorthand notes are entered into the stenotype machine and translated into their English text equivalent by the computer software stored in the reporter's PC. The English text is then transmitted via telecommunication lines and displayed on monitors or stored on PCs within the courtroom (such as at the judge's bench or at counsel tables), and can be transmitted outside the courtroom. This technology can be used to assist hearing-impaired participants in court proceedings.

Communication interfaces (software and hardware) are critical in selecting and implementing a real-time court reporting system in any specific courtroom. Compatibility between systems must be assured, and computer monitors for display must be carefully integrated into the courtroom and coordinated with the monitors needed for the display of other systems. As with any system, data/telecommunication, video outputs, and electrical outlets must be appropriately located, with sufficient and additional outlets as required to support the typical court reporter positions.

Computer-aided legal research (CALR) services. CALR services provide access to traditional legal primary sources, newspapers and journals, and people and public records information. CALR and litigation support systems may be made available to counsel in the courtroom. Litigation support systems can provide quick access to materials and are especially helpful in managing and searching large volumes of case materials.

The locations for computers must be identified early in the process to allow properly placed installation of conduit and recessed floor, furniture, or wall receptacles. To support outside research, receptacles should provide power and data/telecommunication connection to an outside telephone line (POTS) or internal local-area network (LAN).

Integration with HVAC, lighting, and other systems. Advanced technology use in the courtroom dramatically affects the requirements for lighting levels, fixture types and locations, and lighting control. In some courtrooms, control systems should provide integrated control for ceiling-mounted, recessed motorized projection screens. Windows, if provided in courtrooms, should be equipped with shading devices to maintain video image contrasts and may require two levels (light-diffusing and room-darkening) of shading devices. For skylights and for rooms equipped with motorized systems, controls should be integrated with A/V controls at the Clerk's position and the judge's bench.

Assisted listening/simultaneous interpretation systems. Assisted listening systems are typically provided in courtrooms and other large designed spaces in justice facilities to comply with provisions of the Americans with Disabilities Act Accessibility Guidelines (ADAAG). These systems typically feature wall-mounted infrared or radio-frequency emitters, and users of the system are issued headphones.

Jury assembly room

Jury assembly rooms typically require provisions for support of jury assembly and multipurpose/training needs. Consequently, these rooms may be provided with audio sound-reinforcing systems, videoconferencing capabilities, and a variety of display systems (TVs, projection screens, projectors).

Equipment should be provided in these rooms for ADA-compliant assisted-listening and interpretation systems. A/V racks (and rooms) often are provided to support this equipment (see the discussion in the later section "Areas and Spaces," below).

Grand jury room

Grand jury rooms may or may not be provided with audio, video and presentation/display systems. Equipment should be provided in these rooms for ADA-compliant assisted-listening and interpretation systems. A/V racks (and rooms) often are provided to support this equipment (see the discussion in the later section "Areas and Spaces," below).

Roll call/briefing room

Roll call and briefing rooms may or may not be provided with audio, video, and presentation/display systems. In large facilities, these rooms are provided with audio sound-reinforcing systems and a variety of display systems (TVs, projection screens, projectors). Equipment should be provided in these rooms for ADA-compliant assisted-listening and interpretation systems. A/V racks (and rooms) may be required to support this equipment (see the discussion in the later section "Areas and Spaces").

Designated conference or training rooms

Rooms for video training and conferencing should be designed as high-technology classrooms and provided with appropriate audio sound-reinforcing systems, videoconferencing capabilities, and a variety of display systems (TVs, projection screens, and projectors, including ceiling-mounted, ceiling-recessed, and/or other recessed systems). In addition, workstations should be designed with power and LAN or modem jacks, typically incorporated into furniture. Floor boxes should be provided under table locations in conference and meeting rooms, and provisions should be made for data/telecommunication and/or audio-video system drops on the walls of presentation rooms. These rooms should incorporate appropriate lighting and HVAC controls and should be designed for appropriate lecture hall acoustics. Room design should consider camera locations, appropriate colors, and contrast ratios.

Areas and Spaces

Audio-video equipment rooms

Planning for high-technology spaces in justice facilities (including courtrooms and other designed spaces) requires the provision of one or more A/V racks for sound and video equipment, normally located in a small equipment closet adjacent to the particular room. If two large A/V-intensive spaces are located in close proximity, they may share the use of one closet.

These closets should be sized to accommodate sound reinforcement amplifiers, mixers, and related equipment, a court file server, video equipment, patch panels, and so on. Typically, these spaces are 30–50 sq ft, and provided with dedicated outlets, and adequate ventilation to maintain ambient air temperatures is required.

Additional spaces may be required for storage of portable or movable equipment whose use will be shared between two or more assembly areas or courtrooms (for large monitors, SmartBoards, VCRs, and the like).

Court recording center

In court facilities where audio recording is handled from a central location, a room should be provided in the building for a court recording center or suite (central control center, staffed or otherwise). This area should include provisions for workstations and equipment.

Videoconference control center

In facilities planned for extensive video-conferencing capabilities, a video conference control center should be planned and designed to accommodate the staff managing the video conferencing traffic for the building, particularly the traffic associated with exterior connections. The amount of space needed will depend on the systems selected for videoconferencing and video arraignment and should be reviewed during the design phases of the A/V systems for the project.

The following are the typical technology requirements for each station in a single room (a courtroom), as listed in the *Courtroom Technology Manual* developed by the U.S. courts[1]:

A The General Services Administration (GSA) will normally furnish:

1. The judge's bench with:

- A work surface to accommodate a control panel, monitor, and microphones
- Pullout trays on both sides of the judge for laptops and/or keyboards with convenient receptacles
- Modem receptacle box
- LAN (DCN) receptacle box

[1]Administrative Office of the U.S. Courts, *Courtroom Technology Manual,* (Washington, D.C.: AOUSC, August 1999), 1.5–1.7.

- Realtime transcription receptacle box
- Power receptacles
- Conveniently arranged space for the CPU and paper storage
- Access panel in the floor
- Wire management system

2. The clerk's worktable with:

- A work surface that may accommodate a control panel, monitor, and microphone
- Pullout tray
- Box for two phone receptacles
- LAN (DCN) receptacle box
- Real-time transcription receptacle box
- Power receptacles
- Conveniently arranged space for the CPU and paper storage
- Access panel in the floor
- Wire management system
- Space for video printer

3. The reporter's worktable with:

- Space for recording equipment and laptop
- Real-time transcription receptacle box
- Power receptacles
- Access panel in the floor

4. The witness box with:

- Work surface to accommodate a monitor
- Ledge for a fixed gooseneck microphone
- Power receptacles
- Access panel in the floor/receptacle box(es)

5. The jury box with:

- Microphone receptacle boxes
- Railings that do not obstruct the view of portable monitors in the well
- Railings or posts to accommodate small monitors
- Power receptacles
- Access panels in the floor
- Wire management system

6. The lectern with:

- Ledge for a gooseneck microphone
- Sufficient provisions to satisfy the requirements of the Americans with Disabilities Act (ADA)
- Wire management system

7. Attorney tables with:

- Pedestals with boxes and flush doors on the table surface for easy wire management
- Integration of monitors and microphones
- Possible CPU space (should be considered)
- Phone lines for modems

B. The court will normally furnish:

1. An A/V cart with:

- Wheels for portability
- Tabletop for the document camera and papers
- Space for A/V equipment
- Wire management system

2. Monitor stands with:

- Wheels for portability
- The correct height for sight lines
- Internal space for equipment
- Wire management system

SECURITY SYSTEMS

Design for security involves the integrated planning of architecture (barriers, doors and door hardware, and control), devices (control and communication), and staffing. Previous chapters in this book outline the general principles associated with the security planning and design of various justice facilities. Security planning objectives in most justice facilities are integral with the design features of the site and buildings and cannot be separated from the operational and architectural design features.

This chapter focuses on the specific physical and electronic systems required to support the general planning concepts outlined in other chapters.

Design of security in justice facilities involves six major groups of issues:

- General physical and electronic systems (locks, alarms, constructed and natural barriers, and related security equipment) and their respective uses, including weapons screening, access control, alarm system monitoring/central control, site surveillance, night watch, and crisis response

- Specific space and equipment issues, including design provisions for all public, staff, and prisoner areas in the building, plaza areas, parking lots, service and delivery areas, data centers, law libraries and assembly locations, and critical building infrastructures (utilities, data/telecommunication areas, and the like)

- Occupant protection issues—protection for staff (including judges), inmates or prisoners, the public

▲ Guard tower, MSD #5, Lunenburg, Virginia. Virginia Department of Corrections. Photo by Don Eiler, courtesy of HSMM, Inc.

(including victims, witnesses, and jurors), and others

- Records/information/document issues, including protection of hard copy, microform, and computerized files and cash, evidence, and books

- Personnel issues for all general and security staff, including maintenance, housekeeping, and service personnel accessing the building—basic qualifications and background screenings, role assignments, staffing levels, and training requirements

SECURITY SYSTEMS

▶ *The five primary building security objectives for justice facilities regarding protection of staff, other users, the site/building, and the contents of the building.*

DETER
actual/potential
threats

DETECT
security breaks

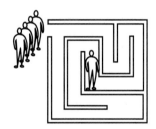

DELAY
to allow staff/
system to
respond

HALT
and control event

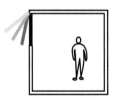

MINIMIZE
or eliminate
danger

- Policy and procedural issues, such as weapons control and screening, access control, security system management structure, security system coordination and planning, threat assessment responsibility, emergency response planning and coordination, and inter-agency agreements and response plans

Good security system design relies on a combination of staff, architectural barriers, and security systems to address the following primary goals regarding protection of the safety and security of the building's users, its functions and operations, and its contents:

- Deter actual or potential threats— allowing the barrier or system to keep a possible activity or event from occurring

- Detect any breaches of security— alerting security staff to an activity or event, providing appropriate coverage and sufficient information to identify the event

- Delay—slowing the movement of an activity or event to allow staff or the building systems to respond to the situation

- Halt and control an event after it has started

- Minimize or eliminate damage arising from such incidents

Regardless of the efficacy of a building's architecture and systems, "People are the main factor in any security program. Equipment, procedures, and architectural security measures are meaningless without capable and trained staff to use them."[1]

[1] James L. McMahon, *Court Security: A Manual of Guidelines and Procedures.* (Washington, D.C.: National Sheriff's Association, April, 1978), 56.

"All security programs must involve human ability in the form of judgment and human responses. Electronic equipment will not solve the majority of security problems."[2]

Designing for appropriate security involves a balancing of the system's costs and its approaches to providing security and safety. Although the use of properly trained and deployed personnel provides optimal security in most situations, using staff is one of the most costly means of providing protection.

Security planning for justice facilities must provide uniform, effective, redundant, and practical systems. The design and use of security systems must be integrated with security-related operations, initial and continued training, and maintenance of the systems. Planning for redundancy is an important aspect of security system design.

The most generally followed method of achieving high reliability at an acceptable cost is to design redundant performance at critical system locations. In general, multiple detectors, particularly when they operate on different principles, are much more likely to perform reliably than any one of them alone.

Properly designed security control and communication systems should be:

- Designed for 24/7/365 continuous operations and an average lifetime of 10–15 years
- Designed to serve specific functions without ambiguity or confusion

2. Alan Abramson. "Electronic Security Systems," Chapter 11 in *Handbook of Building Security Planning and Design,* (New York: McGraw-Hill, 1979), 11-1.

- Permanently installed with proper alignment, sufficient ventilation and cooling, and proper access for maintenance
- Served by power connected to the emergency power and uninterruped power (UPS) systems
- Provided with proper documentation of system design, installation, operation, and maintenance
- Locally supported and serviced

STANDARDS

Most standards applicable to security systems in justice facilities describe the importance of using systems to supplement, rather than replace, staffing. Two major private organizations sponsor and update industry standards related to security and safety equipment. The Underwriters Laboratories (UL) test a wide variety of products for conformance with safety standards. One of the best sources of information on security systems and security electronics is the *Standard Guide for Selection of Operational Security Systems,* ASTM 1465, 1998. (American Society for Testing and Materials, West Conshohocken, Pennsylvania.)

PLANNING CONCEPTS

Security design for many justice facilities focuses on denying access to certain locations through a system of natural or artificial physical barriers and access points, typically involving barriers, walls, gates, doors, locks, fences, and alarms.

The basic principle of denial of access is directly applied in the design of many justice facilities, including detention and correctional facilities, police stations, and others. But they do not exist in a vacuum.

SECURITY DESIGN GUIDELINES*

Component/Function	A	B	C	D	E	F	Comments
Facility administration	√			√			
Health services satellite	√	√	√	√		√	Also other satellite operations (maintenance)
Religious programs	√			√			Academic programs similar
Satellite library	√			√		√	
General visiting							
Contact visiting	√		√	√	√	√	Minimum security
Noncontact visiting	√			√		√	
Search area	√			√		√	
Recreation	√			√	√		
Vocational instruction	√	√	√	√		√	
Food services satellite	√	√	√	√	√		
Canteen	√		√	√		√	
Central library	√			√		√	
Central kitchen/laundry	√	√	√	√		√	
Central health care		√	√	√		√	
Receiving and release				√	√	√	
General warehouse						√	
Central/complex control						√	
Central operations				√		√	
Central maintenance	√	√	√	√		√	
Visitor/staff processing						√	
Central administration					√	√	
Visitor center/gatehouse						√	

Zone A: Inside security perimeter, general areas. Areas included: housing units, cells, and most program areas, including food service.

Zone B: Includes areas with specific security threats and risks, including building maintenance, vocational training, industries, and other areas with access to the outside security perimeter (threat of contraband movement). Entrances and exits to these areas are controlled, and inmates must be searched before and after access into the area. Includes central health, mental health, and receiving and release areas.

Zone C: Located inside the perimeter; includes central and distributed control centers and central operations.

Zone D: Inside security perimeter, most restricted zone. Off-limits to inmates and visitors, under constant visual and electronic surveillance from fixed and roving staff.

Zone E: Outside security perimeter, contains administrative functions, staff services, separate staff and visitor parking, and entrance building.

Zone F: Outside security perimeter. Spaces of this type would include maintenance facility central plant areas and may include some (typically minimum-security) housing, program, or services areas. In some cases, spaces may be provided that are out of sight and sound of supervision staff.

*Similar to state design guidelines in several states. See the applicable ACA, state and local codes and provisions for project-specific design criteria and guidelines.

IMPORTANT: Note that requirements and approaches differ dramatically from state to state and location to location and vary considerably based on the operational and security objectives for a project.

It is clear that detention and correctional facility design is not simply an issue of designing perimeters.

In detention and security facilities, the location of a function within a security zone, the staffing associated with the function, and the type of architectural construction and security features provided within the area are dependent on the following:

- The degree of security needed (considering issues of inmate separation and segregation, escape, contraband movement and detection, and other concerns)

- The location of the facility and physical separation from or connections between other facilities

- The extent to which there is staff observation and supervision

- The amount of access and freedom of movement accorded inmates in a particular area

- The potential that materials, equipment, or the activities themselves in an area can be used as weapons or to make weapons

Designing zones involves designing access and egress points between zones or sectors. In turn, this involves thinking about the degree of restriction or limits placed on access. Access points can be limited (locked and controlled—either locally or from centralized locations) or open, where doors are not locked from the inside, and allow free access—potentially to areas outside a security perimeter. Access points can be restricted, however, and can have delayed access or allow access to only very specific areas (such as a secure and enclosed area or a general movement area).

The table at left—presented for purposes of illustration only—itemizes a number of typical functions and components of correctional facilities and describes potential/typical security zones and access/egress limitations between zones. It is important to note that the advice and strategies presented in the table may or may not apply to your project or situation, and an appropriate strategy should be developed for the security plan for each project.

In all cases, a full and careful review of operations and staffing, architectural systems and barriers, and security equipment provisions should be undertaken before making final decisions related to security requirements.

Within any zone, access between spaces must be carefully reviewed to determine relationships between spaces using the same criteria and requirements listed at left. Typically, design features and construction (materials and systems) at all lines between zones should be developed to meet the more restrictive design requirements.

See Chapters 3 and 5 for additional information related to the typical components/functions listed in Security Design Guidelines.

Zones in Courthouses

Similar concepts of zoning, access, and egress apply to court facilities. In courts, the use of barriers that limit access and free movement is complicated by the fact that courts are public facilities, and our system of laws promotes the sense of free accessibility to the law. Therefore, in the court design environment, "hardening" security tactics are used in more subtle and unobtrusive ways.

In courthouses, the primary security perimeter generally comprises the building envelope/exterior. The security perimeter (and any required doors, windows, or other penetrations) should be designed to restrict and delay unauthorized access and provide notification to security personnel if entry is attempted.

Because the building exterior serves as an initial perimeter, special attention is given to all areas that serve as openings or apertures between the exterior and the walls or roof. Exterior doors and frames are heavy-gauge steel and equipped with security hardware. All exterior windows accessible from the ground or nonsecured areas should be equipped with opaque blinds or drapes. Windows that are located on the lower levels of the building and are visible from outside the building should be protected by security alarms and may be security glazed.

Manholes, sewers, fire escapes, skylights, grates, heating and air-conditioning vents and ducts adjacent to roofs, and any other penetrations into the building envelope should be designed as secure openings (sealed and grouted continuously) and fastened with security fasteners to resist tampering.

Walls and nearby trees that can potentially be places for unauthorized concealment should be reviewed and designed to minimize such opportunities. The "scalability" of a wall, allowing a person to climb up the surface of a building, must be reviewed. The location of a generator or dumpster next to a building, a trellis or horizontal reveals on a building surface, and similar placements may make a surface scalable.

Zones in Law Enforcement Facilities

Similar concepts of zoning, access, and egress apply to law enforcement facilities. In police facilities (as in courthouses), the primary security perimeter generally consists of the building envelope/exterior. The security perimeter (and any required doors, windows, or other penetrations) should be designed to restrict and delay unauthorized access and provide notification to security personnel if entry is attempted. In general, public access is strictly limited and controlled. Although staff are permitted into most areas, access is limited into special areas (prisoner holding, evidence rooms, vaults, armories, and the like).

ARCHITECTURAL AND CONSTRUCTION REQUIREMENTS

The following paragraphs briefly summarize the key architectural and construction requirements for security in detention and correctional facilities. Note that this discussion is intended only as an introduction to these systems and requirements. Appropriate and professional planning, design, construction, commissioning, training, and maintenance requirements for these systems are crucial to successful justice projects, and specific systems and details should be carefully reviewed and approved on a case-by-case basis by project representatives and code agency officials responsible for security and life safety.

Wall Construction

Requirements for security perimeters vary. Consequently, appropriate architectural and engineering systems used in constructing walls that form a portion of a security perimeter will vary. Certain types of materials have been proven effective in withstanding both environmental decay (salts and corrosive elements) and in meeting security perimeter objectives.

In broad terms, concrete construction—whether poured-in-place, precast, or based on concrete masonry units (CMUs)—can be detailed and designed to meet a variety of security construction requirements. Typically, 4,000–4,500 psi minimum compressive strength is used in poured-in-place or precast systems, with appropriate reinforcing in walls 4 in. or greater in thickness. Concrete masonry unit walls can be used for minimum, medium, or maximum security areas, but specific requirements for horizontal and vertical reinforcing and grout must be met. Reinforcing bars and joint reinforcement in all walls must be continuous and securely anchored to floor slabs and ceiling decks.

Steel bar security walls are still used in some correctional and detention facilities; these are created from tool-resistant steel welded to embedded steel plates in walls. Welded wire mesh of various gauges is used in some applications (such as holding areas in federal court facilities), welded to steel tubes that are themselves welded to embedded plates in supporting walls or other wall construction.

In many facilities, inmate-accessible areas are designed to be occupied only for short periods of time or when supervisory staff are present. Wall construction in these areas can consist of nonsecure standard wall construction (drywall on steel studs, often provided with additional layers of drywall for additional resistance to impacts) or can incorporate the use of security gypsum board with heavy expanded wire mesh between layers.

Security Ceilings

Traditionally, security ceilings were constructed of concrete or structural plaster to resist similar levels of attack as corresponding walls and floor systems. More recently, security ceiling designs have focused on restricting access of inmates into areas above the ceiling (beneath the structure) for hiding weapons or contraband or for effecting an escape through an adjoining wall system. Several types of ceiling systems can be used, and final decisions regarding an appropriate system should be based on the following factors:

- The security classification of inmates in the area
- Clear height below the ceiling
- Potential inmate access to the system
- The anticipated level of staff supervision and observation of the space

In addition, ceiling systems should be selected that can clearly indicate when and where unauthorized attempts have been made to gain access to ceiling areas, and policy/procedure should dictate that all ceilings in inmate areas are checked regularly.

Metal panel or plank security ceilings are constructed of 12 in. wide planks that can be mechanically interlocked to prevent removal or concealment of contraband and weapons. Perforated planks with wrapped backing material can be provided to improve acoustics while limiting potential damage to the insulation by inmates. Access panels with security fasteners and hinges should be provided. Lightweight panel systems can be used in lower-security areas or areas with continuous staff observation to slow inmate attempts at gaining access to ceiling spaces.

High-impact-resistant security gypsum board ceiling systems can be provided in lower-security areas, in areas where accessibility to ceiling spaces is very limited, or where supervision is continuous. In these systems, acoustical tiles may be glued directly to the drywall systems. Security-type locked access panels with security hinges, fasteners, and locks should be provided.

Security Hollow Metal Doors and Frames

Security hollow metal doors and door frames are required in many inmate-accessible locations in medium- and maximum-security facilities. In all cases, security hollow metal door frames must be anchored securely to adjoining walls with the use of integrated anchorage and special reinforcing methods. Security hollow metal doors and frames should be constructed of heavy-gauge steel with strong internal door reinforcement designed to resist attack and abuse. In some facilities, wooden doors are used within security perimeters but are mounted to security hollow metal door frames. The hollow door frames should be grouted full to reduce vibration and tie the anchor in the frame to the wall system more securely.

Door Operations

Traditional electromechanical swing door locks are still commonly used for swinging security hollow metal doors because they are cost-effective. However, recent advances in the use of pneumatic systems have led to development of a new generation of security door operators. Instead of electromechanical controls, pneumatic systems are used in sliding door operations, particularly in areas requiring continuous slider cell front designs.

Security Hardware

Security hardware and operators are selected on the basis of door function and required security level. Specific require-ments are dictated by code, including remote release requirements and fire ratings. The development of the door and hardware schedule for any justice facility is an important step in security system design. This process should include a review of each door and door opening, to assess the following:

- Required security level
- Requirements for the function of doors in regard to electrical operation and points of control (primary and secondary)
- Interlocking requirements
- Key type requirements

Appropriate security locks are critical to a facility's day-to-day operations and emergency planning. Manual locks are used in inmate areas where remote operation is not a requirement. Where remote operation is required, electromechanical or solenoid locks should be provided. For fire safety and emergency operations, all doors are required to operate (lock/unlock) manually, as a backup. Recently, pneumatic locks have been developed that rely on compressed air delivered through nylon tubes to activate release mechanisms.

ELECTRONIC SECURITY SYSTEMS

The microprocessor was the driving force behind the revolution in security systems that developed during the mid-1980s. For the first time, the computer was used to integrate all aspects of a security system, allowing all components to communicate and work together. Single positions were used to monitor and control a variety of security, fire, energy management and critical building systems.

Today, there are two common approaches to the design of integrated-control electronic systems in U.S. justice facilities: (1) hard-wired logic and (2) programmable logic controller systems. Hard-wired systems were historically characterized by large wall-mounted relay cabinets that contained electromechanical or solid-state relays, timers, diodes, resistors, and other discrete electrical components. Modern hard-wired systems are modular and easier to configure. This type of system must be complete, custom-wired in accordance with the desired panel function.

Hard-wired systems are fairly reliable but labor-intensive (and thus expensive) to install and costly to change and modify. Because many connections are made by hand, the initial reliability of the system is affected by the installation. Where control-interface functions are complex, hard-wired systems can be difficult for anyone but the original installer to understand and maintain. Consequently, modular hard-wired systems may be best supported by the original installer but can be a long-term maintenance problem inasmuch as manufacturers and installers can change. Similar in configuration to a fire alarm system, a logic controller system is usually a proprietary item (specific to a vendor or company) and may require many modifications to convert, to upgrade, and, sometimes, even to expand the system.

Programmable logic controllers (PLCs) are so named because all of their control logic functions are programmed through the use of handheld devices or through connection to computer terminals. Once programmed, the PLC controller maintains its program with a keep-alive memory device that does not rely on continuous 120V AC power. These devices and systems are reprogrammed only when there is a need to change a

time-delay function, add to the system, or change facility operations.

PLCs can be networked to "talk" to other PLCs in systems, better supporting the designs of integrated or distributed systems. Failures of single PLCs do not affect overall facilities, and the PLC programming process is more readily documented and serviceable by most electronics technicians. System configurations and documentation can be obtained, even when documentation is lost, from the program in memory. PLC-based systems are generally less proprietary in nature. Devices communicate on a series of inputs and outputs (similar to a logic system) signals with components that are commercially available.

Components of Security Systems

All security systems comprise three functional components:

1. The security center
2. The data processing and distribution system
3. Remote sensors and control points

The security center serves as the location for the devices necessary for interaction between staff and systems. Well-designed, this is the only element of the system of which staff are aware. The other components—the central control electronics and the field devices—are permanently located and positioned in closets, above ceilings, in or behind walls, and under floors.

Control panels are the most visible parts of the systems. Control panels and systems should integrate various control and communication systems by function. For example, the gate controls, gate status indicators, intercom select switches, and closed-circuit video equipment (CCVE) select switches for a vehicle sally port should be grouped together. In many facilities, "integrated system" designs are provided, which require only a single interface for each function or task performed by security personnel.

Control panel functions may be displayed on video display terminal screens. If a decision is made to use traditional control panels, they should be fabricated from black anodized aluminum with etched graphics and nomenclature. If provided, these panels will be composed of a combination of control panel components that can include the following: switches, indicators, loudspeakers, television monitor(s), audio annunciators, intercom and microphones, and communication handset.

The data processing and distribution systems (the control electronics) differ according to the type of system used (hard-wired or PLC-based system). Each system has different criteria for the system control electronics. The functional link between the security center and the remote equipment includes many subsystem hardware and software links.

System Structure

Specific requirements at each facility dictate the choice of system. Because of the responsibilities and operational patterns of justice agencies, many, or most, justice facilities are designed with central-station alarm systems (whereby initial signals are relayed to a staffed control center, either on-site or off-site, but controlled by the law enforcement officer responsible for security at the facility).

Access Control Systems

Access control systems are used to automatically limit access at entries to authorized persons and to notify security alarm monitoring systems of valid entries to prevent invalid entrance alarms. A card access control system, with or without keypad, is often provided for staff (and judiciary) use in justice facilities. Typically, access control systems provide a historical record of entries. When access is granted, the door is released by actuation of an electric strike or lock.

All doors from a public circulation system to either a private circulation system or a prisoner circulation system, in any justice facility, should be provided with remote-control electric locks, magnetic locks, or electric strikes. All of these doors, except those permitting access to prisoner holding areas, should have a card-key (or other) access system for entrance by authorized personnel. Doors should be capable of being opened and locked manually in the event of a failure of the power/control system. "Door open too long" (DOTL) alarms should be provided for all monitored security doors to alert the control center that a controlled door has been propped or kept open too long.

Elevators for the use of staff, prisoners, service, and other purposes (judicial elevators in courts, etc.) in most justice facilities should have strict controls and restricted access. Elevator access to restricted areas should be controlled. Secure elevators should be provided with in-cab CCVE cameras and a duress button.

Biometric Identification

The use of a retinal-scan/fingerprint, biometric identification system may be considered for high-security areas. These systems are expensive and require personal information for identification.

Contraband Detection Equipment

In courthouses and other justice facilities, metal detectors and X-ray scanners may be used for entry screening. Provisions should be made for security screening equipment at controlled public entrances. Equipment should include magnetometer(s), an X-ray scanner, at least one handheld metal detector wand, lockers to secure any private property removed from individuals entering the facility (not subject to confiscation), a duress alarm, a telephone, and a portable radio to summon additional help.

This equipment is the most visible security system perceived by the citizenry, and it occupies a prominent place in a designed space that is intended to create a positive first impression. There are different points of view about how obtrusive or unobtrusive the equipment should be. Some design approaches attempt to integrate the equipment in surrounding walls or millwork; others allow it to be free-standing in the entry space.

Life-Safety Code Compliance

Electromechanical locking devices should secure fire stairwell doors outside of the inmate security perimeter consistent with life-safety exiting requirements. Electric locking and unlocking of stairwell doors should be capable of being overridden remotely from the facility's security console (for reasons of security and meeting the fire code).

With the exception of holding cell areas, fire doors should unlock in the event of activation of the main fire alarm panel, the engagement of a local pull station, or loss of power. Subject to the approval of code authorities, unlocking of critical security doors should be time-delayed for several seconds, if required. The use of "resettable" timers for the release of inmates' doors can be very effective in let-

ting staff know when egress pathway doors are open, and then when cell doors will be released. The timers can be reset until the alarm is actually verified.

Perimeter Security Systems

Perimeter security systems in most justice facilities should be designed to alert staff of attempted or actual penetration of any interior or exterior security perimeter. These alarms can activate lighting in the area, CCVE systems, and audible and visual alarm location signals at the control center and (via radio) for mobile patrols.

Although simple systems may be used in some areas of justice facilities, facility perimeters typically must be designed for a high level of security and provided with redundant reliable system designs. In most systems, activation of two detectors in common zones will initiate alarms to the monitoring location.

▼ Prisoner perimeter security fencing, Rivers Correctional Institution, Winton, North Carolina. HSMM, Inc., engineers and production architects; WCC, owner/operator for the Federal Bureau of Prisons and design architect; Hensel Phelps Construction Company, design builder. Photo courtesy of HSMM, Inc.

▲ *MSD #5, Lunenburg, Virginia. Virginia Department of Corrections. Photo by Don Eiler, courtesy of HSMM, Inc.*

access to secure but infrequently accessed areas (e.g., mechanical and electrical rooms, electronic equipment areas, emergency exit doors) and other building entries. The system components are secured and the equipment is located in the control center. These systems should be connected to the door control electronics and receive alarm information from these systems (via network or direct connection).

Control Panels

Control panels serve as an interface between the staff and the electronics by functionally organizing the various switches and indicators under the staff's control. Control rooms may vary in the types of controls used, but should be specifically designed to meet the operations of the various entities that utilize the equipment. Security consoles and alarm reporting systems typically include the following:

- Door control and supervised status annunciation
- Remote elevator control for secure elevator(s)
- CCVE monitoring and video recording of time-delayed egress doors and other critical areas
- Unique and priority annunciation of duress alarms, as well as assistance alarms (from courtrooms, assembly spaces, clerks' offices, probation offices, and various other spaces in justice facilities)
- Intrusion detection annunciation, software-controlled arming and disarming, high security key-operated shunt stations
- Secondary fire protection and life-safety systems annunciation

Security systems are usually installed on or to the side of perimeter fences or exterior building walls. In detention and correctional facilities, these include infrared, photoelectric beam, microwave beam, "e" field, geophone, video motion detection, and fence shaker systems. The systems are zoned to cover discrete three-dimensional areas defined by the range limitation of the equipment and the physical design (geometry, walls, etc.) of the area.

The primary monitoring point for perimeter security systems should be the designated control center, where staff are present and can use CCVE monitors for direct visual observation and to obtain critical information for decision making and response.

Secondary Security Alarms

Secondary security alarm systems are provided in many justice facilities to control

- Dedicated security intercommunications and radio systems (radio systems and antennae)
- Courtroom/jury/witness communications and security
- Management and annunciation of the facility's electronic access control system
- Judges' chambers/suites access control systems
- Monitoring status of standby emergency electrical power and redundancy in system processors

Closed-Circuit Video Equipment

Closed-circuit video equipment (CCVE) is often provided in justice facilities for surveillance of parking areas, the perimeter of the building, prisoner movement and holding areas, and areas where extra security is deemed necessary or where money is collected or handled. Two types of monitoring may be used at staff stations: (1) continuous monitoring of remote areas and (2) selective monitoring of remote areas.

CCVE systems include cameras with detention-grade housings (typically used in inmate-accessible areas) or low-profile housings (in courts, work areas, and public areas), plus mounts, lenses, and other related equipment. The cameras currently used are solid-state color units. Color CCVE accurately identifies people and minimizes fatigue for console operators.

Camera location

There are no firm rules governing camera locations in justice facilities. The law enforcement person responsible for security in a justice facility should direct the design of CCVE systems. In broad terms, CCVE systems should provide surveillance of areas not directly observed by

◀ Control room, Guilford County Juvenile Detention Center, North Carolina. Photo by Don Eiler, courtesy of HSMM, Inc.

staff. In inmate areas, cameras are typically provided at movement control areas (elevators, stairs, doors, sally port entries, etc.) for positive identification, and in areas where alarms may be activated for use of the CCVE cameras for event-driven responses.

In many cases, CCVE surveillance is used to monitor any controlled-access door that penetrates the holding cell area or prisoner security corridor (the "hard line") that cannot be directly observed. In many facilities, all exterior access doors should be monitored and should be activated by field sensors indicating entry. Video recorders (VCRs) can be used to record any events, following a time-delayed unlocking of a door. In addition, CCVE should monitor most, and possibly all, intercom stations located at controlled-access doors.

Digital video motion detection (intrusion detection) can be provided for critical areas with stable lighting levels. Video motion detection can be utilized, or the use of motion detection devices can supplement the signaling of a camera.

Intercom Systems

A hard-wired intercommunications system should be provided, with a master control base station at each control center. A hands-free system is frequently provided that enables any station to call any other station. When located outside offices and similar administrative areas, intercom stations should be flush-mounted wall units with call buttons.

In court facilities, each judge's suite should have an intercom station at any entry; master stations should be provided for the judge, secretary, and law clerk. Intercom stations near judges' chambers should be capable of being muted or silenced. In addition, an intercom station should be provided at each fire stairwell landing.

A public address/paging system should be integrated into the intercom system, to be used for emergency security announcements. The use of the fire speaker system to operate as a public address/paging system (building-wide) should be investigated in order to avoid the cost of having multiple systems.

Personal (Duress) Alarm Systems

Personal/duress alarm systems can be provided to supplement other systems in court facilities. Where provided, these systems consist of static duress buttons at certain key locations, such as at the judges' benches, judges' chambers, money transaction locations, reception desks in clerks' offices, probation offices, the court library, and other spaces. This system can be tied in with the detention area intercom and monitoring systems.

The duress alarm system should also utilize a two-button approach to allow for an assist call in addition to a duress call.[3] In some court facilities, the use of a portable duress alarm system may be considered. These systems use multiple signals—one for communication and one that pinpoints the location of the alarm.

Intrusion Detection System

Intrusion alarms should be installed to protect both real and personal property from burglaries and vandalism occurring after regular business hours. Intrusion

---

[3]System recommendation pioneered by Justice Fred A. Geiger, Second Appellate Court, State of Illinois.

detection system (IDS) sensors should be provided for locations that are not continuously occupied and that require security supervision, such as perimeter doors, hard line doors, evidence storage areas, restricted file rooms, chambers, law library (if not in a secure area), and other areas.

Alarms are typically located in office areas on the first level of a building and those easily accessed from adjoining roof structures. Intrusion alarms will report to the building control center, to a remote monitoring agency, or to another central control location for 24-hours-a-day, 365-days-a-year monitoring. Accessible windows, such as those on the ground floor, should be sealed.

Additional areas that may require intrusion sensors include fire stairwells, electrical rooms, telephone frame rooms, mechanical rooms, other critical building service rooms and their switches and valves, and possibly other areas. Whenever practical, intrusion sensors should be utilized to activate corresponding CCVE cameras.

Radio/Communication Systems

Internal telephone communications between spaces within a courthouse are discussed in the section "Data/Telecommunication Systems" in Chapter 10. Special conditions include the courtroom, where external/internal use should be accommodated, but the telephone should have a visual signal, not an audible signal, for incoming calls.

A building-wide public address system may be coordinated with emergency alarm systems and used to announce any evacuation plan, the closing of the building, or other emergency notices.

Interior Threats

The General Services Administration (GSA) security criteria require protection from interior threats including explosive devices located in a lobby, loading dock, mailroom, or internal parking areas. The primary hazard posed by these interior threats is to the occupants of the spaces immediately adjacent to any screening or prescreened areas. Other hazards include damage to key structural elements, initiating structural failure, or to the critical building components such as electrical or mechanical rooms. Although the charge weight or explosive force for these interior threats is significantly smaller than that associated with exterior threats, the confinement of the explosive by-products produces quasi-static gas pressures that may seriously damage the slabs and walls. These long-duration gas pressure loads are most damaging when confined in small spaces without the ability to vent harmlessly into the atmosphere.

Access to interior parking garages should be strictly limited to judges and designated government employees. All deliveries, whether courtroom parcels or vending machine supplies, must be received at the loading dock and cleared for entry into the building. The admission of uninspected materials and non-government-employee vehicles into the underground spaces for temporary drop-off violates the operational security requirements for a justice facility. Such a violation can undermine the entire physical security design of the facility. A sizable explosion in a parking facility can cause widespread damage and may precipitate a progressive collapse of the entire building.

Lobby/atria

The lobby entrance is one of the most vulnerable locations in a building. All nonemployees must enter through this area, and until the individuals are screened, everyone is considered to pose a threat. The real threat is a satchel bomb, defined by the GSA security criteria. A satchel bomb may easily be concealed in a large briefcase or duffel bag and surreptitiously placed anywhere in the structure prior to screening. The introduction of a satchel-sized charge into a prescreened lobby area may result in two distinct hazards. First, there is the large amount of glass in the lobby area that can be transformed into lethal projectiles. Second, the adjacent spaces, particularly above the lobby, may be heavily occupied and vulnerable to blast pressures.

All untreated glass in a lobby/atrium area can be expected to fail in the event of any moderately sized blast either within the facility or at the exterior secured perimeter. Therefore, the interior glass should also be designed to minimize the amount of secondary fragments created by such a blast event. The vulnerable interior glazing should be laminated annealed glass adhered to an improved framing system with structural silicone, following the same protective design approach developed for the exterior glazing.

The slabs or walls protecting the adjacent areas should be able to withstand the blast loads caused by a satchel-sized charge at the screening desk without breaching. If possible, the egress passageways should be situated to limit the direct blast pressures entering the occupied spaces.

Mailroom/loading dock

The mailroom and loading dock are additional locations where package bombs can be introduced into a facility by mail or delivery by a third party. To prevent package bombs from entering the facility, scanning equipment, including an X-ray machine and a magnetometer, should be located at the loading dock to scan all incoming parcels. It is important for all deliveries to be screened, whether presented by a government employee, a U.S. postal employee, or an outside party. In addition, the loading dock walls and slabs should be hardened to resist the effects of a package bomb. If the mailroom is colocated with the loading dock, it should be hardened to resist the same explosive charge. The walls of these areas must be constructed from heavily reinforced, fully grouted and detailed CMU block or cast-in-place reinforced concrete.

Critical building components

There are a number of critical building components within a justice facility that directly affect the operation of the building, as well as the functioning of the building under emergency conditions. The operation of these components is crucial to providing for evacuation and rescue after a terrorist bombing. The GSA security criteria require that critical building components not be located within 50 ft of the loading docks or receiving and shipping areas. Among these building components are utility rooms, utility mains, and service entrances, including electrical, telephone/data, fire detection/alarm systems, fire-suppression water mains, and cooling and heating mains. Where the required separation distance is not available, the walls and slabs around these critical building components must be hardened to isolate such areas from the presumed threat locations. While the GSA security criteria do not require hardening the main electrical room and the mechanical rooms when they are in close proximity to a prisoner sally port, prudent design would provide the same level of protection to these areas.

Interior parking

Interior parking constitutes an extreme vulnerability in any facility. To reduce the hazard presented by this threat, only vehicles driven by select government employees should be permitted to park in a garage located within the lower levels of a building. At no time should public parking be allowed in the facility. Because private vehicles are not protected at all times, it would be very easy for a terrorist to place a bomb in an authorized vehicle and thereby have a judge or government employee unknowingly transport the bomb into the building. Therefore, the interior parking section should be designed to withstand the effects of a surreptitiously placed explosive device. To accomplish this, the interior parking area must be isolated from the rest of the critical or occupied spaces with walls and slabs capable of withstanding the specified threat. Furthermore, the columns based in the underground parking areas must be designed to withstand an explosion. Concrete columns may be protected with a steel jacket or, to a lesser extent, with closely spaced spiral reinforcement, and steel columns may be protected with a concrete encasement.

Other/Special Security Systems

Vaults and safes

Provision of fire- and burglar-resistant vaults or safes in the facility may be necessary for the storage of dangerous or valuable items and evidence. In police facilities, evidence storage areas require special design features and systems.

In court facilities, a separate burglar-resistant safe may be required for the storage of funds collected at the fine-payment area and in the clerk's office. Motion detectors should be installed in any secure rooms that have breakable walls.

Emergency power generator

In the event of a power disruption, an emergency power generator should automatically operate key lights, heat/smoke alarm and duress alarms, the public address system, and other essential operating equipment in the facility. Status monitoring of the emergency generator should be provided ("problem" and "running" annunciation) in the building's central control. In addition to the facility's emergency power system, uninterruptible power supply (UPS) and standby batteries should be provided for the security

---

DETENTION AREA CONTROL SYSTEMS/PANELS/COMPONENTS

An electronics control system for a detention facility should provide for the following at a minimum:

- Panel power/lamp test
- Silence switches
- Vehicle gates with intercoms
- Interlock overrides
- Motion detector alarms
- Closed-circuit video equipment (CCVE) systems
- Roll-up doors
- Local intercom/paging systems
- Perimeter security
- Emergency shut-down switch
- Power shut-down restore
- General housing cell
- Disciplinary housing cell
- Shower area/door
- Emergency group release (both swing and sliding doors)
- Control room door
- Movement doors (both swing and sliding doors)
- Visiting booth door
- Visiting area intercoms
- Washroom door
- Door status alarm (standard and interruptible)
- Interior lighting control
- Cable television (CATV)
- Supplemental smoke/heat alarm
- Electromechanical interlocks
- Man gate/vehicle gate (with intercoms)
- Perimeter lighting control
- Elevator shut-down
- Position monitor
- Control point overrides

system. See Chapter 9, "Mechanical, Electrical, and Structural Systems," for additional information.

Movement/location tracking systems

In inmate areas, systems can be provided that allow tracking of inmates throughout the facility. Common technologies include bar- or radio-coded wristband systems.

AREAS AND SPACES

Building Control Center

In justice facilities designed without a prisoner holding area, a building control center should be provided to serve as the location where alarm annunciator panels, closed-circuit television monitors, the public address system, and other security equipment are housed.

This area will be the primary security control center and will serve as headquar-

ters during an emergency. The area may also serve as the central reporting station to which police and fire agencies will report in an emergency.

Specific functions and controls provided in a building control center should include:

- Alarm annunciation
- Secure/access switching
- Remote controls
- Video monitors
- Video controls
- Audio inputs
- Audio monitors
- Audio controls
- Access system controls
- Radio communication controls

Central Control

Among the requirements of the second edition of the ACA *Standards for Adult Local Detention Facilities* is that "the facility maintain[s] a control center." The standards specify that Central Control, also known as Master Control, must be staffed 24 hours a day, that access to it must be limited, and that it should monitor and take responsibility for inmate counts, key control, and coordination of the internal and external security network. The ACA standards note that the functions to be accommodated within Central Control include the following:

- Monitoring all security perimeter systems
- Control and communication with people at all entries to, and exits from, the primary security perimeter

▼ Control room, James River Juvenile Detention Center, Virginia. Photo by Don Eiler, courtesy of HSMM, Inc.

- Control and communications with people at many key access points between various security zones within the facility

- Monitoring building systems, security/safety systems and equipment, and the like

- Handling facility control, monitoring shift changes and identification checks

- Communication with facility staff at all posts, whether fixed/stationary or moving

Central Control should be designed as its own security zone with a security vestibule entry and security glazing into areas where direct monitoring by control center staff is anticipated. The security glazing is typically designed to withstand a 45-minute or longer attack. Pass-through openings should be provided for keys, packages, and paperwork, and heating, ventilating, and air-conditioning (HVAC) systems should be secured. All power, data, and telecommunication service to and from Central Control should also be secured.

Historically, control centers were glazed and enclosed high-security rooms positioned to allow direct observation of some areas and relying on CCVE systems to monitor other areas. Design criteria related to the durability of walls, ceilings, floors, and glazing (attack ratings) were based on the estimated time that a control center would need to withstand a concerted attack before assistance would respond. Typically, intercom systems were used for communications between virtually all areas, supplemented by radio.

With advances in designs for direct supervision, open control centers have been developed (with override capability provided from the open centers to

▲ Control room, Norfolk Juvenile Detention Center, Virginia. Photo by Don Eiler, courtesy of HSMM, Inc.

Central Control). In some cases, fixed control centers have been eliminated in favor of wireless remote communication and control devices.

Even in facilities that employ direct supervision, however, the design requirements for the last point of refuge—Central Control—is typically governed by estimates of expected response in the event of an emergency, and the systems and materials are designed to surpass these estimates by a worst-case safety factor. The critical issue remains the definition of appropriate security levels for each control center, consistent with objectives for staff safety and overall institutional security.

In small facilities or complexes, some or all of the functions of the building control center may be consolidated with the functions accommodated in this area. In large facilities and those in which prisoners may not be present during all hours (such as court facilities), the Central Control room may serve as the control center for prisoner-related security and access, but with the building control center serving as the hub of perimeter security monitoring and control.

Where provided, especially in small and mid-sized facilities, Central Control may function as a staffed supervision point for monitoring special holding or housing units or other processing, public, or inmate activity areas. In some facilities, it may be combined with the law enforcement dispatch function and may monitor or assist in public reception.

The design of consoles is critical to the effective function of the control room. Prefabricated and custom millwork solutions can be provided. Where custom-designed consoles are provided, designs should consider workstation ergonomics, access for maintenance and service, and operator positions related to sight lines.

Secondary Control Centers

Secondary control centers are located in various areas of detention and correctional facilities. These centers support the operation of Central Control by controlling and restricting movement and monitoring systems and emergency equipment within defined areas, such as medical areas, housing units, educational and vocational centers, visitation areas, and the like. In general, all control centers should be designed to provide optimal views of areas under the supervision and control of the control center staff.

Security Equipment Rooms

Rooms housing security electronics equipment are typically located outside inmate or public areas and should be easily accessible to maintenance personnel. Equipment rooms should be located directly above (or below) each other to provide vertical alignment of communication risers.

▲ Control room, Beaumont Juvenile Correction Center, Virginia. Photo by Don Eiler, courtesy of HSMM, Inc.

▲ Control room, Beaumont Juvenile Correction Center, Virginia. Photo by Don Eiler, courtesy of HSMM, Inc.

CHAPTER 12
COSTS, FINANCING, AND PROJECT DELIVERY

The questions, "How much will a justice facility cost?" "Where will the money to pay for it come from?" and "How will it be designed and constructed?" are complicated, and their answers are interdependent. Design decision makers are advised to proceed carefully and to consult specialists in these areas. There is no magic formula or one-size-fits-all approach.

If one imagines a matrix consisting of the variety of justice facility types, from police stations to large courthouses, combined with the different levels of government—federal, state, county, and municipal—as well as the many thousands of geographic localities in the country with their own public decision-making authorities in place, it is apparent how varied and even idiosyncratic the processes of developing a project can be.

Consistent terminology and clarity of definitions are key to effective development in any project. The word *facility* may be understood differently by different people, depending on the jurisdiction or circumstance. Some people may understand it to include an annex, branch office, support building or kiosk site, whereas others may not. The project to be developed may be the renovation of existing space, an addition, the new construction of a freestanding building, or all of these together. The terms of occupancy involved may entail owning, renting, or renting with a lease-purchase agreement.

PROJECT COSTS

Hard and Soft Costs
Project costs have two major components

—construction costs and nonconstruction costs—often referred to as "hard costs" and "soft costs," respectively. The hard costs are those typically included in the general contractor's bid: site utilities; landscaping and site finishes; building(s), from foundation to roof, including interior tenant construction; and general contractor's and subcontractors' overhead and profit.

The nonbuilding construction, or soft costs, are those for the acquisition of the site; architectural and engineering design services; specialty consulting, studies, surveys, testing, permits, and associated reimbursable expenses; the cost of financing, public proffers, and so forth.

In addition, a project's soft costs can include furnishings, fixtures, and equipment (FF&E) and information technology systems that are not typically included in standard design and construction contracts.

Contingencies and Escalation

Design contingency
An allowance for undefined work (commonly known as a "design contingency") should be included in the initial hard-cost budget in anticipation of undefined requirements that are identified during the design phase. Traditionally, this contingency is identified by the architect and owner and ranges from 10 to 15 percent at the start of a project. The contingency should reflect the size, complexity, and level of uncertainty surrounding the project. A small historic renovation project constructed in several phases should carry a higher design contingency than a very

large standard office building constructed on a site with favorable soil conditions. The allowance for undefined work is reduced, during the course of design, from 10–15 percent at the start of the project to 0 percent at 100 percent completion of the construction documents (CDs). At the 100 percent CD phase, all work will have been defined and the contingency will have been redistributed appropriately within the budget.

Construction contingency

A construction contingency should be included in the owner's soft cost budget in anticipation of unforeseen conditions encountered from the time the construction contract is let through project completion. Traditionally, this contingency is identified by the owner and ranges from 3 to 5 percent for new construction and 5 to 10 percent for renovation, depending on the owner's sensitivity to risk.

Phasing contingency

Projects that will be built in phases should include a phasing contingency to cover the cost of temporary partitions, multiple mobilizations and demobilizations, additional cost of labor for work done other than during normal working hours, and other costs incurred during a phased construction project.

Project contingency

A project contingency should also be considered in the owner's soft cost budget to cover owner-directed changes during the course of design and construction. This contingency is identified by the owner and depends on how well the owner has defined his or her expectations and project scope. A unique or first-of-its-kind facility is more likely to require a project contingency than a familiar build-

ing type that has been replicated many times.

Escalation

Traditionally, agencies of the federal government have used a construction cost escalation rate defined by the Office of Management and Budget (OMB). This rate has been fixed nationwide, regardless of geographic location. It reflects general escalation rather than escalation in a location-specific construction market basket. However, the escalation rate should reflect location-specific conditions. The U.S. General Services Administration (GSA) has recognized this need and since 1998 has included a location-specific escalation factor in its *General Construction Cost Review Guide* (GCCRG).

Public projects often escalate construction cost projections to the date that bids are scheduled to be received. In the private sector, it is more common to escalate to the midpoint of construction, which better reflects how the general contractor and subcontractors actually price work on the day they submit their bids. Some trades do not even begin their work until halfway through construction. These subcontractors escalate their prices to the date they will actually perform the work. This is especially the case in a robust construction market. The construction period for a mid-rise federal courthouse, for example, is approximately 36 months. The project budget should include escalation to the midpoint or to 18 months beyond the anticipated construction award date.

Budget formulation for a project can begin with a fixed allowable budget figure for all costs, within which decision makers then determine what can be afforded and should be done. Alternately, a budget can be built up beginning with studies to determine the need for the project, followed by the development of a program to identify scope and quality requirements and probable costs before then seeking the necessary financing and approvals to proceed.

Cost, Expectations, and Scope

Three dimensions of a project—cost, expectations (quality and schedule) and scope—must be aligned to achieve a successful outcome. The cost includes all hard and soft costs of the project, as well as an understanding of operational and life-cycle costs. The quality involves the design, materials, construction methods, and detailing. The schedule is the time required to carry out the design, documentation, construction, and occupancy processes. The scope of the project is its size and programmatic objectives.

If one dimension of the project changes, the others will be affected. If the scope of the project is enlarged, it can mean that the quality may be reduced unless the overall budget can be adjusted upward to accommodate the change.

Life-cycle costing

Decision makers should look beyond the initial costs of design and construction to evaluate performance over the course of a project's full useful life. The operations and maintenance costs for public facilities intended to have a 50–100-year life may be significantly reduced if higher-quality or more durable materials, assemblies and equipment are selected. Personnel costs may also be reduced through thoughtful design. If the design for a correctional facility allows for a reduction in the required number of guards, then person-

nel costs are saved every year the facility is in operation. Higher first costs can be recovered, often very quickly, in long-term savings. Design strategies that build in extra flexibility for a facility may incur higher initial costs, but these are offset by providing for quicker, easier, less disruptive, and less expensive renovation and maintenance.

Best value is achieved when initial and future costs, added together, yield the best life-cycle cost within acceptable quality limits.

The false economies of lowest-first-cost budgeting are a chronic problem in the building industry, and in the past projects have been plagued by inflexibility and needlessly high future costs for the sake of saving money in the beginning.

Public sector projects involving community interests and taxpayer dollars inevitably have a political aspect. If budget decisions are made by people whose sense of the applicable time line is limited to their terms of office as elected officials, rather than the full 50–100-year life-cycle of a building, such short-sightedness can compromise the value of a project. This puts an added burden on the project team, which must then present trade-offs between first and future costs during the approvals process. Knowing the trade-offs makes it possible for decision makers to intelligently choose or reject solutions aimed at achieving the best life-cycle value .

Life cycle of building components

Although public buildings are designed to realize a 50–100-year life, many building components have shorter life expectancies. The useful life of most mechanical equipment is 25–30 years; of carpet, 5 years; and so forth. Funding for facility recapitalization (the scheduled replacement of capital improvements that have reached the end of their useful lives) has been habitually ignored by government officials. Studies of the long-term cost of ownership indicate that an annual commitment of 2–4 percent of a project's current replacement value should be set aside to cover recapitalization costs. A recapitalization funding plan should be developed for every project to identify the probable replacement costs of equipment and material as they reach the end of their useful lives, and to identify a funding strategy to meet these requirements.

Scope and cost "creep"

Justice facilities take a long time to develop from inception to occupancy. A large court project may take 7 or more years. A long time line increases opportunities for the unexpected to happen. Various projects in development in the 1990s were taken by surprise when unilateral budget cuts were enacted, when building security was heightened, and when information technologies transformed design requirements. Security and technology issues, particularly, led to an upward creep in the original scope of some projects. Project costs increase when functional programs are amended and construction schedules stretched out. Reducing chances of a surprising cost "creep" over a long development process requires the best possible planning at the predesign stage and careful management throughout the design process.

Major Cost Drivers

Italian economist Wilfredo Pareto has observed that 80 percent of the cost of anything resides in approximately 20 percent of its component parts. This observation is known as "Pareto's law."

Using this logic, it is possible to influence 80 percent of a project's cost by watching a relatively limited number of cost drivers. The following list identifies the drivers that influence project cost significantly, which should be measured and managed during the design process:

- Site-specific concerns such as poor soil conditions, the presence of rock, road and utility realignments, demolition of existing structures, hazardous material abatement, environmental mitigation, adjacency to subways and other underground structures, and availability of utilities

- Owner-driven initiatives and mandates, such as blast resistivity in the wake of the Oklahoma City bombing and September 11 attacks, enhanced internal security, and energy-efficient and "green" building design

- Owner standards and guidelines

- Code requirements and zoning restrictions

- Project-specific requirements

- Building configuration

- Program/mix of functions

- Efficiency (ratio of usable to gross area)

- Quality of systems and materials

- Procurement methods and contract documents

- Market conditions

- Schedule

- Special labor and/or purchase requirements, such as the purchase of U.S.-manufactured products, not imported ones.

The roles played by different cost drivers will vary considerably from one project to another. Some, like market conditions, may be contingent on both geographic location and timing. Those described in the following paragraphs are especially important.

Building efficiency

The relationship of usable/occupiable/net area to the gross area (or gross square feet, GSF) indicates the efficiency of the building, including its "core" and "back-of-the-house" space. Interestingly, all other factors being equal, projects that are more efficient cost more on a cost/GSF basis.

When a building is configured efficiently, the space that is saved is typically excess circulation space. Circulation space is relatively inexpensive to construct. By deleting inexpensive excess space, the overall cost is reduced, but the cost per GSF increases. (Because the cost/GSF is a fractional relationship, in which GSF is the denominator, the total cost of a project is divided by less area, thereby increasing the cost/GSF.) It is important for the project team to understand this dynamic when communicating cost data to funding authorities. The success of a project should not be judged exclusively on a cost/GSF basis.

A generally accepted method for calculating area has been developed so that the efficiency of a building can be identified. (See the discussion of ANSI/BOMA guidelines later in this chapter.) At each project milestone, efficiency should be measured using a consistent protocol. The importance of monitoring efficiency cannot be overstated. In the construction of a recent judicial facility, the efficiency of the project at 100 percent complete design was measured at 61 percent. The target efficiency for this type of project is 67 percent. The project was 6 percent less efficient than targeted, meaning that 6

percent more nonprogram space was constructed than planned. The project was bid at $15–$20 million over the funding allocation. Almost all of the overage could be attributed to the inefficiency of the design. Conversely, another judicial facility managed to achieve the targeted efficiency while providing a relatively large public atrium space. This was done by using a compact building form—the square, locating the atrium in the middle, and designing very efficient secondary circulation systems. The configuration of this project "bought" the ability to provide a large public space without exceeding its targeted efficiency.

In some cases, the site configuration, programmatic requirements, and other factors combine to cause the efficiency of a building to be less than targeted. Small buildings, a complex of small buildings, and very tall slender buildings are generally less efficient than compact mid-rise structures. The mix of space also affects efficiency. Courthouses are less efficient than federal office buildings because of the need for appropriate public circulation space on court floors, and because of security requirements that separate judicial and public circulation spaces.

Monitoring efficiency should be part of the design process and should continue from the concept phase throughout the design process. It is especially important to evaluate the efficiency of each scheme presented at the concept phase so that efficiency and the attendant cost ramifications can be taken into consideration during the design process.

There is no single metric for evaluating success. The dollars-per-square-foot figure does not necessarily say anything about the fitness of a facility or the quality of its space.

Mix of tenant space

The cost of a project is determined not just by its size, but also by its degree of complexity. The more complicated the programmatic mix on the site and within the building envelope, the more costly the project will be to design and construct.

The design process should identify the relative amounts of expensive space (such as courtrooms), less expensive space (such as standard open office space), and inexpensive space (such as parking). The mix of space has a great impact on the overall cost per GSF. Courthouses constructed in the early 1990s typically included visitor parking. Security concerns have led to the development of newer courthouses that provide very little parking, serving only the judges and official vehicles. Newer courthouse projects will immediately appear to be more costly on a cost/GSF basis because they include less inexpensive parking space. For this reason, cost/GSF should be calculated both with and without parking.

Just as with the calculating of usable and gross space, a protocol should be established for calculating space by type. Space should be calculated by classification as opposed to (or in addition to) user. Users may request a different blend of types of space to meet different needs in different buildings. A U.S. marshal's service or a sheriff's department will need proportionately more detention space in a 2-story courthouse than in an 8-story one, because both require a sally port. In the larger building an economy of scale is realized where the sally port can be used to support a greater number of courtrooms.

In evaluating the relative cost of judicial facilities, it is helpful to monitor cost on a cost per unit basis other than cost/GSF. For courthouses, this metric may be the cost per courtroom or cost per chambers (especially in shared-courtroom buildings). For correctional facilities, the metric may be cost per inmate or cost per bed.

Public space

Public space is defined here to include main public entry lobbies and public elevator lobbies and waiting areas. This cost driver is of greater consequence to the costs of courthouses and other judicial structures where citizens move freely in and out of the building. The amount, volume, and configuration of public space affect cost. Because public space is not generally considered to be "tenant space," these factors also impact efficiency. Small buildings typically have proportionately more public space because there is a minimum threshold of public space required to serve a building. Once this threshold is passed, a project can benefit from economies of scale, needing relatively less public space in proportion to tenant space.

The configuration and size of public space are changing as a result of new security requirements. The need for magnetometers at most public buildings changes the entry sequence and often adds space. Public space should be managed by identifying and quantifying its extent. It should be estimated as a subset of nontenant space, and a cost per square foot (SF) of public space should be identified. Cost per cubic foot (CF) of public space is another useful measure, as most public spaces are at least partially double-height volumes or higher. The ratio of public space to total project GSF is most useful in comparing a project to another of equal size and scope.

Site conditions

Site conditions have a significant impact on the cost of construction. A small site, or one that has low or uneven load-bearing capacity, may require a taller building on a smaller footprint or in a contorted shape. The cost of improving the site in terms of utilities, landscaping, and other site finishes can be monitored by costing these items and dividing them by the site area or by the gross area of the building.

The ratio of site area to building area for urban sites is typically smaller than that for suburban sites. The cost of improving sites in urban areas is often higher in cost per SF of site area because the finishes for hardscape (sidewalks, retaining walls, etc.) are generally more expensive than those for less developed suburban sites. However, suburban sites are generally bigger, and more area is improved. Correctional facilities have special site requirements, including type, number of rows, and extent of perimeter fence.

In some instances, utilities and public roadways are not accessible within the site perimeters of correctional projects. Off-site utility costs and roadway improvements for these projects become an important consideration.

The geological composition of the site is one of the greatest unknowns in forecasting construction cost and is important to understand as early as possible—even before a site is acquired. A geotech report will reveal the assumed soil-bearing capacity of the site, the presence of rock, and any existing or adjacent structures. It will identify site locations that are more favorable for construction and indicate the type of foundation system(s) that is appropriate. The soil conditions should inform the design process in terms of positioning buildings on the site. Trade-

offs between alternate design schemes and the attendant site and structural costs should be explored before a scheme is accepted at the end of the concept phase.

The more the task of construction is complicated by inadequate staging areas or other difficult site conditions, the higher the final cost. Building off the backs of trucks in a dense urban area, or on a steeply sloping hillside with existing structures that get in the way, drives up the expense.

Structure

In addition to soil conditions, there are code requirements, seismic zone and dead load requirements, and security considerations that influence the structural design of a building. Most projects have the option of considering more than one structural solution for a building. Each should be evaluated in terms of cost. Generally, long-span schemes in oddly configured buildings are more costly to construct than shorter-span compact structures.

The relative cost of building in concrete versus building in steel varies from locality to locality, project to project, and general contractor to general contractor. General contractors who supply their own concrete can offer it at a lower cost than a competitor who must purchase concrete from a subcontractor. Correctional facilities have a broad variety of structural options, as they range programmatically from almost residential, campus-type construction to high-security structures.

Projects that are constructed of steel can be monitored by evaluating the pounds of steel per GSF and the cost per ton of steel.

In the wake of the Oklahoma City bombing, all federal courthouses are designed to resist progressive collapse. Recent events have brought the question of blast-resistant glazing to the fore. Blast-resistant design actually goes beyond considerations of the type of glass needed and involves the design of the entire perimeter wall. The facade of Pentagon Wedge One that was the site of the September 11 attack had been reinforced with a steel "grid," along with blast-resistant punched windows. The windows alone reportedly cost $10,000 each. A comparable conventional aluminum window would cost approximately $800–$1,000.

Exterior closure

The cost of the exterior closure of a project is driven by the extent of the exterior wall, or "skin," enclosing the building and the selected material palette. The amount of skin is affected by the configuration of the building (perimeter), the height of the building, and the articulation of the façade. The skin area can be calculated by multiplying the perimeter of each floor by its height. This quantity can then be multiplied by a modifier that takes into account the undulations in the plane of the façade, otherwise known as its articulation.

The articulation also takes into account the returns at the windows, doors, pilasters, and so forth, that require finishing by the trade. The precast concrete subcontractor sets a price based on "finished area" of precast. This includes all edges surrounding windows—not just to where a window sits, but also all the way to where the return ends. Perimeter × height × modifier for articulation = the "developed area of the exterior closure." The modifier for articulation can range from 5 percent for a very smooth, shallow façade to upwards of 25 percent for a building with heavy cornices, deep-set windows, and other such features.

A building that is long and narrow will require more skin than a building that is very compact. The most compact geometry a building can achieve is a cylinder. Because constructing curved surfaces presents a further set of complexities and costs, the most efficient conventional construction geometry is a cube. The lower the floor-to-floor height, the less skin required per floor. A perfectly flat façade requires less of a modifier for articulation than a medieval cathedral, for example, with its carved ornamentation and flying buttresses.

A useful way to understand how much skin is being built is to calculate the "skin ratio." The skin ratio is the developed skin area per gross area. The smaller the skin ratio, the less skin being built and the more efficient the building configuration. A very compact warehouse building may have a skin ratio of 20 percent. An office building in a city where height restrictions encourage the use of low floor-to-floor heights may have a skin ratio of 30–50 percent. A federal courthouse can have a skin ratio of 45–75 percent.

Solid versus glazed wall

The cost of the exterior closure is affected by the types and mix of materials selected. Another useful relationship to analyze is the ratio of solid wall to glazed area. A recent study of four completed courthouses for the Courthouse Management Group of GSA revealed a broad range of solid/glazed ratios. The ratios varied from 49 percent solid/51 percent glazed to 81 percent solid/19 percent glazed. This relationship will become increasingly important as security requirements are highlighted and bullet-resistant and/or blast-resistant glazing is incorporated more extensively into the design of public buildings.

With blast-resistant punched windows costing about 10 times as much as conventional punched windows, there will be increasing pressure to reduce the proportion of glazed area. The challenge to balance the "openness" of our institutions with security concerns will be played out—in a very public way—in the façade design of public buildings and in their cost.

Vertical circulation

The cost of vertical circulation systems can be monitored by identifying the elevator ratio: total GSF per number of elevators; and by unit cost: total cost of elevators per number of elevator openings. The elevator ratio helps to determine whether the quantity of elevators is typical. The cost per opening helps to illuminate how relatively expensive the system is. Elevator ratios for small buildings and those with multiple circulation systems will tend to be higher than those for office buildings. Larger buildings benefit by economy of scale.

Most small buildings will require that two elevators be installed for maintenance reasons, even when the population of the building does not otherwise support a second elevator. Courthouses, with their three separate circulation systems, require a minimum of two elevators for each system, judicial, public and prisoner, and may have an elevator ratio as low as 25,000 GSF/elevator. In contrast, an office building may have an elevator ratio as high as 55,000 GSF/elevator.

The cost per stop will vary according to the type, speed, capacity, number of front and rear openings, quality, special features, and cab finish allowance.

Elevators serving 5 or fewer floors are usually hydraulic elevators, and those serving 5–13 floors may be geared traction elevators; for buildings with elevators serving more than 13 floors, the use of gearless traction elevators should be considered. This selection scheme is based on the capability and speed of each system. Hydraulic elevators are slow and are impractical for serving more than 6 floors. The increased speed of a gearless elevator cannot be realized in a building of fewer than 12 floors because there is no acceleration advantage until a cab travels more than 12 floors.

These systems range in cost from hydraulic (at the low end) to gearless traction (at the high end). The cost of each elevator is further affected by its rate of travel or speed, the weight it can transport, and the number of openings (front and/or rear) required. The cab allowance covers the finishes and fittings in the elevator cab and varies according to the elevator's use. An elevator cab allowance in the public cabs of a federal courthouse can be in the $35,000–$45,000 range. In a service elevator it may be as low as $5,000–$10,000.

It is advisable to work with an elevator consultant to identify the correct number and types of elevators necessary to accommodate the needs of the building's population. The cost of the vertical circulation system can be managed by tracking the elevator ratio and the cost per stop in each cost estimate.

Mechanical

Mechanical costs include heating, ventilating, and air-conditioning (HVAC) systems, the building management system, and the plumbing and fire protection systems. HVAC costs can be monitored by watching the GSF/ton of cooling and the cost/ton. Plumbing can be monitored by the cost/fixture. The controls system that manages the mechanical and electrical systems can be monitored by the number of control points and the cost per point. Fire protection can be monitored by cost per sprinkler head.

Electrical

Electrical costs have traditionally been monitored by the ratio of watts/GSF. This metric is misleading, because factors other than power have a significant impact on cost. Electrical costs are best compared on the basis of cost of electrical work/GSF. It is useful to break out the cost of lighting (and associated wiring and controls)/GSF. Lighting accounts for about a quarter of all electrical costs. Data and telecommunications costs vary widely.

Most construction budgets include the cost of conduit and raceways for data and telecommunications. The costs of wiring and the necessary devices are typically carried as part of the owner's soft costs budget. It is essential to understand where the funding for data/telecom work is carried in the overall project budget and to coordinate the data/telecom work with the general construction work to avoid installation problems, delays, and the attendant extra costs.

Bid and construction terms

The requirements established in the "front end" bid documents and construction contract affect the overall project cost. When the bid and contract terms are clear, fair, and equitable, the general contractor typically responds with a competitive bid. When this is not the case, or when projects have been bid several times

or funding has not been approved, the members of the contracting community respond by increasing their bids. With the use of standardized, equitable, and clear contracts for construction, general conditions and fees can be projected more consistently.

Method of Measurement: The Impact of ANSI/BOMA Measurement Guidelines

On October 14, 1996, in an effort to better align the federal government's real estate practices with those of the private sector, Congress mandated that federal agencies use private sector terminology and standards to measure and report space. In May 1998, the Public Building Service document, PBS B-100.1, was revised to incorporate the guidelines of the American National Standards Institute/Building Owners and Managers Association (ANSI/BOMA). This private sector methodology replaced the old method used exclusively by the federal government. The intent was to simplify and standardize definitions so that the federal government and the private sector would speak the same language and so that meaningful comparisons could be made between rental rates.

This alignment of federal and private sector terminology will eventually simplify real estate management on many levels. However, the ramifications of this transition are significant. The implications of BOMA methodology for space procurement requests and management are only now being realized.

The federal government's old methodology of measurement reported space in terms of "occupiable" and "gross" square feet. The newly adopted methodology is based on that of BOMA, as defined in the ANSI/BOMA publication Z65.1-1966, "Standard Method for Measuring Floor Area in Office Buildings." BOMA's methodology reports space in 18 categories. The BOMA categories that are most similar to GSA's old categories are Usable Area (for occupiable) and Gross Building Area (for gross).

"Usable Area" differs from "occupiable" in several ways. It is measured to the "dominant surface" of the exterior wall and it includes corridor deviations. In addition, slab penetrations or voids that are specifically made to serve a tenant are measured as if the slab were still there. Examples of these voids, or "ghost floors," include two-story spaces such as courtrooms, private (judge's and prisoner's) elevators, communicating stairs between floors but outside the building core, and the like. Finally, according to the ANSI/BOMA standard, on single-occupancy floors (and buildings), circulation corridors—other than those required by code for fire egress—are part of the office usable area.

In all, ANSI/BOMA guidelines artificially inflate the gross area, which artificially increases efficiency and reduces the cost per GSF. This makes the statistics look better even though the overall cost of construction remains the same.

The use of ANSI/BOMA guidelines as a commonly understood methodology is a laudable mandate. Its impact on the government's understanding of unit costs, efficiency, and other real estate metrics is just becoming apparent. Such effects should be analyzed in greater detail so that the new metric is applied equitably and the associated guidelines are adjusted accordingly. Care should be taken to illustrate the difference in reporting area when the different measurement methods are used, so that misunderstanding is avoided.

Cost Management as a Design Tool

The members of a project team should use their understanding of cost drivers to inform the design process. Cost management should not be treated as something that happens after design when the cost of a project has exceeded the available funding. It should be integrated into the design process from its initial inception and used as a tool throughout design and construction to make informed decisions. Value engineering principles should also inform the process, allowing the project team to make best-value decisions as design progresses. These may entail, in some cases, investing more, not less, in initial costs to take advantage of life-cycle savings. Value engineering should not be confused with crudely reactive cost cutting. True value management helps to align costs by spending project funds strategically and knowingly.

Best value can be derived by:

- Developing a value management plan that includes "value alignment" sessions, starting as early as the program phase
- Clearly defining available funding
- Clearly defining owner and user expectations
- Clearly defining project goals and objectives
- Defining and evaluating program requirements
- Managing the schedule
- Managing claims and change orders
- Empowering decision makers and demanding accountability

FINANCING

Financing the design and construction of new facilities for justice operations is the responsibility of government, chiefly the executive branch, often at several levels operating in concert. Individual facilities at the municipal and county levels may be financed as part of a coordinated capital budgeting program that includes a number of facilities.

Federal projects are generally financed through appropriations. At other levels of government, when a commitment is made to embark upon a major capital building project that requires incurring a long-term debt, the agency of government responsible for retiring the debt often takes a bond marketing approach. The funds required to pay for the design and construction of the facility are raised through general obligation or limited obligation bonds.

Bonds

General obligation bonds involve a political process almost by definition, because most states require that they be approved by the voters. The government raises the money with the promise that it will be paid back, principal and interest, with general tax revenues from the public coffers. In contrast, limited obligation bonds of various kinds relieve the government of the need to commit its general tax revenues as a financial guarantee, and voter approval is not required. Two noteworthy types of limited obligation bonds are those for lease-rental and lease-purchase arrangements.

Lease-rental bonds generate funds for capital expenditures through arrangements that bind an occupant to pay enough rent over the long term to retire the principal and interest, as well as to absorb the ongoing costs of operation and maintenance of the facility.

Lease-purchase bonds, in contrast, generate funds to cover capital expenditures through arrangements that begin with a partnership between a public authority and a private funding source (or other public source). The public authority identifies its facility needs and specifies the requirements to be met by the new construction. The private, or other, developer then pays for the construction, absorbing all the initial capital costs. The occupant(s) then pays back the capital costs plus interest through rent fees over the length of a long-term lease. At the end of the lease, the title for ownership of the facility is transferred to the occupant.

Lease-purchase arrangements featuring public-private partnerships for the construction of new justice facilities—and, in some instances, for the privatized operations and maintenance of them as well—may become a more familiar financing approach in the coming years. Foreign governments, notably in the United Kingdom, are gaining more experience with larger roles for the private sector, and the approach is now being explored by the Canadian government to a notable degree.

PROJECT DELIVERY METHODS

Project delivery methods involve the terms of agreement between the major parties in the design and construction process for a facility and the rules that govern how the process is to be conducted. The major parties are the owner, the architectural and engineering (A/E) design professional, and the contractor. Other parties may be added and the lines of responsibility between them may be altered, depending on the method of project delivery that is selected.

The delivery methods are varied and evolving. There can be disagreement among the parties in a project about which method is best. One party may prefer one approach over another, and one approach may actually be more effective than another for a particular facility type or situation. The approach taken to develop a general jurisdiction courthouse in an urban area may be entirely different from that used to develop a correctional facility on a remote site.

Design-Bid-Build

The traditional approach to design and construction is characterized by a linear, step-by-step sequential process that begins with extensive predesign analysis and planning and subsequently proceeds through the schematic, design development, and construction documentation phases to produce drawings and written specifications for the project,which are then put out to bid. A contractor is selected, and construction is carried through to completion and building commissioning.

A weakness of the traditional method is that the triangular relationship between owner, A/E, and contractor depends on a high level of mutual trust, which can sometimes be tested severely under the pressures that can develop when things go wrong in a complicated project that takes a long time to complete. It can also be more difficult to "nail down" the final cost of a project until late in the process.

In the past, implicit in the design-bid-build approach was the assumption that the lowest responsive bid was able to address all the requirements of a project satisfactorily. In the current effort to encourage construction excellence, source

selection procedures and best-value construction procurement is ensuring that those in the field of bidders are qualified for the work and that they intend to construct a high-quality project in accordance with project documents.

The strength of the traditional approach is that it can increase the likelihood of a high-quality outcome, because the design process allows time to analyze key issues at the planning stage, especially, and because the users of the facility can be engaged for their critical input throughout the process. The owner of the facility is very often not the same entity as its user. Securing the necessary input of the user may be easier to accomplish when the project delivery method features a linear, sequential approach. In addition, more thorough design oversight through the construction process may be possible —an important consideration in projects where craft and fine-grained articulation are priorities. In cases where those in the field of bidders all are properly qualified, the design-bid-build approach may prove to be the most competitive.

Construction Management

Efforts within the building industry to accelerate and streamline design and construction processes began more than a generation ago, when the costs of doing business became excessively high with double-digit interest rates. During the same period, there were also reductions in in-house staff and in the level of expertise in many agencies, and owners turned to construction managers, forging various kinds of relationships and granting them responsibility for handling the more complicated costing and scheduling.

In most construction management (CM) relationships, the A/E continues to have an independent relationship with the owner, but the manager may be heavily involved in design decision making, with authority to let multiple contracts for different pieces of work undertaken concurrently. The step-by-step sequential process associated with the design-bid-build approach is replaced in CM by fast-track scheduling, whereby a number of things are done in parallel.

In some arrangements, the details of the initial CM contract are modified in mid-stream when the design has been developed to a point at which the contractor is comfortable with committing to a fixed time line and guaranteed maximum cost for construction. This approach can provide an earlier commitment of cost through a guaranteed maximum price (GMP) delivered approximately at the design development phase on prefinal documents.

Design-Build

A more completely turnkey process, from the owner's point of view, is provided by the design-build approach, a delivery method in which a single full-service entity takes responsibility for all phases, from the initial predesign tasks of planning and programming through construction and move-in occupancy. The full-service design-build organization may offer a design-build-operate option, and even private financing as well, as part of a comprehensive design-build-lease-purchase package.

The great appeal of the design-build method to an owner may be the simplicity of the process. A potential pitfall may be the sacrifice of control over the quality of design materials and methods. In this process, unlike the traditional design-bid-build process, there is no independent design advocate who is looking out for the interests of the owner.

Criteria-based design-build

Modifications of the design-build process include at least two ways in which owners have refined it. The first, criteria-based design-build, is achieved through the development of specific criteria for the project prior to selection of the design-build team. The team selected then has a relatively free hand to proceed, but only within the terms of the preestablished criteria.

Bridging

The other variation on the design-build approach, bridging, appears to be more satisfactory to many design professionals who are otherwise concerned that the delivery method may undermine, rather than enhance, design quality. Bridging typically calls for the owner to work with an A/E to formulate a design concept that responds to the owner's needs before selecting the design-build team to develop and implement the concept.

The variations that are possible within each of the three mainstream project delivery options noted earlier are considerable, and they continue to grow as the design and construction industry becomes more experienced with new techniques. There are distinct advantages and disadvantages to each of the options,[1] and none can be said to work best in every instance for a particular justice facility type. The interrelated issues of costs, financing, and project delivery will combine to drive different decisions in each case.

1. See Michael D. Dell'Isola, "Know Your Options: The Impact of Different Delivery Systems on the Management of Contracts," *Construction Specifier* (September 2001): 38–45.

APPENDIX
SPACE REQUIREMENTS FOR JUSTICE FACILITIES

	GENERAL SPACE REQUIREMENTS FOR LAW ENFORCEMENT FACILITIES		
AREA/ROOM	**AREA (SQ FT)**	**RECOMMENDED MINIMUM DIMENSION (LINEAR FT)**	**COMMENTS**
A Administration (All Areas)			
1 Offices (all areas of facility)	150	Min. 10	Natural light; appropriate security.
2 Cubicle or open-office workstations	64	Min. 8	Multitask workstation; 4 ft interior workstation clearances for staff with weapons.
3 Shared workstations (e.g., field officers or report writing stations	48	Min. 6	4 ft interior workstation clearances for staff with weapons.
4 Training/assembly	25/seat	Min. 30	Standard conference/classroon with additional clearances for staff with weapons; consider A/V systems.
5 Conference rooms	30/seat		Consider A/V systems.
B Operations (Patrol, Investigations, Traffic, Other)			
1 Roll call	30/seat	Min. 12	Standard assembly/classroom areas with additional clearances for staff with weapons.
2 Armory; weapons	100 min. typical 150	Min. 8	Restricted access; secured internal storage with work areas.
3 Equipment; equipment storage	100 min. l typical 150	Min. 8	Restricted access; secured internal storage with work areas.
4 Interviewing	Varies	Min. 10	Various requirements, including special/direct observation, A/V systems, etc.
5 Lineup	40/position	Min. 8 on lineup side; min. 12 on observer side	Direct access from public, staff, and in-custody areas; special acoustic separation; glazing, lighting, and design requirements.
6 Lockers	10/locker, toilet/shower additional	Min. 8 clearances	Full-height, full-size lockers; provide acoustic/sight line privacy; separate officers/staff.
7 Toilet/shower	Per standards	Min. 4 clearance all areas	Adequate clearance for armed staff during routine and emergency use.
8 Physical training	400	15 min. any direction	Room configurations should accommodate fixed equipment with separate area for instructional training with mats.
C Support Services (Records, Communications, Property, Evidence, Lockup)			
1 Records areas	Varies	NA	Computerized and physical records; typically heavy floor load requirements.
2 Communication center	300 + 120 per station	Min. 15	Various configurations; supervisor should observe/backup; 3 ft clearance to service equipment in place
3 Equipment areas	100 min.	Min. 8	per ANSI/EIA/TIA standards.
4 Evidence drop	Varies	Min. 10	Include through-wall lockers (to evidence processing areas).
5 Lab; processing areas	Varies	Min. 12	Standard lab module dimensions, clearances, equipment, and special requirements (HVAC systems, chemical storage, security, and more).
6 In-custody holding/ processing areas	Varies	Min. 8 within areas; min 6 in circulation	National and state standards govern; specific security, fire, occupant/staff safety, observation requirements.
7 Building support areas	Varies	Varies	Must not be vulnerable to outside attack.

GENERAL SPACE REQUIREMENTS FOR DETENTION FACILITIES

AREA/ROOM	AREA (SQ FT)	RECOMMENDED MINIMUM DIMENSION (LINEAR FT)	COMMENTS
A Administration (All Areas)			See Chapter 2.
B Intake/Transfer/Release Areas			
1 Inmate holding areas (includes open supervised waiting)	80 min.	Min. 8	National and state standards govern; specific security, fire, occupant/staff safety, observation requirements.
2 General inmate processing areas (photo, fingerprint, initial property, initial screening)	120 min. (enclosed); 80 (open stations)	Min. 8	Provide and maintain crucial minimum clearances for custody control and observation.
3 In-custody movement/circulation, including sally ports	Varies	Min. 6	Maintain 6 ft min. corridors (assumes one-way); 8 ft min. if two-way circulation.
4 Staff offices/interview areas (typical of all staff offices within security perimeter)	120 min. (enclosed); 80 open stations	Min. 8	Maintain separation and design for staff safety, backup and supervision, and access.
5 Vehicle sally port	500 min., to 4,000	Min. 20	Accommodate hdcp transport vehicles, all expected current and potential future vehicle clearances, incl. buses.
C General Program Areas (Central or Distributed)			
1 Classroom, multipurpose, specialty programs	25–30/seat	Min. 30	Standard conference/classroom with additional clearances for response and emergency separation; consider A/V system requirements.
2 Contact visitation (if provided; general/nonofficial)	25–30/position	15 min., clear line of sight crucial	Direct observation/view by officer of most visitor/in-custody activity; design for response to emergency.
3 Contact visitation (official)	70–80 typical	Min. 8	Restricted access; for confidential attorney visits; typical to have direct view of areas; design for response to emergency.
4 Noncontact visitation	40/position	Min. 5 (handicapped)	Monitored/supervised by officer; total separation of visitor from secure areas.
5 Hearing/multipurpose rooms	800 min.	Min. 20	Needs vary; define purpose. Formal hearings may require full courtroom design provisions (see Chapter 4).
D Control Rooms/Central (or Master) Control			
1 Master/central control	250 min.; 150 each additional station	Min. 15	Stringent security, sight line, ergonomic, and equipment requirements; 24-hour control of internal and external systems; hub in emergency situation and response.
2 Secondary control centers (housing units and other locations)	120 min.; range to 200	Min. 10	Multitask workstation; 4 ft interior workstation clearances for staff; may be open positions.
3 Equipment areas	100 min.	Min. 8	Secure; room layouts per ANSI/EIA/TIA standards.

E Medical/Psychiatric Treatment Areas

1	Exam/treatment	150 min.; additional for office, supplies	Min. 10	Stringent security, sight line, ergonomic, and equipment requirements. Monitored/supervised access; design for staff safety; emergency access, incl. nonambulatory patients.
2	Clean/soiled linens, supplies	100 min.	Min. 8	ACA and other national/state standards; bio-hazardous material handling.
3	Supplies/equipment, including controlled substances	Varies	Min. 8	Stringent security and inventory control requirements; comply with ACA and other national/state standards; bio-hazardous material handling.

F Inmate Housing

1	Cells/sleeping areas	35 unencumbered/occupant and bed, writing surface, fixtures (as req'd)	Min. 7	Stringent security, sight line, ergonomic, and security/communication equipment requirements. Comply with ACA and other national/state standards; inmates/staff safety critical; emergency situation design considerations.
2	Dayrooms	Per standards	Min. 10	ACA and other national/state standards; inmate/staff safety critical with emergency situation design
3	Showers/other areas	Per standards	Min. 5 (hdcp)	Specific sight line requirements (access, during use); durability, maintenance, safety crucial.
4	Program areas at units	Per standards; in most cases, not less than 400–600 per individual housing unit	Min. 15	Common in detention facilities to reduce movement; multipurpose area (classroom, religious programs, light activities, visitation purposes).
5	Recreation area at units	Per standards; typically 750, 1,000, or 1,500 per unit	Min. 25	Common in detention facilities, particularly for units with more than four subunits (separate "pods" or "modules" are provided, to limit required movement to hour or more of required recreation).

G Support

1	Food service, laundry	Varies	Min. 12	Food service and laundry design must meet all federal, state, and local codes and regulations. Comply with ACA and other standards for detention/correctional services.
2	Staff/worker areas	Varies	Min. 10	Sanitation and break areas monitored and supervised; designed for safety and emergency access.
3	Building support areas	Varies	Varies	Restricted/secure system; not accessible or vulnerable.

GENERAL SPACE REQUIREMENTS FOR COURT FACILITIES

AREA/ROOM	AREA (SQ FT)	RECOMMENDED MINIMUM DIMENSION (LINEAR FT)	COMMENTS
A Adjudication Areas			
1 Courtrooms	1,500–2,400 or more	28–32 width for nonjury; 36 or greater for jury	Comply with national and state standards. Stringent security, safety, access control, and separation requirements. Litigation area should be designed for handicapped access to witness stand, jury box, attorney tables, all public areas, and all points of access or exit. Other positions in the courtroom should be "adaptable" to allow future access if/as required.
2 Chambers	Varies; typically 250–500 for judge's personal office	Min. 12	Chambers, or the full judicial suite of private offices, typically accomodate a secretary, clerk, court reporter, and space for legal research and conferencing, in addition to the judge's personal area.
3 Mediation/hearing rooms	600–1,200	Min. 20	Verify requirements for millwork, sight lines, and flexibility. Verify use; may be stringent security, safety, separation, and access control requirements. Proximity to breakout rooms in ADR/mediation functions crucial.
4 Attorney/client conference	100 min.	Min. 8	Number and distribution per standards; typically two or more per courtroom. Verify need for additional spaces for mediation, pretrial conferences with prosecutor, other uses.
5 Public waiting	100/court min.	Min. 6	Per standards; queuing critical to courtroom use/case processing
6 In-custody holding	80/area; typically two holding rooms per area, min.; other areas required	Min. 8	Separate, distinct, and secure access to prisoner holding; direct access to courtroom. Stringent security, safety, and separation requirements. Acoustical separation and absorption required; comply with federal, state, other standards.
7 Jury deliberation suite/room	300 for 12-person panel	Min. 12	Access, security, and separation requirements. Sound-lock vestibule typical; stringent acoustic separationrequirements; comply with federal, state, and other standards.
B Work Processing Areas			
1 Offices (all areas of facility)	150	Min. 10	Natural light; appropriate security.
2 Cubicle or open-office workstations	64	Min. 8	Multitask workstation; 3.5 ft interior workstation clearances (min.)
3 Shared workstations (e.g., field officers or report writing stations)	48	Min. 6	4 ft interior workstation clearances for staff with weapons.
4 Conference/training/assembly	25/seat	Min. 30	Standard conference/classroom with appropriate D/T, A/V (distance learning, remote conferencing) systems.
5 Storage/equipment	Varies	Min. 8, if enclosed or designated area	Special requirements for evidence, exhibits, records, confidential records, specialized equipment. Verify use.

C Customer Service Areas

1 Lobby/security screening	500 lobby min.; 200 min screening + 150 per additional station	Min. 20 (entrance/exit flow)	Public entry, weather vestibule, prescreening queueing, screening process, and postscreening distribution points. Comply with national, state standards for processing, security, and safety; stringent hdcp and life-safety access and egress; area monitored/controlled.
2 Public information/kiosk	80 min.; airport-type displays typical in large facilities	Min. 12 depth unless side alcove	Per recommended standards; directional signage, wayfinding, court docket monitor, and other court information may be provided; verify use — station designs differ.
3 Public counter/transaction area	120 min. (public/staff side included) for position assigned to counter; 40 for standup position	Min. 5.5 width typical	State/national guidelines; should comply with Crime Prevention Through Environmental Design (CPTED) standards for personal space, transaction-processing areas. May use automatic queuing/distribution systems; variety of standing, seating, communication systems.
4 Pro se/self-help center	Varies	Varies	Space requirements per intended use.

D Court Support Areas

1 Jury assembly area	15 in lecture format (10 per person in large groups); plus other waiting/staff areas	Varies; based on size of call, panels moving to court, assigned full- or part-time jury staff	Typically provided with staff work area, check-in, group waiting, secondary waiting/work areas, rest rooms and coffee area, storage (for equipment/tables/chairs — to allow jury assembly room to be used as multipurpose area).
2 Central holding	Varies	Min. 8	Stringent security, sight line, ergonomic, and security/communication equipment requirements. Comply with ACA and other national/state standards; inmates/staff safety critical; emergency situation design considerations.
3 Court-related office areas	Varies, see text	Min. 10 in offices; 6–8 in open office/cubicle areas	Comply with applicable state, national, federal, or local standards. Detailed standards for visitor access and screening in probation, prosecuting attorney, and other offices. Design for safety, security, and separation of staff, public, victim-witness, and other users.
4 Building support areas	Varies	Varies	Restricted/secure systems; not accessible or vulnerable.

GENERAL SPACE REQUIREMENTS FOR CORRECTIONAL FACILITIES

AREA/ROOM	AREA (SQ FT)	RECOMMENDED MINIMUM DIMENSION (LINEAR FT)	COMMENTS
A Administration (Executive, Operations, Other)			
1 Offices/training/lockers/other	Varies	Min. 10	See Chapter 2. Natural light; appropriate security. Correctional administrative offices are typically within the outer perimeter, but in areas with access restricted from inmate areas.
B Control Centers			
1 Master/central control	250 min.; 150 each additional station	Min. 15	Master control typically located near reception center, with direct control of most pedestrian movement through perimeter (visitor access, staff moving to post assignments).
2 Secondary control centers (housing units and other locations)	120 min.; range to 200	Min. 10	Multitask workstation; 4 ft interior workstation clearances for staff, may be open positions.
3 Equipment areas	100 min.	Min. 8	Secure; room layouts per ANSI/EIA/TIA standards.
C Inmate Housing			
1 Cells/sleeping areas	25–35 unencumbered/occupant, plus bed, writing surface, fixtures (as req'd)	Min. 7	Stringent security, sight line, ergonomic, and security/communication equipment requirements. Comply with ACA and other national/state standards; inmates/staff safety critical; emergency situation design considerations.
2 Dayrooms	Per standards	Min. 10	ACA and other national/state standards; inmate/staff safety critical with emergency situation design.
3 Showers/other areas	Per standards	Min. 5 (hdcp)	Specific sight line requirements (access, during use); durability, maintenance, and safety crucial.
D Visitation			
1 Contact visitation (if provided; general/nonofficial)	25–30/position	15 min., clear line of sight crucial	Direct observation/view by officer of most visitor/in-custody activity; design for response to emergency.
3 Contact visitation (official)	70–80 typical	Min. 8	Restricted access; for confidential attorney visits; typical to have direct view of areas; design for response to emergency.
4 Noncontact visitation	40/position	Min. 5 (hdcp)	Monitored/supervised by officer; total separation of visitor from secure areas.
5 Search/screening ares	100 min. typical	Min. 8	Per ACA and other national/state standards; consistent with needs for institutional security, for inmates and (some) visitors.

E Programs and Industries

1	Academic, multipurpose areas	25–30/seat	Min. 30	Standard conference/classroom with additional clearances for response and emergency separation; consider A/V system requirements.
2	Industry program areas	25–30/seat plus special/adjoining industry areas	Min. 30	Industry program areas specially designed for use; typically separate areas with entry security and screening for users, staff, and supplies. Special observation, screening, and control.
3	Religious programs	15–20/seat in assembly, plus offices and program/broadcast areas	Min. 30	Special requirements for staff, volunteers, programs, and development of broadcast or special programs. Often directly accessible to inmates, based on security/safety needs, supervision type, classification, and security status.
4	Library/law library	25–30/seat; stacks, staffwork areas additional	Varies	Combination of centralized program and delivered services, based on security/safety requirements, inmate supervision type, classification, and security status.
5	Recreation	Key feature of prison design — see diagrams in Chapter 5	Varies	Combination of active indoor, active/passive indoor, and passive indoor activities. Major program and site organizational determinants.

F Central Medical/Psychiatric Services

1	Examination/treatment	150 min.; additional for office, supplies	Min. 10	Stringent security, sight line, ergonomic, and equipment requirements. Monitored/supervised access; design for staff safety; emergency access, including nonambulatory patients.
2	Infirmary	Varies	Varies	Stringent security, sight line, ergonomic, and security/communication equipment requirements. Comply with ACA and other national/state standards; inmates/staff safety critical; emergency situation design considerations.
3	Clean/soiled linens, supplies	100 min.	Min. 8	ACA and other national/state standards; biohazardous material handling. Design for infirmary/delivered care support.
4	Supplies/equipment, including controlled substances	Varies	Min. 8	Stringent security and inventory control requirements; comply with ACA and other national/state standards; biohazardous material handling.

G Other Support

1	Food service/laundry	Varies	Min. 12	Food service and laundry design must meet all federal, state, and local codes and regulations. Comply with ACA and other standards for detention/correctional services.
2	Staff/worker areas	Varies	Min. 10	Sanitation and break areas monitored and supervised; design for safety and emergency access.
3	Facility/site warehouse/central plant	Varies	Varies	Restricted/secure system; not accessible or vulnerable.

BIBLIOGRAPHY AND RESOURCES

PROFESSIOAL AND GOVERNMENTAL ORGANIZATIONS

American Institute of Architects (AIA)
1735 New York Avenue, NW
Washington, DC 20006-5292
202.626.7300

The Committee on Architecture for Justice, a professional interest area of the AIA, publishes annually the *Justice Facilities Review*, "the red book," a juried compilation of projects featuring all facility types.

American Correctional Association (ACA)
4300 Forbes Road
Lanham, MD 20706-4322
1.800.222.5646

Publishes updated standards supplements to the following documents:

Standards for Adult Local Detention Facilities. 3rd edition, 1991.
Standards for Adult Correctional Institutions. 3rd edition, 1990.
Standards for Adult Juvenile Community Residential Facilities. 3rd edition, 1994.
Standards for Juvenile Detention Facilities. 3rd edition, 1991.
Standards for Juvenile Training Schools. 3rd edition, 1991.
Standards for Small Jail Facilities. 3rd edition, 1989.
Directory of Juvenile and Adult Correctional Departments, 1997.
National Jail and Adult Detention Directory, 1996–1998.

The ACA also publishes *Corrections Today*, seven times a year. It features articles on operational and facilities-related issues.

American Jail Association (AJA)
2053 Day Road, Suite 100
Hagerstown, MD 21740-9795
301.790.3930

Publishes bimonthly *American Jails*, featuring articles on current operational issues, facility designs, and technological advances for jail facilities.

National Sheriff's Association (NSA)
1450 Duke Street
Alexandria, VA 22314-3490
703.836.7827

Publishes bimonthly *Sheriff*, featuring articles on current issues.

International Association of Chiefs of Police (IACP)
515 N. Washington Street
Alexandria, VA 22314
703.836.6767

Publishes monthly *Police Chief: The Professional Voice of Law Enforcement*, featuring articles on current issues, as well as the planning guidelines publication cited below.

National Center for Juvenile Justice (NCJJ)
701 Forbes Avenue
Pittsburgh, PA 15219
412.227.6950

Publishes numerous reports and funded studies, as well as the courts design guidance publication cited below.

National Center for State Courts (NCSC)
300 Newport Avenue
Williamsburg, VA 23187
757.253.2000

Publishes various documents and reports, including papers and proceedings from the Court Technology Conferences (CTC), convened every three years, as well as the state courts design guidelines publication cited below.

Federal Bureau of Prisons (FBOP) Office of Facilities Development and Operations
320 First Street, NW
Washington, DC 20534
202.514.5942

Makes available design and construction information to professionals upon request.

National Institute of Corrections Information Center (NIC)
1860 Industrial Circle
Longmont, CO 80501
1.800.995.6429

Makes available a variety of publications dealing with operational and facilities design issues.

National Criminal Justice Reference Service (NCJRS)
National Institute of Justice (NIJ)
P.O. Box 6000
1600 Research Boulevard
Rockville, MD 20850
301.251.5063

An international clearinghouse for criminal justice-related information and the primary research agency for the Department of Justice. Access for professionals is available by appointment.

Office of Juvenile Justice and Delinquency Prevention (OJJDP)
Office of Justice Programs, U.S. Department of Justice
810 Seventh Street, NW
Washington, DC 20531

Produces numerous reports and funded studies, including *Conditions of Confinement: Juvenile Detention and Corrections Facilities*, a research report prepared by ABT Associates, Inc., under a grant from OJJDP, 1994.

National Commission on Correctional Health Care (NCCHC)
2105 North Southport, Suite 200
Chicago, IL 60614
312.528.0818

Makes available *Standards for Health Services in Juvenile Detention and Confinement Facilities* (1999), *Standards for Health Services in Jails* (2003), and *Standards for Health Services in Prisons* (2003).

Criminal Justice Institute, Inc.
Spring Hill West
South Salem, NY 10590
914.533.2000

Publishes annually a document containing extensive statistical information pertaining to adult and juvenile corrections.

LAW ENFORCEMENT FACILITIES DESIGN

Law Enforcement Agency Accreditation Program. *Standards for Law Enforcement Agencies*. Alexandria, VA: Commission on Accreditation for Law Enforcement Agencies, 1994.

Rosenblatt, Daniel N. et al. *Police Facility Planning Guidelines: A Desk Reference for Law Enforcement Executives*. Alexandria, VA: The International Association of Chiefs of Police, 2002.

DETENTION AND CORRECTIONS DESIGN

Kimme, Dennis A. et al. *Small Jail Design Guide: a Planning and Design Resource for Local Facilities of up to 50 Beds*. Washington, DC: U.S. Department of Justice, Office of Justice Programs, National Institute of Corrections, 1988.

Kimme and Associates, Inc. *Jail Design Guide: A Resource for Small and Medium-Sized Jails*. Washington, DC: U.S. Department of Justice, Office of Justice Programs, National Institute of Corrections, 1998.

Krasnow, Peter C. *Correctional Facilities Design and Detailing*. New York: McGraw-Hill, 1998.

Witke, Leonard R., ed. *Planning and Design Guide for Secure Adult and Juvenile Facilities*. Lanham, MD: American Correctional Association, 1999.

COURTS DESIGN

The U.S. government has developed extensive design guidance material for federal courts, and approximately half of the states have prepared state court guidelines for themselves over the years. Some states have recently updated their standards and are now in the forefront of good planning and design practice. These include California, Colorado, Michigan, Utah and Virginia.

Judicial Conference of the U.S. *U.S. Courts Design Guide.*
Washington, DC: Administrative Office of the U.S. Courts, 1997.

Public Buildings Service. *Standard Level Features and Finishes for U.S. Courts Facilities.* Washington, DC: U.S. General Services Administration, 1996.

————. *Facilities Standards for the Public Buildings Service* (PBS-P100). Washington, DC: U.S. General Services Administration, 2000.

————. *Green Courthouse Design Concepts.* Washington, DC: U.S. General Services Administration, 1997.

Hardenbergh, Don, Michael Griebel, Robert Tobin, and Chang-Ming Yeh. *The Courthouse: A Planning and Design Guide for Court Facilities.* Williamsburg, VA: National Center for State Courts, 1991, 1998.

Hurst, Hunter, et al. *Shaping a New Order in the Court: A Sourcebook for Juvenile and Family Court Design.* Pittsburgh, PA: National Center for Juvenile Justice, 1992.

Sobel, Walter, ed. *The American Courthouse: Planning and Design for the Judicial Process.* Chicago: The American Bar Association, 1973.

Sobel, Walter and Daiva Peterson, eds. *Twenty Years of Courthouse Design Revisited. Supplement to The American Courthouse.* Chicago: The American Bar Association, 1993.

Wong, F. Michael, ed. *Judicial Administration and Space Management. A Guide for Architects, Court Administrators, and Planners.* Gainesville, FL: University Press of Florida, 2000.

ACCESSIBILITY DESIGN RESOURCES

Accessibility Guidelines for Buildings and Facilities; State and Local Government; Final Rule. Section 11 Judicial Facilities; Section 12 Detention and Correctional Facilities. Federal Register, Part II, 36 CFR Part 1191. January 1998.

ADAAG Manual: A Guide to the Americans with Disabilities Act Accessibility Guidelines. Washington, DC: U.S. Architectural and Transportation Barriers Compliance Board, 1998.

Uniform Federal Accessibility Standards (UFAS). Federal Register (FR 31528). August 1984.

American Bar Association / State Justice Institute. *Into the Jury Box: A Disability Accommodation Guide for State Courts.* Washington, DC: American Bar Association, 1994.

American Bar Association / National Judicial College. *Court-Related Needs of the Elderly and Persons with Disabilities: A Blueprint for the Future.* Washington, DC: American Bar Association, 1991.

Dooley, Jeanne, Naomi Karp, and Erica Wood. *Opening the Courthouse Door: An ADA Access Guide for State Courts.* Washington, DC: American Bar Association, 1992.

SECURITY DESIGN RESOURCES

U. S. Marshals Service. *Requirements and Specifications for Special Purpose and Support Space Manual.* Washington, DC: U.S. Department of Justice, 1997.

Griebel, Michael A. and Todd S. Phillips. "Architectural Design for Security in Courthouse Facilities." *Annals of the American Academy of Political and Social Science* 576 (July 2001).

McMahon, James L. *Court Security: A Manual of Guidelines and Procedures.* Washington, DC: National Sheriff's Association, 1978.

Thomas, Michael F. *Courthouse Security Planning: Goals, Measures, and Evaluation Methodology.* Columbia, SC: Justice Planning Associates, Inc., 1991.

ADDITIONAL RESOURCES / GENERAL INFORMATION

Alfini, James J., and Glenn R. Winters, eds. *Courthouses and Courtrooms: Selected Readings.* Chicago: American Judicature Society, 1972.

Craig, Lois, et al. *The Federal Presence: Architecture, Politics, and Symbols in United States Government Buildings.* Cambridge: MIT Press, 1978.

Dell I'Sola, Michael. "Know Your Options. The Impact of Different Delivery Systems on the Management of Contracts." *The Construction Specifier,* September 2001, pp. 38–45.

Dell I'Sola, Michael and Brian Bowen. *Architect's Essentials of Cost Management.* New York: John Wiley & Sons, 2002.

Greenberg, Allan. *Courthouse Design: A Handbook for Judges and Court Administrators,* Chicago: American Bar Association, Commission on Standards of Judicial Administration, 1975.

Griebel, Michael, et al. "New Generation Smart Courthouses." From proceedings, Fifth National Court Technology Conference (CTC 5). Williamsburg, VA: National Center for State Courts, 1997.

Hardenbergh, Don, ed. *Retrospective of Courthouse Design, 1980–1991.* Williamsburg, VA: National Center for State Courts, 1992.

Hardenbergh, Don and Todd S. Phillips, eds. *Retrospective of Courthouse Design, 1991–2001.* Williamsburg, VA: National Center for State Courts, 2001.

Pare, Richard, ed. *Courthouse: A Photographic Document.* New York: Horizon Press, 1978.

Phillips, Todd S. "Courthouses: Designing Justice for All." Architectural Record, March 1999, pp. 105–164.

Phillips, Todd S., Lawrence Webster, and Charles Boxwell. "Technologies and Courthouse Design: Challenges for Today and Tomorrow." *The Court Manager* 12, no. 3 (Summer 1997): pp. 7–10.

CODES AND STANDARDS, SPONSORING ORGANIZATIONS

American Society of Heating, Refrigerating and Air-Conditioning Engineers, Inc. (ASHRAE)
1791 Tullie Circle, N.E.
Atlanta, GA 30329
404.636.8400

American Society for Standards Testing and Materials (ASTM)
100 Barr Harbor Drive
West Conshohocken, PA 19428-2959
Especially ASTM Committee F-33 on Detention and Correctional Facilities.

International Code Council
5203 Leesburg Pike, Suite 600
Falls Church, VA 22041
703.931.4533

National Fire Protection Association (NFPA)
One Batterymarch Park
P.O. Box 9146
Quincy, MA 02269-9959
1.800.344.3555
Life Safety Code Handbook (NFPA 101). 8th edition, 2000. Specific related detention and correctional facilities chapters.
National Electrical Code (NFPA 70), various editions.

National Institute of Building Sciences (NIBS)
1201 L Street, NW
Washington, D.C. 20005
202.289.7800

Publishes *Construction Criteria Base (CCB)*, an exhaustive compilation of building codes and standards. Also hosts on its website, www.nibs.org, the Whole Building Design Guide (WBDG), a gateway for building professionals to information on integrated, "whole building" design techniques and technologies. It is especially useful for information pertaining to federal courts.

Underwriters Laboratories, Inc. (UL)
333 Pfingsten Road Northbrook, IL 60062-2096

Other Sponsors

ACI	American Concrete Institute
AISI	American Iron and Steel Institute
ANSI	American National Standards Institute
ASCE	American Society of Civil Engineers
BOCA	Building Officials and Code Administrators International
CABO	Council of American Building Officials
HMMA	Hollow Metal Manufacturers Association
NAHB	National Association of Home Builders
NCMA	National Concrete Masonry Association
NCSBCS	National Conference of States on Building Codes and Standards
NIST	National Institute of Standards and Technology
PCA	Portland Cement Association
SBCCI	Southern Building Code Congress International
Voice of Safety	VOSI
WFCA	Western Fire Chiefs

INDEX

DATE DUE

DEMCO, INC. 38-2931

BUILDING TYPE BASICS FOR JUSTICE FACILITIES:

1. Program (predesign)

What are the principal programming requirements (space types and areas)? Any special regulatory or jurisdictional concerns?

3, 4, 7, 11–21, 23–29, 37– 41, 43, 46– 50, 53–54, 56, 75, 77– 83, 85–96, 117–19, 121–22, 124–29, 131–36, 147–52, 154–56, 158, 160, 162–68, 184–85, 188–89, 192–94

2. Project process and management

What are the key components of the design and construction process? Who is to be included on the project team?

6, 7, 148, 288–90

3. Unique design concerns

What distinctive design determinants must be met? Any special circulation requirements?

29–31, 57, 59, 64–65, 70, 82, 136–37, 172, 176, 232, 257–62, 273

4. Site planning/parking/landscaping

What considerations determine external access and parking? Landscaping?

9–10, 31–32, 34, 60–61, 64–65, 70, 72–74, 96–98, 100, 108–9, 137, 139–43, 145–46, 163, 169, 172–77, 179, 182, 185, 188–89, 192, 255–56

5. Codes/ADA

Which building codes and regulations apply, and what are the main applicable provisions? (Examples: egress; electrical; plumbing; ADA; seismic; asbestos; terrorism and other hazards)

31, 49, 70, 80–82, 96, 126, 137, 172, 175, 219–21, 223, 231–32, 257–73, 283

6. Energy/environmental challenges

What techniques in service of energy conservation and environmental sustainability can be employed?

228–29, 284

7. Structure system

What classes of structural systems are appropriate?

229–34, 262–64, 28

8. Mechanical systems

What are appropriate systems for heating, ventilating, and air-conditioning (HVAC) and plumbing? Vertical transportation? Fire and smoke protection? What factors affect preliminary selection?

83, 209, 212–19, 222–26, 228, 285

9. Electrical/communications

What are appropriate systems for electrical service and voice and data communications? What factors affect preliminary selection?

41, 88, 134, 194, 213, 219–22, 224, 226–28, 236–48, 250–56, 264–73, 286